DARK SIDE OF THE MIND

STAR WARS

PSYCHOLOGY

THE BOOK YOU'RE LOOKING FOR....

edited by

TRAVIS LANGLEY

Travis Langley

STERLING
New York

STERLING
New York

An Imprint of Sterling Publishing
1166 Avenue of the Americas
New York, NY 10036

ISBN 978-1-4549-1736-6

Distributed in Canada by Sterling Publishing
c/o Canadian Manda Group, 664 Annette Street
Toronto, Ontario, Canada M6S 2C8
Distributed in the United Kingdom by GMC Distribution Services
Castle Place, 166 High Street, Lewes, East Sussex, England BN7 1XU
Distributed in Australia by Capricorn Link (Australia) Pty. Ltd.
P.O. Box 704, Windsor, NSW 2756, Australia

For information about custom editions, special sales, and premium and corporate purchases, please
contact Sterling Special Sales at 800-805-5489 or specialsales@sterlingpublishing.com.

Manufactured in Canada

2 4 6 8 10 9 7 5 3 1

www.sterlingpublishing.com

To my grandfathers
Vernie Langley, Jr. and (in memory)
William "Bill" Mills

Science fiction was never their big thing, but that first Star Wars movie is a cowboy story, "from a certain point of view," as Ben Kenobi might say.

Special Thanks
to George Lucas for giving us heroes a long time ago and far far away, and to the designers, actors, film crew, game developers, and many others who helped populate his galaxy in the beginning and keep things going today.

Contents

3. »»» Journeys

4. »»» Paths

5. »»» Awakenings

Acknowledgments:
The Rebel Alliance

I never stopped expecting an *Episode VII*. Admittedly, I did start to wonder if it would happen during George Lucas's lifetime. Long before Lucasfilm announced that the Star Wars cinematic series would finally resume, I started planning the book that would become *Star Wars Psychology: Dark Side of the Mind*. Its time has come, thanks to Lucasfilm, Disney, and New York Comic Con. Minutes after I mentioned my previous book's editor, Connie Santisteban, to illustrator Marc Nadel, we crossed paths with her in the hallway at NYCC. Connie had just added popular culture to her repertoire at Sterling Publishing, I had just prepared a popular culture psychology series proposal, and we immediately agreed that we wanted to work together again. "Remember that Star Wars book I wanted to do?" I asked Connie. "It's time!"

Thanks to Connie Santisteban, Lauren Tambini, Sari Lampert, and so many other fine folks at Sterling Publishing, *Star Wars Psychology* and *The Walking Dead Psychology* are here, with more titles on the way. Such an ambitious series would never be possible without the chapter authors, a group of professionals who know how to bring psychology and popular culture together in informative and entertaining ways. Because I met most of them at conventions or through our *Psychology Today* blogs, I must thank *The People versus George Lucas* interviewee Matt Smith, whose research led me to my first Comic-Con, and Kaja Perina, my editor at PsychologyToday.com. Different fan conventions' organizers have created opportunities for me to meet fascinating people and develop my ideas on the psychology of popular culture: Randy Duncan, Peter Coogan, and Kate McClancy, my fellow Comics Arts Conference organizers; Eddie Ibrahim, Sue Lord, Adam Neese, Gary Sassaman, and more who run Comic-Con International; Lance Fensterman (New York Comic Con); Mark Walters and Ben Stevens (Dallas Comic Con); Jimmy and Kara Dyer (ComiCon-Way); and the most excellent Christopher Jansen, Peter Katz, Donna Chin, Mo Lightning, Madeleine McManus, Jerry Milani, Victoria Schmidt, Brittany Walloch, and others who have organized the Wizard World conventions.

Of the hundreds of speakers who have appeared on convention panels with me, noteworthy for this book are those who presented OuterPlaces.com's first "Science of Star Wars" panel: Kieran Dickson, Jenna Busch, Steve Huff, Emily Manor-Chapman, and Eliot Sirota. That's when Eliot and I figured out how to make lightsabers work. (Just wait until we crowdsource their production!) I finally met Carrie Goldman, who wrote this book's foreword, in person after Chase Masterson (*Star Trek: Deep Space 9*) invited me to join the two of them, Joe Gatto, Matt Langdon, Ashley Eckstein (*Star Wars: The Clone Wars*), and others on their "End Bullying Now!" panel at New York Comic Con. Noteworthy friends who also played important parts in that eventful NYCC trip include Athena Finger, Danny Fingeroth, Irwin Hasen, Chelle Mayer, Michael Uslan, and Nicky Wheeler-Nicholson. Adam Savage deserves a shout-out for throwing the Comic-Con after-party (as does Grant Imahara for telling us to go) where Matt Munson made sure everyone made friends and I met great people like Fon Davis, who worked on visual effects for the Star Wars Special Editions and prequels.

Teaching at Henderson State University, I am truly fortunate to enjoy the support of administrators like President Glen Jones, Provost Steve Adkison, and Dean John Hardee, who welcome creative ways to teach. It's a good thing librarian Lea Ann Alexander similarly welcomes my weird acquisition requests. Eric Bailey made sure I got to rewatch Episodes IV–VI in their original theatrical versions. Active, enthusiastic students in our

Comics Arts Club, the Legion of Nerds, and related classes keep the educational experience exciting. Legion founders Ashley Bles, Dillon Hall, Coley Henson, and Bobby Rutledge created their campus club where more than a hundred students meet, read, trade, game, LARP, laugh, and share all kinds of nerdy passions. Our faculty writers group (Angela Boswell, Martin Halpern, Vernon Miles, Suzanne Tartamella, David Sesser, Michael Taylor) reviewed proposals and portions of this manuscript. My fellow psychology faculty members offer endless encouragement, and it's a genuine pleasure to work with people I both like and respect: Aneeq Ahmad, Paul Williamson, Rafael Bejarano, Emilie Beltzer, and Rebecca Langley. Rebecca gets additional credit as my sounding board, proofreader, best friend, and the person who keeps up with all kinds of things when I must immerse myself in exploring these fictional worlds.

Our brain trust of nonpsychologists provide important outlooks on and input for all the books in this series: "Action Flick Chick" Katrina Hill, Alan "Sizzler" Kistler, and Legion of Leia founder Jenna Busch. Katrina and Alan served as editorial assistants on the first of these books, *The Walking Dead Psychology*, and Jenna filled that role this time around. Although wikis are tricky because any idiot can edit them, I must praise StarWars.wikia.com, a.k.a. Wookieepedia, where conscientious contributors have created one of the best collaborative encyclopedias on the web. We always check the original sources, but Wookieepedia sometimes helped us determine which sources we needed to check and what we needed to find in them.

My literary agent Evan Gregory of the Ethan Ellenberg Literary Agency tends to more details than most readers want me to explain. Bonnie Burton, Chris Gore, Nicholas Langley, Linda Mooney, Peter Mayhew, and Billy Dee Williams deserve mentions for reasons diverse and occasionally bizarre. We especially thank actor Sam Witwer for sharing his thoughts on Darth

Maul and writer Don Glut for recounting the experiences he had novelizing *The Empire Strikes Back*.

We owe an ongoing debt to George Lucas and literally thousands of people who have crafted the Star Wars saga over time. Roy Thomas and Howard Chaykin told the first *Star Wars* comic book stories. Novelist Alan Dean Foster effectively launched the Expanded Universe when he wrote *Splinter of the Mind's Eye*.

Film Credits

Story: George Lucas (Episodes I–VI); various (television and other films).

Production Company: Lucasfilm Ltd.

Distribution: 20th Century Fox (Episodes I–VI); Warner Bros. Pictures (*Star Wars: The Clone Wars* theatrical motion picture).

The Original Trilogy

- *Star Wars* (1977), retitled *Star Wars: Episode IV A New Hope* (1981). Screenplay/Director: George Lucas. Producer: Gary Kurtz.
- *Star Wars: Episode V The Empire Strikes Back* (1980). Screenplay: Leigh Bracket, Lawrence Kasdan. Director: Irvin Kershner. Producer: Gary Kurtz.
- *Star Wars: Episode VI Return of the Jedi* (1983). Screenplay: Lawrence Kasdan, George Lucas. Director: Richard Marquand. Producer: Howard Kazanjian.

The Prequels

- *Star Wars: Episode I The Phantom Menace* (1999). Screenplay/Director: George Lucas. Producer: Rick McCallum.

More adventures keep coming. Arguing about which tales are "canon" doesn't change the fact that many great stories have made their marks and left more than a few of us wanting to wield lightsabers or fly X-Wings through the stars.

- *Star Wars: Episode II Attack of the Clones* (2002). Screenplay: George Lucas, Jonathan Hales. Director: George Lucas. Producer: Rick McCallum.
- *Star Wars: Episode III Revenge of the Sith* (2005). Screenplay/Director: George Lucas. Producer: Rick McCallum.

Animation

- *Star Wars: Clone Wars* (television series, 2003–2005). Screenplays: Various. Director: Genndry Tartakovsky. Producers: Genndry Tartakovsky, George Lucas, Claudia Katz, Rick McCallum, Brian A. Miller. Original Network: Cartoon Network.
- *Star Wars: The Clone Wars* (motion picture, 2008). Director: Dave Filoni. Producers: George Lucas, Catherine Winder.
- *Star Wars: The Clone Wars* (television series, 2008–2014). Screenplays/Directors: Various. Producers: George Lucas, Catherine Winder. Original Network: Cartoon Network.
- *Star Wars Rebels* (television series, premiered 2014). Screenplays/Directors: Various. Producers: Dave Filoni, Simon Kinberg, Greg Weisman.Original Network: Disney XD.

Foreword:
Why Star Wars Matters

CARRIE GOLDMAN

author of *Bullied: What Every Parent, Teacher, and Kid Needs
to Know about Ending the Cycle of Fear* (HarperCollins, 2012)

" Why do we have wars, if everyone is always wishing for
peace? Why do some people do bad things to others?"
a four-year-old girl asked me last year. There are the usual
answers—lengthy explanations of land, politics, power, and religion—but the elegant simplicity of the young child's question
deserved an equally direct answer. "I think it comes down to two
things," I told her. "The first is fear, and the second is a lack of
empathy, which means the ability to truly understand and share
the feelings of another person."

"Fear of what?" she persisted.

A good question, because not all fear is bad. Fear of danger
is what keeps us alive, just as fear of hunger motivates us to
work and provide food for our families. But fear can morph and
distend and become maladaptive. Fear of those who are different
can lead to mistreatment; fear of losing power and privilege can
lead to inequality; fear of change can lead to close-mindedness;
and fear of pain can lead to desperation and betrayal.

When you combine unhealthy fear with a lack of empathy,
you open a psychological door that allows people to harm
others without pangs of conscience. In milder forms, fear without empathy leads to attitudes of entitlement and unkindness,
manifested as bullying behaviors. In its most extreme forms,
this lethal psychological combination leads to severe bullying or
even genocide, as we saw in Hutu Rwanda or Nazi Germany.

When you view another person as less than human, you feel entitled to do whatever you want to that person.

In puzzling through how to explain these concepts to a small child, I turned to an ancient form of education: storytelling. People learn better through stories. If you want to convey the full breadth of the human condition, create an epic story that allows a large cast of characters to feel all the feelings. Share that story far and wide, so that different people with diverse life experiences can hear the same story and identify with the complex range of human emotions. If the story is good enough, it will have staying power, and it will be told for generation after generation.

The very best tales will transcend cultures and languages. These rare triumphs of storytelling often include common elements: a hero's journey; a fight between good and evil; the navigation of fear and grief; an exploration of family loyalty, love, and attachment; power and ambition; and the limits of human endurance in the face of misfortune and injustice.

Star Wars has achieved a level of immortality that few epic stories can claim. Due to its widespread audience, people across cultures and generations have a shared understanding of the characters and the plot. Based on the instant recognition of what it means to be Darth Vader or Princess Leia or Luke Skywalker, we can have enduring discussions in our own world about the experiences of the characters in the fictional Star Wars world.

For example, the central figure in the first six theatrical Star Wars films is Anakin Skywalker. The progression of his character serves as a metaphor to help people understand the role that fear plays in acts of war and the role that finding empathy plays in opening the heart to acts of redemption.

I used the story arc of Anakin to explain the motives behind war to the curious four-year-old, who has seen every Star Wars movie, but I kept the analogies very simple. As we all know,

Star Wars contains a depth that fosters high-level adult conversations about much-studied topics, such as gender identity, masculinity, anxiety, attachment, grief, loyalty, and resilience. You will find examples in this book of how the Star Wars saga allows us to examine psychological states, diagnoses, and treatments of people in our everyday world. It is a gift to have a story that lends itself to rich discussions with toddlers and PhDs alike.

Star Wars matters because it gets people *talking* to each other. On our digital planet, where it seems as if everyone is constantly obsessed with a smartphone, it is easy to feel isolated by the lack of face-to-face interactions. Star Wars is heavily followed online, but it also leads to real-life gatherings of people at conventions, at charity events, and at screenings. For example, when a new Star Wars film is released, there will be a sense of camaraderie as fans don their favorite costumes and set out in great spirited groups to line up at theaters, awaiting a chance to share the experience of learning what happens next in the story. Much of the fan bonding at theaters will take place through small talk and chitchat, but these interactions can be just as important to a feeling of connectedness and well-being as the intellectual discussions we cherish. Star Wars is a vehicle that creates a sense of belonging.

When people feel as if they belong, they are able to provide support and help to other members of society. This saga has become a jumping-off point for meaningful actions offline. There is no better example of this than the 501st Legion, a charitable organization that raises millions of dollars for charity each year. The members of the 501st Legion build intricate costumes that are exact replicas of those worn by characters in the Star Wars movies. Nicknamed the "Bad Guys Doing Good," the 501st Legion pays special attention to children's causes and has garrisons around the world.

In 2010, when my then first-grade daughter Katie was bullied at school for being a female Star Wars fan, the response from the Star Wars community was instant and emphatic. Star Wars is for everyone, she was told, and thousands of people from far-reaching nations sent her messages of kindness and acceptance. With the help of strangers who became friends, we created a charity event that takes place each year on the second Friday of December, called Wear Star Wars Share Star Wars. People around the globe are invited on that day to wear something Star Wars—related *and* to make a donation of a Star Wars toy to a child in need. The one stipulation is that they attach a sticky note to the toy specifying that it can go to a girl *or* a boy. We even got Hasbro involved!

Star Wars matters. It matters to the little girl who would rather wield a lightsaber than wear a tiara. It matters to the young man who is isolated at home but finds camaraderie at conventions. It matters to the father who is trying to find a way to bond with his growing teenager, and one of the few things on which they agree is to watch Star Wars together. It matters to the sick child who sees the members of the 501st Legion in full armor at a Make-A-Wish Foundation event. It matters to the psychologists who are seeking to connect with their patients. And it matters to the four-year-old children who seek to understand why people have wars.

We are so fortunate as a society to have Dr. Travis Langley and his outstanding contributors' new book, *Star Wars Psychology: Dark Side of the Mind*. May the Force be with you as you read, learn, and rediscover why you love Star Wars.

Carrie Goldman is the award-winning author of *Bullied: What Every Parent, Teacher, and Kid Needs to Know about Ending the Cycle of Fear* (HarperCollins, 2012). She is a regular blogger for the *Huffington Post*, ChicagoNow, and *Psychology Today.com*. Goldman works with schools, corporations, and community groups on bullying prevention, intervention, and reconciliation. Together with Chase Masterson, she cofounded the Anti-Bullying Coalition. Goldman received her BS from Northwestern University and her MBA from the Kellogg School of Management.

Introduction:
Lights in the Dark Side

TRAVIS LANGLEY

A movie called *Star Wars* took our world by surprise. Four years before it would be rereleased with the subtitle *A New Hope*, George Lucas's ambitious "space opera" combined many kinds of storytelling in a sprawling sci-fi setting and quickly became the most successful movie ever made to date. In a decade when disaster movies, heart-tugging dramas, crazy comedies, gritty action flicks, and one very hungry shark had ruled the box office, a science-fiction epic changed moviemaking. The film's success made me, a nerdy bookworm who felt lonely in the midst of other kids, feel less alone in the world. Its sheer popularity meant that there were plenty of other people out there who loved the fantastic things I loved, even if I did not yet know who they were, and it said that the world was changing. *Star Wars* really was a new hope.

The Star Wars saga has reached billions of beings who populate this spot in the universe. The characters and their stories tap into something primal. They resonate with us for reasons we might not even understand. Star Wars thrills and inspires. That's a good thing. Life on this planet is too brief to plod mundanely through it when our minds can appreciate so much more. You're reading this book and we're writing it as occupants of a vast universe full of possibilities and, thanks to our imaginations, impossibilities as well. Wondering about impossible things sometimes lets us redefine possibilities. Once upon a time, the ability to light a fire was merely a fantasy dreamed by a distant ancestor in a cave. That ancestor was not alone. Dreamers in other caves and fields and forests and icy plains shared that hope without necessarily knowing it was shared. When Luke Skywalker gazes across the desert to watch his world's double sunset, after his friends have already left their out-of-the-way world, he feels isolated and yearns for something more. Other people on his . and other worlds wish for change, too, or there would be no rebels fighting to be free.

The rebels who have written this book's chapters are psychology experts and Star Wars fans. Through the lens of psychology, we look at the characters and stories. We also peek back through that lens the other way to look at psychology itself through the characters and stories. With Star Wars, that is particularly appropriate because psychology itself shaped the saga. Unsure how he was going to complete his interstellar tale, George Lucas got a bit stuck until he discovered the works of mythologist Joseph Campbell. Extending the ideas of psychiatrist Carl Jung,[1] Campbell had outlined the archetypal Hero's Journey, the *monomyth* ("one myth") underlying myths and legends of heroes throughout our world and across time.[2] Jung and Campbell had observed that people in every place and time tell tales of heroes who face darkness, win victories, and returned transformed. "It was very eerie," Lucas said, "because in reading *The Hero with a Thousand Faces*, I began to realize that my first draft of *Star Wars* was following classical motifs."[3] Once he saw his heroes' journey, he knew how to take them through it. He'd found his map through the stars.

When Jung described the dark side of the mind, he referred to the part that is shadowed and hidden deep inside. It might not be evil at all. Even as Emperor Palpatine tries to bring Luke's darkness out into the open, Luke believes that Darth Vader has good in him, light hidden deep inside the dark lord's shadows. While we are certainly not all Jungians, all of us bringing you this book do believe that the hidden, unrevealed part of human nature is worth exploring. Both the light and the dark sides unite us all.

The Jedi are not alone in arming themselves with light. The Sith with their own lightsabers and even characters who would prefer "a good blaster at your side"[4] all wield light.

It's time for us to shine a light on them all.

> "The unconscious is not just evil by nature, it is also the source of the highest good: not only dark but also light, not only bestial, semihuman, and demonic but superhuman, spiritual, and, in the classical sense of the word, 'divine.'"
>
> —psychiatrist Carl Jung[5]

References

Campbell, J. (1949). *The hero with a thousand faces.* Princeton, NJ: Princeton University Press.

Jung, C. G. (1953). *The practice of psychotherapy: Essays on the psychotherapy of the transference and other subjects.* Princeton, NJ: Princeton University Press.

Jung, C. G. (1964). *Man and his symbols.* New York, NY: Doubleday.

Larsen, S., & Larsen, R. (2002). *Joseph Campbell: A fire in the mind.* Rochester, VT: Inner Traditions.

Notes

1. Jung (1964).
2. Campbell (1949).
3. Larsen & Larsen (2002), p. 541.
4. Han Solo in *Star Wars: Episode IV A New Hope* (1977/1981).
5. Jung (1953), p. 364.

1 »
Tales

Once upon a time, in a land far away . . .

Every Star Wars film opens with the science-fiction equivalent of those time-honored words. Cowboys, pirates, and knights of old race to adventure—especially knights. Does it really matter that technology supplies the magic that makes their swords shine or that computerized brains, not ghosts or magic, make the suits of armor venture forth on their own?

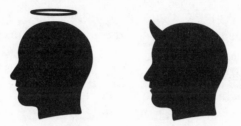

The Good, the Bad, and the Scruffy: Can We Define Good and Evil?

TRAVIS LANGLEY

"We are all ready to be savage in some cause.
The difference between a good man and a
bad one is the choice of the cause."
—psychologist William James[1]

The Star Wars saga regales us with tales of rebels opposing oppression, heroes fighting villains, and individuals' best qualities struggling against their worst. When the Jedi characterize the Force as a dichotomy of light and dark sides without shades of gray, are they oversimplifying matters of good and evil for everyone, or does sensitivity to the Force make them uniquely vulnerable to the allure of their own power?

What are good and evil?

Several chapters in this book examine how good people wind up committing evil deeds, but what is a good person? Can people, not just actions, be evil? Defining good and evil largely falls within the realm of philosophy or theology and is outside the domain of empirical science, and yet psychologists study it all the time. Even when they avoid using the word *evil*, many psychologists look not only at the origins of the best and worst in human behavior but also at the personality traits that accompany inclinations to do good and bad things. When circumstances bring out the worst in many people, some people still try to do the right thing. There are also those, however, who revel in cruelty and destruction in any situation. Why?

Naming the Darkness

"Evil is knowing better, but willingly doing worse."
—psychologist Philip Zimbardo[2]

Psychopathy refers to a set of traits largely defined by a person's lack of empathy or the emotional aspects of a conscience. Psychopaths can know about other people's feelings without sharing them. They also can know the difference between right and wrong without having the kinds of feelings about moral issues that other people experience. This lifelong personality pattern is high in fearlessness and callousness; low in empathy, inhibition, and remorse; and potentially hazardous to the people in a psychopath's way.[3] The related term *sociopathy* has been defined in many different and inconsistent ways. Professionals who compare it with psychopathy tend to view the psychopath as someone who never developed empathy or a conscience in the first place and the sociopath as a psychopathic-seeming individual whose emotional and moral concerns for others stopped developing when that person's environment crushed him or her, usually early in life. Whether this means the sociopath's good side has died altogether or simply lies dormant becomes *Return of the Jedi's* central question: Whereas Ben Kenobi believes that the good in Anakin Skywalker to be dead in Sith Lord Darth Vader, Luke feels sure that the Jedi in his father can return.[4]

Neither psychopathy nor sociopathy appears as a standard diagnosis in the *Diagnostic and Statistical Manual of Mental Disorders* (DSM). The related DSM diagnosis, *antisocial personality disorder*, describes a "pervasive pattern of disregard for and violation of the rights of others, occurring since age 15 years" with evidence of frequent, related misconduct before that age.[5] Although it includes remorselessness as a symptom, the diagnostic criteria largely focus on the individual's behavior rather than on ingrained personality traits. Except for a few younger children, Star Wars characters—especially the villains—are typically adults and are not prone to chatting about their adolescent days. Anakin Skywalker does not appear to have embarked on any rights-violation sprees during his adolescence (between *The Phantom Menace* and *Attack of the Clones*). Among the three overlapping disorders of psychopathy, sociopathy, and antisocial personality disorder, sociopathy may best describe Anakin as he grows to become Darth Vader: The Sith Lord has psychopathic traits but did not start out that way.

Psychopathic qualities are insufficient to account for the range of evil, though. Simply lacking empathy does not necessarily mean that a sociopath delights in harming others. Some psychopathic individuals (whether psychopaths or sociopaths) can become productive members of society, channeling their fearlessness and lack of inhibition into constructive activities. The so-called James Bond personality refers to a high-functioning individual with some psychopathic traits, *subclinical narcissism* (being egotistical but not malignantly so), and *Machiavellianism* (being pragmatic and manipulative).[6] Han Solo tries to act this way, probably as a front to protect himself in a dangerous galaxy. Despite all his roguish bluster and occasional antisocial actions, however, he cares too much about others to qualify as any kind of psychopath at heart. Darth Vader, in contrast, shows many psychopathic traits, is dangerously egotistical, and manipulates others through intimidation and by making bargains that he revises as he sees fit. Vader meets the three criteria of the *dark triad*, a particularly volatile combination of psychopathy, narcissism, and Machiavellianism at more extreme, maladaptive levels.[7]

Emperor Palpatine is even worse. A person can coldly exploit others without experiencing delight over controlling and hurting others. The dark triad falls short of describing Palpatine's *malignant narcissism*, the vicious sort of grandiose selfishness that psychologist Erich Fromm called "the quintessence of evil."[8] Some of the researchers who first studied the dark triad began looking at *sadism* (gleefully hurting others) as a fourth component in a *Dark Tetrad*.[9]

How can basic human emotions such as fear and anger, all of which serve a variety of adaptive survival functions, send someone down the path to the dark side? Good people can lose touch with their own moral concerns for many reasons beyond their control:

- Despite the many fiction writers who feel the need to give their villains tragic origins, a single tragedy does not by itself turn kind, empathetic adults with well-developed personalities into depraved, "insane" monsters. It can alter people in ways that make them vulnerable to other influences. Posttraumatic stress can leave a person emotionally numb, restricting the range of emotions that that person previously felt.[10]
- Substance abuse, especially in cases of addiction, can both numb emotions and increase selfishness in abusers.[11]

- Traumatic brain injury can alter the way a person acts, feels, or thinks.[12] In a few cases, brain injury can cause a condition known as *acquired psychopathy*, in which a previously nonpsychopathic individual loses qualities such as self-restraint, sensitivity, and the ability to care what happens to others.[13]

Force power that can lift a spaceship up from a swamp[14] or convince a Stormtrooper he's looking for other droids could potentially alter the Force-user's own cognitive and emotional processes much like stress, drugs, brain injury, or that magnetic field.

The same psychic abilities that give Force-sensitive individuals advantages over others also make them particularly vulnerable to mental influences from others. A normally empathic individual will be particularly prone to experiencing sadness when others around him or her feel blue, fear when others get scared, or happiness when others are upbeat. Imagine how psychic abilities might magnify this. The Jedi who uses anger to wield Force powers risks tapping into the anger of all living things. Confidence and experience may lead a particular Jedi Knight to believe that he or she has sufficient willpower to use emotions safely as a shortcut to accessing Force powers. That Jedi may maintain self-control no better than does a person who says, "I'm not drunk," while staggering from having nine drinks too many. "'Roid rage" would barely light a candle compared with the firestorm that dark side–fueled fury might unleash.

Looking for the Light

"The opposite of a hero isn't a villain; it's a bystander!"
—educator Matt Langdon[15]

Han Solo tries to be a bystander, to stay out of the skirmish between the Rebel Alliance and the Empire as neither hero nor villain, but he cannot. Rising to the occasion when his friends and others need him most, he shows that he is, in spite of himself, heroic. Why does he help them, though? Making sense of Han's heroism may be no less important than trying to understand why others follow a path of evil—especially in the case of Darth Vader, the hero turned villain who turns hero once again rather than stand idly by while the Emperor attacks Vader's son. Where do heroism and other positive qualities come from?

Although the term *positive psychology* dates back at least as far as Abraham Maslow's 1954 book *Motivation and Personality*, positive psychology emerged as a distinct area within psychology only after American Psychological Association president Martin Seligman challenged his fellow psychologists in 1998 to "create a science of strength and virtue" that would "nurture what is best within ourselves."[16] Psychology still needed to examine the worst aspects of human nature, he said, but ought to stop neglecting the best. Seligman, renowned for his pioneering work on the potentially debilitating effects of trauma and learned helplessness,[17] wanted to look at something better. Others would follow. Social psychologist Philip Zimbardo launched himself into fame with a prison simulation study that showed how cruelly people might act when given authority and how harshly those assigned to be their prisoners might suffer.[18] After spending several decades looking at human evil, culminating in his 2007 book *The Lucifer Effect*, Zimbardo launched the Heroic Imagination Project so that he also could investigate heroism.[19]

Whereas the DSM categorizes and describes mental illnesses, positive psychologists developed the *Character Strengths and Virtues* manual (CSV)[20] to identify people's better qualities scientifically. The list of virtues looks much like a path to becoming a Jedi:

- Wisdom and knowledge.
- Courage.
- Humanity.
- Justice.
- Temperance.
- Transcendence.

Different strengths contribute to each virtue. The virtue *humanity*, for example, includes the strengths *bravery, persistence, integrity,* and *vitality.* Of course, some of those traits could make both heroes and villains better at what they do. What, then, is goodness?

Doing the right thing at great risk or cost to oneself strikes us as more heroic than doing good in a way that benefits oneself. Riding out into freezing weather to save Luke despite high odds that he himself might never make it back alive proves that Han Solo is a hero.[21] Arriving in time to protect Luke during the rebels' attack on the Death Star[22] is no one-time-only good deed. Standing up to evil only after he realizes Darth Vader is cheating him does not yet convince viewers that Lando Calrissian is a good guy, after all.[23] In other words, people judge heroic acts in terms of how *altruistic* those actions are, the degree to which they involve selflessly helping others.

The members of the Jedi Order believe that their knights should care for everyone equally, as though caring more for specific individuals is too selfish and makes the Jedi vulnerable to the dark side. Anakin seems to prove them right when he commits evil deeds because of his feelings of attachment: Devotion to his mother prompts him to slaughter Tuskens,[24] and

The Mark of Altruism

"To attain the Mark of Altruism, you must
selflessly help a soul in need."
—Hermit[25]

In the online game *Star Wars Galaxies: An Empire Divided*,
the Mark of Altruism is a sculpture that a player-character
receives after assisting a poor farmer. The character needs
to collect the Marks of Courage, Honor, Intellect, and Altruism
to become the Hero of Tatooine. Embarking on these quests
to achieve personal status and reward hardly seems selfless,
though.

Rather than debate with those who consider all helpful
acts to be *egoistic* (self-serving), some professionals differentiate between different kinds of motivations and rewards.
Intrinsic motivation involves having the drive and desire to
perform an act for its own sake, as opposed to *extrinsic
motivation*, in which an individual performs an act to receive
some kind of external reward. Helping the farmer in order
to achieve the Mark of Altruism is an extrinsically motivated
act; this makes the mark's name ironic because people
(even the helpers themselves[26]) consider helpfulness to be
less altruistic and more selfish when the person is helping
mainly to achieve an ulterior purpose.

later his fear of losing his wife inspires him to pursue greater
power.[27] His son Luke, however, proves them wrong through
his pattern of accomplishing great things because of his feelings for others: Even though Yoda and Ben both expect the
worst when Luke leaves Dagobah to save his friends[28] and again
when he tries to redeem Darth Vader,[29] Luke succeeds each
time through hope, faith, loyalty, and compassion. Condemning
attachments for fear of potential consequences may be a mistake
if it means overlooking the deeper motivations behind them,
that is, whether the person values others for self-serving versus
other-serving reasons.[30]

Cynical people can argue that there is no true altruism because every benevolent act involves potential benefit to oneself, even if that benefit is merely feeling good about helping others.[31] That argument is a word game no one can win. Altruism exists if we count the intent to help others despite personal risk or cost, and it does not exist if we define it more narrowly. It's a term that people define to try to summarize a concept that is too big to be described in one word. In *The Phantom Menace*, Jar Jar Binks and nine-year-old Anakin are the characters most eager to help others even before either sees how doing so can help himself, as though helpfulness without obvious benefit requires naive innocence.[32] Helping appears to go with the natural need to interact with others.[33]

Empathy, that deep emotional concern whose absence can indicate psychopathy, is one of the greatest predictors of altruistic behavior.[34] Empathy is more complex than it may sound. *Affective empathy* involves feeling sympathy, compassion, or even distress in line with the way others feel.[35] *Cognitive empathy* entails knowing and understanding how others feel, whether that means taking the perspective of real people or identifying with fictional characters. Feeling and knowing pave the way for the actions we call altruistic. Good people endeavor to do good things.

A False Dichotomy?

Denying oneself to benefit others, we call good. Exploiting others to benefit oneself, we call bad. Tormenting others to achieve selfish satisfaction, we call evil. Empathy plays an important role in altruistic behavior and its absence features prominently in a psychopathic personality, but we tend to perceive the greatest evil when monsters such as Emperor Palpatine and Jabba the Hutt actively enjoy their cruelty.

The Jedi Order and the Empire each operates in its own methodical way—order. Rebels and many of the galaxy's criminals shake things up—chaos. Order and chaos are separate issues from right and wrong. Could it be similarly possible that neither light nor dark is inherently good or evil? The Jedi's wariness of experiencing the full range of emotions felt by Luke, who accomplishes great things directly because he cares, may cheat them out of living fuller lives. By eschewing positive emotions such as love and joy, Jedi Knights may deprive themselves of true light.

References

American Psychiatric Association (2013). *Diagnostic and statistical manual of mental disorders* (DSM-5) (5th ed.). Washington, D.C.: American Psychiatric Association.

Baron-Cohen, S. (2011). *The science of evil*. New York, NY: Basic.

Batson, C. D., Sager, K., Garst, E., Kang, M., Rubchinsky, K., & Dawson, K. (1997). Is empathy-induced helping due to self-other merging? *Journal of Personality and Social Psychology, 73*(3), 495–509.

Buckels, E. E., Jones, D. N., & Paulhus, D. L. (2013). Behavior confirmation of everyday sadism. *Psychological Science, 24*(11), 1–9.

Chabrol, H., Van Leeuwen, N., Rodgers, R., & Sejourne, N. (2009). Contributions of psychopathic, narcissistic, Machiavellian, and sadistic personality traits to juvenile delinquency. *Personality and Individual Differences, 47*(7), 734–739.

Chakrabortty, A. (2010, March 8). *Brain food: The psychology of heroism*. The Guardian: http://www.theguardian.com/science/2010/mar/09/brain-food-psychology-heroism.

Cromer, J. N. (2012, March 9). *After brain injury: The dark side of personality change, part 1*. Psychology Today: https://www.psychologytoday.com/blog/professor-cromer-learns-read/201203/after-brain-injury-the-dark-side-personality-change-part-i.

Damasio, A. R., Tranel, D., & Damasio, H. (1990). Individuals with sociopathic behavior caused by frontal damage fail to respond autonomically to social stimuli. *Behavior Brain Research, 41*(2), 81–94.

DeWaal, F. B. M. (2008). Putting the altruism back into altruism: The evolution of empathy. *Annual Review of Psychology, 59*(1), 279–300.

Dovidio, J. F., Allen, J. L., & Schroeder, D. A. (1990). Specificity of empathy-induced helping: Evidence for altruistic motivation. *Journal of Personality and Social Psychology, 59*(2), 249–260.

Forsyth, D. R., Berger, R. E., & Mitchell, T. (1981). The effects of self-serving vs. other-serving claims of responsibility and attribution in groups. *Social Psychology Quarterly, 44*(1), 59–64.

Fromm, E. (1964). *The heart of man*. New York, NY: Harper & Row.

Gorlick, A. (2008, November 5). *For kids, altruism comes naturally, psychologist says*. Stanford Report: http://news.stanford.edu/news/2008/november5/tanner-110508.html.

Hansen, J. M. (2003). *The lost promise of patriotism: Debating American identity, 1890–1920*. Chicago, IL: University of Chicago Press.

Hare, R. D. (1993). *Without conscience: The disturbing world of the psychopaths among us.* New York, NY: Guilford.

Hetzel-Riggin, M. D., & Harbke, C. R. (2014). Hierarchical convergence of PTSD symptom clusters: A comparison of the numbing, dysphoria, and dysphoric arousal models of PTSD. *Traumatology, 20*(4), 302–312.

Jakobwitz, S., & Egan, V. (2006). The dark triad and normal personality traits. *Personality and Individual Differences, 40*(2), 331–339.

James, W. (1895, December 24). *Letter to E. L. Godwin.* Cited by Hansen, p. 14.

Jonason, P. K., Li, N. P., & Teicher, E. A. (2010). Who is James Bond? The Dark Triad as an agentic social style. *Individual Differences Research, 8*(2), 111–120.

Lembcke, J. (2013). *PTSD: Diagnosis and identity in post-empire America.* Lanham, MD: Lexington.

Maslow, A. (1954). *Motivation and personality.* New York, NY: Harper & Row.

Meiring, L., Subramoney, S., Thomas, K. G. F., Decety, J., & Fourie, J. (2014). Empathy and helping: Effects of racial group membership and cognitive load. *South African Journal of Psychology, 44*(4), 426–438.

Mendez, M. F., Owens, E. M., Jimenez, E. E., Peppers, D., & Licht, E. A. (2013). Changes in personality after mild traumatic brain injury from primary blast vs. blunt forces. *Brain Injury, 27*(1), 10–18.

Mercer, M. (2001). In defense of weak psychological egoism. *Erkenntnis, 55*(2), 217–237.

Mitchell, D. G. V., Avny, S. B., & Blair, R. J. R. (2006). Divergent patterns of aggressive and neurocognitive characteristics in acquired versus developmental psychopathy. *Neurocase, 12*(3), 164–178.

Patrick, C. (2005). *Handbook of psychopathy.* New York, NY: Guilford.

Paulhus, D. L., & Williams, J. M. (2002). The dark triad of personality: Narcissism, Machiavellianism, and psychopathy. *Journal of Research in Personality, 36*(6), 556–563.

Peterson, C., & Seligman, M. E. P. (2004). *Character strengths and virtues.* Washington, D.C.: American Psychological Association.

Popova, M. (n.d.). *The Heroic Imagination Project.* Brain Pickings: http://www.brainpickings.org/2011/02/07/philip-zimbardo-heroic-imagination-project/.

Rao, V., Spiro, J. R., Schretlen, D. J., & Cascella, N. G. (2007). Apathy syndrome after traumatic brain injury with deficits in schizophrenia. *Psychosomatics: Journal of Consultation and Liaison Psychiatry, 48*(3), 217–222.

Rossi, A. S. (2001). *Caring and doing for others: Social responsibility in the domains of family, work, and community.* Chicago, IL: University of Chicago Press.

Scherrer, H. (2003, August 27). *Professor Philip Zimbardo: The interview.* http://forejustice.org/zimbardo/p_zimbardo_interview.htm.

Seligman, M. E. P., (1972). Learned helplessness. *Annual Review of Medicine, 23*(1), 407–412.

Seligman, M. E. P. (1998). Building human strength: Psychology's forgotten mission. *APA Monitor, 29*(1), 1.

Seligman, M. E. P., & Maier, S. F. (1967). Failure to escape traumatic shock. *Journal of Experimental Psychology, 74*(1), 1–9.

Shamay-Tsoory, S. G., Aharon-Peretz, J., & Perry, D. (2009). Two systems for empathy: A double dissociation between emotional and cognitive empathy in inferior frontal gyrus versus ventromedial prefrontal lesions. *Brain, 132*(3), 617–627.

Stanton, G. H. (2007). Foreword to the second edition. In J. Waller, *Becoming evil* (2nd ed., pp. vii–ix). New York, NY: Oxford University Press.

Stone, M. H. (2009). *The anatomy of evil.* Amherst, NY: Prometheus.

Thomas, G., & Batson, C. D. (1981). Effect of helping under normative pressure on self-perceived altruism. *Social Psychology Quarterly, 44*(2), 127–131.

Tonigan, J. S., Rynes, K., Toscova, R., & Hagler, K. (2013). Do changes in selfishness explain 12-step benefit? A prospective lagged analysis. *Substance Abuse, 34*(1), 13–19.

Wakefield, J. C. (1993). Is altruism part of human nature? Toward a theoretical foundation for the helping professions. *Social Service Review, 67*(3), 406–458.

Waller, J. (2002/2007). *Becoming evil.* New York, NY: Oxford University Press.

Warneken, F., & Tomasello, M. (2009). The roots of human altruism. *British Journal of Psychology, 100*(3), 455–471.

Zimbardo, P. G. (1969). The human choice: Individuation, reason, and order versus deindividuation, impulse, and chaos. In W. J. Arnold & D. Levine (Eds.), *Nebraska Symposium on Motivation* (Vol. 17). Lincoln, NE: University of Nebraska Press.

Zimbardo, P. G. (1971, October 25). *The psychological power and pathology of imprisonment.* A statement prepared for the U.S. House of Representatives Committee on the Judiciary, Subcommittee No. 3: Hearings on Prison Reform, San Francisco, CA.

Zimbardo, P. (2007). *The Lucifer effect: Understanding how good people turn evil.* New York, NY: Random House.

Notes

1. James (1895).
2. Sherrer (2003).
3. Baron-Cohen (2011); Patrick (2005); Stone (2009); Waller (2002/2007).
4. *Star Wars: Episode VI Return of the Jedi* (1983 motion picture).
5. American Psychiatric Association (2013), p. 659.
6. Jonason et al. (2010).
7. Jakobwitz & Egan (2006); Paulhus & Williams (2002).
8. Fromm (1964), p. 37.
9. Buckels et al. (2013); Chabrol et al. (2009).
10. Hetzel-Riggin & Harbke (2014); Lembcke (2013).
11. Tonigan et al. (2013).
12. Mendez et al. (2013); Rao et al. (2007).
13. Cromer (2012); Damasio et al. (1990); Hare (1993); Mitchell et al. (2006).
14. *Star Wars: Episode V The Empire Strikes Back* (1980 motion picture).
15. Chakrabortty (2010).
16. Seligman (1998), p. 1.
17. Seligman & Maier (1967); Seligman (1972).
18. Zimbardo (1969; 1971).
19. Popova (n.d.).
20. Peterson & Seligman (2004).
21. *The Empire Strikes Back* (1980 motion picture).
22. *Star Wars: Episode IV A New Hope* (1977 motion picture).
23. *The Empire Strikes Back* (1980 motion picture).
24. *Star Wars: Episode II Attack of the Clones* (2002 motion picture).
25. *Star Wars Galaxies: An Empire Divided* (2003 massively multiplayer online role-playing game).
26. Thomas & Batson (1981).
27. *Star Wars: Episode III Revenge of the Sith* (2005 motion picture).
28. *The Empire Strikes Back* (1980 motion picture).
29. *Return of the Jedi* (1983 motion picture).

30. Forsyth et al. (1981); Rossi (2001).
31. Mercer (2001); compare Wakefield (1993).
32. Gorlick (2008).
33. Warneken & Tomasello (2009).
34. Batson et al. (1997); deWaal (2008); Dovidio et al. (1990); Meiring et al. (2014).
35. Shamay-Tsoory et al. (2009).

2

So You Want to Be a Jedi?: Learning the Ways of the Force through Acceptance and Commitment Therapy

JENNA BUSCH AND JANINA SCARLET

Obi-Wan Kenobi: *"Master Yoda says I should be mindful of the future."*
Qui-Gon Jinn: *"But not at the expense of the present moment."*[1]

"Mindfulness means paying attention in a particular way; on purpose, in the present moment, and nonjudgmentally."
—biomedical scientist Jon Kabat-Zinn[2]

Sure, it looks cool to wield a lightsaber and fight against the Imperial Stormtroopers, but what does it actually take to become a Jedi? Which Jedi practices resemble mental health practices currently used to help people with various mental health disorders? What are the main differences between a Jedi and a Sith, and how do they relate to mental health?

The Jedi Knights study and serve the Force, a mystical energy that connects all things. They fight as a last resort. They are guided by the Force and follow principles of non-attachment and self-discipline. The Jedi also value mindfulness, acceptance, and compassion, all of which have been shown to help people with various psychological disorders, such as anxiety, depression, and posttraumatic stress disorder (PTSD), chronic pain, substance addictions, and other disorders.[3] Therapies that specifically focus on some of these "Jedi" skills are known as *mindfulness-based therapies*, and include acceptance and commitment therapy (see sidebar), mindfulness-based cognitive therapy, and dialectical behavior therapy.[4]

Learning Psychological Flexibility

Mindfulness

Each Jedi spends a lifetime training to use and be one with the Force. The Force is a kind of metaphysical power that guides the Jedi. It is said to be everywhere and in everything. The Jedi Masters teach their Padawans from an early age to quiet their minds in order to be able to connect with the Force. This connection with the Force is a form of *mindfulness*, which refers to paying attention to the present moment on purpose, without judgment or distraction.[5] It turns out that the Jedi might have been onto something. Jedi or not, mindfulness has many physical and psychological benefits.[6] In fact, regular mindfulness practice can reduce anxiety and depression,[7] reduce symptoms of PTSD,[8] improve mood,[9] improve brain functioning,[10] and potentially prolong life.[11]

Many people spend a great deal of time feeling devastated about the past, as Anakin Skywalker does about not being able to see his mother anymore after she dies, and worrying about the future, as Anakin does when he fears losing Padmé.[12]

Acceptance and Commitment Therapy

Acceptance and commitment therapy (ACT) is a type of therapy that uses similar skills to those that the Jedi teach. The primary idea behind ACT is that mental disorders stem from psychological *inflexibility*, such as thinking only in absolute terms[13] (as the Sith do)—"If you're not with me, then you're my enemy."[14] To help people who struggle with psychological inflexibility, ACT focuses on the following six skills to increase psychological flexibility:

1. *Mindfulness*—paying attention to the present moment, something Yoda and other Jedi Masters spend a lot of time doing. For example, Yoda encourages Luke to be mindful as he tries to help him balance rocks and lift the X-Wing from the swamp in Degobah.[15]
2. *Acceptance*—the willingness to feel and connect with any sensations and experiences a person has. Obi-Wan accepts his fate when he fights Darth Vader and lets Vader strike him down on the Death Star.[16]
3. *Self-as-context*—focusing on non-attachment to a specific outcome or identity. After the Clone Wars, Obi-Wan did not present himself as a Jedi

Instead, mindfulness focuses on the present moment.[18] This practice may include noticing the sounds that are present in the environment, observing emotions, or paying attention to one's own breath or other physical sensations that arise naturally in the body. The key is to notice when the attention drifts away from the intended focus and to bring it back nonjudgmentally, *accepting* the experience as it is.[19] Sometimes when a person is engaging in an unpleasant task, such as cleaning out the refrigerator, or is feeling a painful emotion, like sadness or anxiety, focusing on this experience might be difficult.

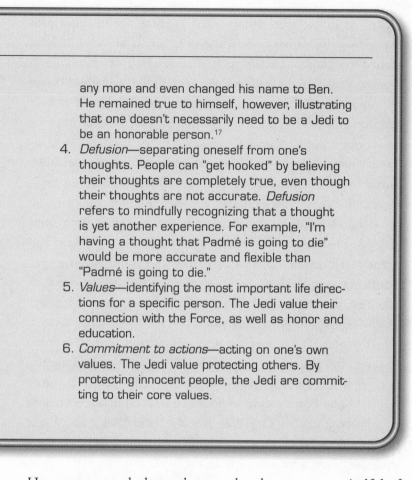

any more and even changed his name to Ben. He remained true to himself, however, illustrating that one doesn't necessarily need to be a Jedi to be an honorable person.[17]

4. *Defusion*—separating oneself from one's thoughts. People can "get hooked" by believing their thoughts are completely true, even though their thoughts are not accurate. *Defusion* refers to mindfully recognizing that a thought is yet another experience. For example, "I'm having a thought that Padmé is going to die" would be more accurate and flexible than "Padmé is going to die."

5. *Values*—identifying the most important life directions for a specific person. The Jedi value their connection with the Force, as well as honor and education.

6. *Commitment to actions*—acting on one's own values. The Jedi value protecting others. By protecting innocent people, the Jedi are committing to their core values.

However, research shows that people who are more mindful of their experiences, who connect with their feelings and tasks, even if they are unpleasant, are generally significantly happier than people who try to distract themselves or focus on something more pleasant.[20]

In the Star Wars series, the more mindful one is about his or her experience, pleasant or unpleasant, the more that person can connect with and use the Force. For example, when Yoda initially trains Luke Skywalker on Dagobah, Luke struggles with lifting the X-Wing out of the swamp because of his lack of focus.[21] It might seem strange that focusing on an unpleasant experience, like anxiety or frustration, might be more helpful than distracting oneself from it. The research on mindfulness suggests that it might lead to an increase in the "feel good" brain responses by releasing neurotransmitters, such as endorphins[22] and dopamine.[23] In addition, mindfulness practice can improve the person's physical health, especially when it comes to telomere length. *Telomeres* are the end parts of the human DNA found in each of our living cells. The longer someone's telomeres, the longer one's lifespan and the healthier a person can be. Telomeres shorten naturally with age, as well as with stress and disease. People with chronic stress, anxiety disorders, and Alzheimer's disease tend to have shorter telomeres. However, practicing mindfulness seems to slow down the process of telomere shortening and might essentially improve someone's psychological and physical health.[24]

In the Star Wars series, stronger connection with the Force (through the practice of mindfulness) does seem to prolong the lives of Jedi. The Jedi who have an especially strong connection with the Force can in some way transcend death, returning as a Force ghost, as Obi-Wan Kenobi[25] and Yoda[26] do. When they return as Force ghosts, the Jedi can continue to guide their Padawans, even after apparent death.

Non-attachment

One of the fundamental lessons a Jedi needs to master is non-attachment. The Jedi are forbidden to marry or hold strong attachments, as they believe that any emotion might lead one to the dark side of the Force. Non-attachment refers to allowing things to be as they are. For example, Anakin is attached to becoming a Jedi Master and when the Jedi Council refuses to appoint him as such, he becomes furious.[27] In this example,

Anakin's attachment to the specific outcome causes him to become angry, a trait of the dark side.

Attachment refers to the expectation of pleasurable experiences (for example, always being around loved ones) and the unwillingness to experience changes or let go of changes.[28] Attachment to people or the expectation of specific outcomes may cause the individual additional suffering.[29] A way to practice non-attachment is through the process of *acceptance*. *Acceptance* refers to the willingness to mindfully experience one's feelings, as well as any life events that one does not have control over.[30] This does not mean that the individual has to enjoy these experiences, but rather that the person does not struggle against them. Very often the struggle against something that cannot ultimately be avoided (*experiential avoidance*) only increases a person's psychological distress.[31]

Acceptance is one of the Jedi qualities that Anakin struggles with the most. In his failure to practice acceptance and his attempts to control his own fate, as well as the fates of his loved ones, Anakin becomes increasingly obsessed with the fear of losing the people closest to him. Anakin's unwillingness to experience fear leads him to engage in Sith-like attempts to avoid or control these emotional experiences. Experiential avoidance and disconnection from one's values are tied to many psychological disorders, such as addiction and impulsivity,[32] depression and anxiety disorders,[33] PTSD,[34] and even suicide.[35] People driven by experiential avoidance often become impulsive, angry, and even violent, all of which violate the practice of the Jedi. For example, when Tusken Raiders kill Anakin's mother, he not only kills those responsible but takes his anger out on innocent Tuskens as well.[36] Failure to practice acceptance, as evidenced in Anakin's fear of losing Padmé, drives him to try to control his and Padmé's fates, which results in him joining the dark side.[37]

Self-Discipline

Along with being one with the Force, the Jedi must learn to conquer arrogance, overconfidence, and defeatism. Above all else, the Jedi need to master *self-discipline* in order to master the rest of their training. Some of the guiding principles of self-discipline might include patience, restraint, and trust in the Force. Patience is an especially important quality, as the absence of patience, like the lack of acceptance, can lead to anger, impulsivity, and, as in the case of Anakin, making poor choices, which is a sure way to the dark side.

In psychology, self-discipline is sometimes taught in terms of following one's *values*, which means personal life directions, such as spending time with friends and loved ones, receiving education, and being kind and compassionate to others.[38] Most of these principles seem to align with those of the Jedi.

The Jedi are honorable warriors, who must only use the Force to gain knowledge and as a form of a defense against an enemy, but never to attack. They must use their knowledge and abilities to protect others and should practice compassion toward other beings, including prisoners. Despite having only a limited training, Luke Skywalker not only understands these concepts, he embodies them. Even when his life is in danger, he refuses to kill his worst enemy, Darth Vader, and when an injured Vader is dying, Luke shows compassion.

Compassion refers to acknowledging the suffering of another being, having a desire to alleviate that suffering, and taking some kind of action or expressing the intention to reduce the suffering.[39] Luke recognizes that Darth Vader is in pain and, wishing to alleviate his suffering, he comforts him and honors Vader's last wish of helping him take off his helmet.

Sometimes erroneously believed to be a weakness, compassion toward others requires great strength of character and has even been found to be helpful in reducing psychological suffering. For example, practicing compassion for just a few months has been shown to drastically reduce the symptoms of PTSD and depression in war veterans, suggesting that compassion is beneficial for mental health.[40]

Jedi versus Sith: Psychological Flexibility versus Inflexibility

Overall, the differences between the Jedi and the Sith can be compared to the differences between psychological flexibility and inflexibility. According to the six skills of acceptance and commitment therapy, psychological flexibility comes from practicing acceptance, mindfulness, non-attachment to thoughts and identity labels (i.e., defusion and self-as-context), and following one's values, such as protecting others and being compassionate, all of which the Jedi are encouraged to practice. For example, in the video game *Knights of the Old Republic*, the Jedi Bastila Shan's compassion leads her to save the life of the Sith Lord Darth Revan after he is betrayed by his apprentice. In fact, this act of compassion brings him back to the light side.[41]

On the other hand, a Sith, who does not practice acceptance and commitment therapy skills, is likely to use his or her power to further personal ambitions. The Sith are stereotypically dealing "in absolutes,"[42] lack acceptance, and tend to be impulsive. They try to control life and death, as well as fate and their experiences, and usually lack compassion. The Sith are generally willing to commit a murder in order to gain or maintain power. Emperor Palpatine, for example, trains Count Dooku as his apprentice, despite later planning to have Anakin kill Dooku. This is all part of Palpatine's plan to get Anakin to join the dark side.[43]

Overall, it seems that most of the skills taught to the

Jedi—mindfulness, compassion, acceptance, and helping others—can be helpful in overcoming or possibly preventing various psychological disorders. While the Sith qualities—striving for personal gain, lack of compassion, and lack of acceptance—generally seem associated with psychological disorders. It might be more tempting to be on the dark side, but the way of the Jedi and the light side seems to offer the most benefits and to lead to mental health and stability.

References

Anderson, K. J., & Moesta, R. (1996). *Lightsabers*. New York, NY: Boulevard

Bormann, J. E., Hurst, S., & Kelly, A. (2013). Responses to Mantram Repetition Program from veterans with posttraumatic stress disorder: A qualitative analysis. *Journal of Rehabilitation Research & Development, 50*(6), 769–784.

Carlson, L. E., Beattie, T. L., Giese-Davis, J., Faris, P., Tamagawa, R., Fick, L. J., Degelman, E. S., & Speca, J. (2015). Mindfulness-based cancer recovery and supportive-expressive therapy maintain telomere length relative to controls in distressed breast cancer survivors. *Cancer, 121*(3), 476–484.

Chow, Y. W., & Tsang, H. W. (2007). Biopsychosocial effects of qigong as a mindful exercise for people with anxiety disorders: A speculative review. *The Journal of Alternative and Complementary Medicine, 13*(8), 831–840.

Davidson, R. J., Kabat-Zinn, J., Schumacher, J., Rosenkranz, M., Muller, D., Santorelli, S. F., Urbanowski, F., Harrington, A., Bonus, K., & Sheridan, J. F. (2003). Alterations in brain and immune function produced by mindfulness meditation. *Psychosomatic Medicine, 65*(4), 564–570.

Epel, E. S., Puterman, E., Lin, J., Blackburn, E., Lazaro, A., & Mendes, W. B. (2013). Wandering minds and aging cells. *Clinical Psychological Science, 1*(1), 75–83.

Forman, E. M., Herbert, J. D., Moitra, E., Yeomans, P. D., & Geller, P. A. (2007). A randomized controlled effectiveness trial of acceptance and commitment therapy and cognitive therapy for anxiety and depression. *Behavior Modification, 31*(6), 772–799.

Gilbert, P. (2005). *Compassion: Conceptualisations, research and use in psychotherapy*. London, UK: Routledge.

Hanh, T. N. (1999). *The heart of the Buddha's teaching: Transforming suffering into peace, joy and liberation—The four noble truths, the noble eightfold path, and other basic Buddhist teachings*. New York, NY: Random House.

Hayes, S. C. (2003). Buddhism and acceptance and commitment therapy. *Cognitive and Behavioral Practice, 9*(1), 58–66.

Hayes, S. C., Luoma, J. B., Bond, F. W., Masuda, A., & Lillis, J. (2006). Acceptance and commitment therapy: Model, processes and outcomes. *Behaviour Research and Therapy, 44*(1), 1–25.

Hayes, S. C., Pistorello, J., & Levin, M. E. (2012). Acceptance and commitment therapy as a unified model of behavior change. *The Counseling Psychologist, 40*(7), 976–1002.

Kabat-Zinn, J. (1990). *Full catastrophe living: Using the wisdom of your body and mind to face stress, pain, and illness*. New York, NY: Delacorte.

Kearney, D. J., Malte, C. A., McManus, C., Martinez, M. E., Felleman, B., & Simpson, T. L.

(2013). Loving-kindness meditation for posttraumatic stress disorder: A pilot study. *Journal of Traumatic Stress, 26*(4), 426–434.

Killingsworth, M. A., & Gilbert, D. T. (2010). A wandering mind is an unhappy mind. *Science, 330*(6006), 932.

Kjaer, T. W., Bertelsen, C., Piccini, P., Brooks, D., Alving, J., & Lou, H. C. (2002). Increased dopamine tone during meditation-induced change of consciousness. *Brain Research: Cognitive Brain Research, 13*(2), 255–259.

Litvin, E. B., Kovacs, M. A., Hayes, P. L., & Brandon, T. H. (2012). Responding to tobacco craving: experimental test of acceptance versus suppression. *Psychology of Addictive Behaviors: Journal of the Society of Psychologists in Addictive Behaviors, 26*(4), 830–837.

Luoma, J. B., & Villatte, J. L. (2012). Mindfulness in the treatment of suicidal individuals. *Cognitive and Behavioral Practice, 19*(2), 265–276.

LucasArts: (2006). *Star Wars: Knights of the Old Republic* [Xbox video game]. San Francisco, CA: Lucasfilm.

Roemer, L., Lee, J. K., Salters-Pedneault, K., Erisman, S. M., Orsillo, S. M., & Mennin, D. S. (2009). Mindfulness and emotion regulation difficulties in generalized anxiety disorder: Preliminary evidence for independent and overlapping contributions. *Behavior Therapy, 40*(2}, 142–154.

Scarlet, J., Lang, A. J., & Walser, R. D. (in press). Acceptance and commitment therapy (ACT) for posttraumatic stress disorder. In G. Wynn & D. Benedek (Eds.), *Complementary and alternative medicine for PTSD.* Cambridge, MA: Oxford University Press.

Stover, M. W. (2005). *Star Wars: Episode III Revenge of the Sith.* London, UK: Century.

Twohig, M. P. (2009). Acceptance and commitment therapy for treatment-resistant posttraumatic stress disorder: A case study. *Cognitive and Behavioral Practice, 16*(3), 243–252.

Windham, R., Trevas, C., & Edwards, T. L. (2007). *Star Wars: Jedi vs. Sith: The essential guide to the Force.* New York, NY: Del Rey.

Notes

1. *Star Wars: Episode I The Phantom Menace* (1999 motion picture).
2. Kabat-Zinn (1990).
3. Hayes (2003); Hayes et al. (2006); Scarlet et al. (in press).
4. Hayes et al. (2012).
5. Roemer et al. (2009).
6. Hayes et al. (2006); Roemer et al. (2009).
7. Roemer et al. (2009).
8. Bormann et al. (2013).
9. Epel et al. (2013).
10. Davidson et al. (2003).
11. Carlson et al. (2015); Epel et al. (2013).
12. *Star Wars: Episode III Revenge of the Sith* (2005 motion picture).
13. Hayes (2003); Hayes et al. (2006); Hayes et al. (2012); Scarlet et al. (in press).
14. *Revenge of the Sith.*
15. *The Empire Strikes Back.*
16. *A New Hope.*
17. *A New Hope.*
18. Hayes et al. (2006); Kabat-Zinn (1990).
19. Epel et al. (2013).
20. Killingworth & Gilbert (2010).
21. *Star Wars: Episode V The Empire Strikes Back* (1980 motion picture).

22. Chow & Tsang (2007).
23. Kjaer et al. (2002).
24. Carlson et al. (2015); Epel et al. (2013).
25. *Star Wars: Episode IV A New Hope* (1977/1981 motion picture).
26. *Star Wars: Episode VI Return of the Jedi* (1983 motion picture).
27. *Revenge of the Sith.*
28. Hanh (1999).
29. Hayes (2003).
30. Hayes et al. (2006).
31. Hayes et al. (2006).
32. Litvin et al. (2012).
33. Forman et al. (2007).
34. Twohig (2009).
35. Luoma & Villatte (2012).
36. *Star Wars: Episode II Attack of the Clones* (2002 motion picture).
37. *Revenge of the Sith.*
38. Hayes et al. (2012); Scarlet et al. (in press).
39. Gilbert (2005).
40. Kearney et al. (2013).
41. LucasArts (2006).
42. *Revenge of the Sith.*
43. Stover (2005).

3

From Phantom Menace to Phantom Limbs: Speculations about Amputations, Neuroprosthetics, and Darth Vader's Brain

E. PAUL ZEHR

"And that mechanical arm—revolting. A gentleman
would have learned to fight one-handed."
—Count Dooku[1]

> "At some point in every person's life you
> will need an assisted medical device....The
> prosthetic generation is all around us."
> —American athlete Aimee Mullins[2]

Against a hellish backdrop replete with lava flows on the
bleak planet Coruscant, Anakin suffers defeat at the hands
of Obi-Wan Kenobi. This defeat includes dismemberment in
the form of lightsaber amputation of both of Anakin's legs above
the knee and his left arm below the elbow. The man soon to be
known as Darth Vader, though surely a Lord of the Sith and a

master of the dark side of the Force, still has a human flesh-and-blood body and brain. What responses would be occurring in that brain during this trauma? Next, Anakin Skywalker's flesh is subjected to surgeries in which three advanced cybernetic neuroprosthetics are attached, giving rise to the features that forever mark him as the icon of evil—Darth Vader. What beneficial and pathological changes in physiological function probably have occurred inside the brain of Darth Vader? Examining the science of this Sith Lord means going back to appreciate the development of his body from infancy.

Even before birth, while baby Anakin develops inside his mother, Shmi, on Tatooine, sensations arising from his developing arm and leg movements are busy providing "calibrations" for his brain. Throughout life, this process of calibration continues and is shaped by one's experiences, resulting in a loose form of "mapping" of brain cells (*neurons*) in the parts of the brain that sense one's body parts (*somatosensory cortex*) and house the neurons that control muscles (*motor cortex*). In Darth Vader these body maps contribute to his sense of himself and his body "image"—brooding, dark, and threatening as it is.

While he is growing up on Tatooine, changes in Anakin's brain refine these sensory and motor maps as a result of all his activities and experiences, including pod racing. After Anakin's battle with Obi-Wan in *Episode III: Revenge of the Sith*,[3] amputation of those three limbs probably causes an immediate cascade of changes throughout his body, with dramatic effects on his brain. This chapter focuses on what this could do to Darth Vader's brain and body.

What Would Limb Amputation Do to Darth Vader's Brain?

Limb amputation causes large and powerful changes in the sensory and motor maps in the human body. We can speculate that

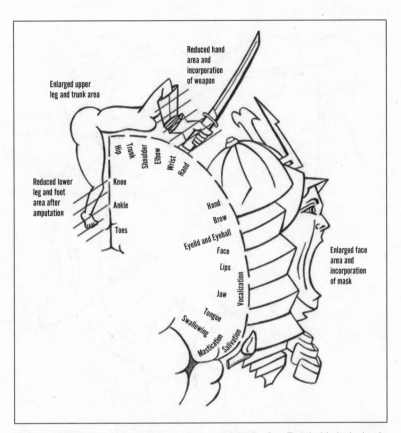

Figure 1: Cortical body map as shown originally for Darth Vader's brain before injury (inspired by Pennfield and Rasmussen[4]).The map is distorted because the size of the body part on the map represents the number of neurons devoted to that part, not the physical size of the part itself. The map shown here indicates the relative number of neurons devoted to that area of Darth Vader's brain before his defeat and limb amputations. Note how close the hand and the face areas are to each other, with the thumb coming just up against the forehead. *Image courtesy of Chelsea Kaupp.*

the same thing holds true even for the brain of a Sith Lord such as Darth Vader. A brain map assessed before his injuries probably would look like the one shown in Figure 1. Amputation reduces sensory and motor traffic for the limbs that are lost. This leads to emptying of the territory in the maps, which is then taken over by brain cells from other nearby regions. Regions that suddenly have useless inputs from and outputs to missing body parts are

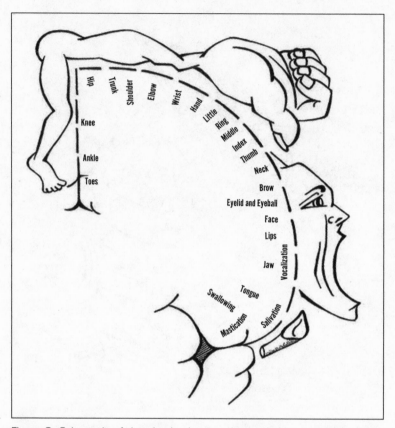

Figure 2: Schematic of the plastic changes that probably occurred in Darth Vader's somatosensory cortex after he lost three limbs in his lightsaber battle with Obi-Wan Kenobi. The expansion of brain regions resulting from the use of Vader's tools (weapon and helmet) and the regions of phantom limbs are shown. *Image provided by Chelsea Kaupp.*

repurposed. This allows a functional reorganization of the brain that includes taking up functions and territories from body parts (such as the face) that are nearby within the map. When a part of the body (such as Luke's hand) is lost as a result of amputation, the neurons in the brain devoted to that part of the body basically weaken. Other parts of the brain then make different and stronger connections and take over the part of the brain that used to be devoted to the amputated limb.

Losing those three limbs to the deft cuts of Obi-Wan Kenobi's lightsaber is the most traumatic thing that ever happens to Anakin Skywalker's body. Sensory inputs present since his life began are suddenly gone, and muscles that used to be activated easily by his nervous system no longer exist. Because the neurons in the brain are still intact and waiting to send and receive information and signals, the absence of his body parts creates a disparity between what these sensory and motor systems expect and what actually happens (see Figure 2).

Bizarre issues probably arise in Darth Vader's body because nervous systems aren't very good at forgetting about disappearing body parts. In Anakin's somatosensory cortex, connections between neurons and receptors on the now amputated index finger of his left hand are suddenly gone. Those neurons in the somatosensory cortex still exist, though, and are anticipating information from his body.

When that input disappears and fails to reappear, an "expansion" of the maps probably occurs. Areas near the now disconnected brain regions essentially connect, take over, and make use of the neurons in the old area that contains neurons for the amputated finger. This will lead to "miswiring" of the connections from the old territory to the new territory on the maps. Touching Darth Vader's face (if you dare and before you die) gives him sensations of his fingers in the area where his left hand used to be but that now connects to his cheek.

This *neuroplastic renovation*—the pruning of some and the expansion of other connections between neurons—within Darth Vader's brain occurs in both sensory and motor areas and represents his body's attempt to accommodate the needs of his nervous system. Often, though, very much darker adaptations can arise that affect the sensory maps and sensory perception. Enter the phantom limb and phantom pain syndromes.[5]

These syndromes arise when the cortical representations for the amputated limb do not recede and are functionally remapped by other areas. Instead, there remains a persistent sensation that the limb exists (*phantom limb*), and it is possible that the absent limb feels intense pain (*phantom pain*). In phantom limb syndromes, people can have the very realistic sensation that the limb exists and is still there. Itching, tingling, and perceived weight in the limb are all sensed.

With phantom pain, Darth Vader will feel painful sensations coming from his legs and left arm. Even though these limbs no longer exist as part of his body, his brain continues to keep a representation of them. In addition to this being a very troubling thing to experience and probably contributing to his often foul mood and hair-trigger temper, it is also difficult to treat in the Death Star sick bay. The most effective treatment Vader probably would be advised to take would be to trick his brain into thinking his missing body parts continue to exist by providing false visual information.[6]

In light of the traumatic nature of Darth Vader's amputations and the fact that the prosthetic surgeries apparently are performed without anesthetic (thereby increasing the trauma), he probably experiences phantom limb pain. A long time ago, in a galaxy far away, Imperial physicians use a split mirror setup to help Darth Vader. For issues with his left arm, a split mirror allows him to see the other (intact) side of his body on the mirror side (the one with the amputation). Careful study by the physicians of his movements during different tasks with the intact limb while looking in the mirror would allow Darth Vader to experience the perception that his amputated hand is actually moving and feeling sensation. Over time, his phantom limb sensations slowly abate or disappear altogether because Vader's brain, like all human brains, puts the most emphasis on vision. The only way to resolve the illusion is for his brain to conclude that there is a real hand there and that it isn't in pain. Darth Vader's extensive phantom limb and phantom pain syndromes are probably worse than most others would be because of his talented and adaptable brain. All his Jedi training has primed his nervous system to adapt quickly even if the change is, in fact, a maladaptation.

Darth Vader's Reach Extends Well Beyond His Steely Grasp

Going back to the time when he begins Jedi training, Anakin's sensorimotor maps experience profound changes. Tool use—a lightsaber is definitely a tool—significantly alters these brain maps. We humans use tools only when we need them, but we always need our bodies. Tools, even those he might use a lot, such as a lightsaber, aren't literally part of Anakin's body and aren't with him all the time. At least not physically.

A representation of Vader's lightsaber probably remains with him in his brain, though. Sensory maps of human bodies in human brains can be reshaped to include parts of the way we use tools. All that Jedi training changes the functional ability of Anakin's body, and this alters the organization of the neuronal maps in his brain.

The neuroplastic processes that occur in Darth Vader's brain when he practices using the lightsaber and the Force probably are heavily influenced by the physical sensations of moving the tools and the visual input that he gets from seeing himself in action. Even the acts of manipulating objects by using the Force generate a percept of functional "reach" beyond his body.

Back on Earth, scientists working in the complete absence of any input from the light side or dark side of the Force (although how would we know?) confirmed brain plasticity from tool use. They used a clever but simple study that relates to sensorimotor remapping by lightsaber training.[7] People

The Real Reason Luke Wins:
Darth Vader Needs to Feel the Force

"Prosthetics offer sensation and do everything flesh can. They're ideal substitutes in every way, except for requiring maintenance."
—Jedi Knight Valin Horn[8]

If he is going to function at the level of a true Sith Lord, Darth Vader needs the highest-quality control of his neuro-prosthetic limbs. Sensory feedback is a natural and critical part of producing movement. Sensory feedback also increases learning in brain-machine interfaces and in neuro-prosthetics. Fully incorporating a neuroprosthetic into the brain requires artificial sensors in the devices that can be relayed back into the brain. Back on Earth, "sensory sleeves" placed over a monkey's arm helped improve his ability to move a computer cursor by using brain activity.[9] Through the use of Vader's state-of-the-art prosthetics during his post-surgical rehabilitation, visual and somatosensory feedback together probably are employed to optimize his learning.

Key to this are electrodes for recording motor commands in Darth Vader's brain but also electrodes that send sensory information directly into the brain by stimulating the sensory cortex during accurate movements. This provides patterns of electrical stimulation to his brain that mimic sensory signals in movement with an intact body. His brain gets the kind of sensory feedback it would get if the movements were made by his real limbs.

practiced using a long handheld "grabber" like those used to clean up trash from parks, streets, and Death Star corridors without the user having to bend over. After using the grabber to pick up and move things around, the participants thought their arms were actually longer! From a functional perspective, within the brain, their arms really were longer since they could reach farther with the grabbers. Practice using the grabbers even led to changes in arm movements performed

But all of this works only up to a point, and there's an implication of all these brain maps for Vader's use of the Force. Proper application of the Force (whether on the light side or the dark side) seems to require some coincident use of the body. Certain limb gestures and body postures help with concentration when one is conjuring the Force, whether it's Darth Vader, Luke Skywalker, or Yoda doing the conjuring. This suggests that changes in the intact function of the brain that result from traumatic body damage such as limb amputation probably affect the fidelity with which the Force can be wielded.

This means that Darth Vader, with his three amputated limbs and reshaped brain maps, has much more difficulty exerting fine control over his actions when using the Force. By accident, he probably kills more henchmen and rebel forces than he means to. This also weakens him when he is fighting his son Luke in *Return of the Jedi*.

Luke Skywalker has a limb amputation of his right forearm during his battle with Vader on Cloud City in *The Empire Strikes Back*. However, because Vader has three limbs amputated compared with Luke's one, he has more control issues. This is almost certainly a factor that contributes to Luke defeating—and amputating another limb from—Darth Vader.

later without the tool. This meant that some persistent and plastic brain adaptation was activated by using the grabber. A comparison with observations in nonhuman primates made it seem that the plasticity was due to changes in somatosensory maps of the body in the brain as a result of using the tool.[10] Tools—whether grabbers, hockey sticks, martial arts weapons, or lightsabers—give people abilities that extend beyond those abilities that are normally part of the body.

These changes in functional ability in the use of tools cause neuroplastic adaptations in the brain, but the strength and duration of such plasticity is not completely known. Could the changes become durable enough to become real memories for a new representation or map for lightsaber fighting? Importantly for Darth Vader, does his brain take on the functional qualities—with many different properties from those of the original—of the three new "alien" prosthetic limbs?

The New Hope of Neuroprosthetics

Darth Vader has some pretty fancy prosthetics with robotic motors and interfaces to his nervous system to control them. With much practice and long-term use, Vader's brain stores *prosthetic motor memories*—long-term memories for movement—created by using his cybernetic left arm and legs. Here on Earth, primate research using neuroprosthetics controlled directly by the brain has led to strong changes in only a few weeks.[11]

On his right side, when Darth Vader decides to produce a deliberate movement—reaching out to grasp the throat of an adversary, for example, with or without the Force—complex neural commands related to motor planning and organization send signals to the motor output areas of his brain. These commands then travel down his spinal cord to the level appropriate for the muscles needed to produce the action: higher up for arm movements and lower down for leg movements.

Once at the appropriate spinal cord level, the neurons activate the muscles that are needed. This chain of events, though very rapid, takes time even in a Sith Lord. When it comes to the brain, spinal cord, and peripheral nervous system, sensory and motor signals can move around as rapidly as 180 to 220 miles per hour. Vader's nervous system integrates all these signals on a millisecond time scale, producing changes in tens and hundreds of milliseconds, and Vader consciously perceives them over seconds.

After that surgical intervention on Coruscant, Darth Vader would need practice to control his neuroprosthetics by using the commands from his brain that are relayed and detected as electrical activity in his muscles. To use his new prosthetic limbs effectively, Darth Vader's nervous system must control his limbs directly by using brain-machine interface. Sith and machine merge to truly be one, but this requires surgical implanting of multiunit electrode arrays into the brain and the spinal cord of Darth Vader.

An illusion known as the "rubber hand" shows the ability brains have for incorporating foreign parts into body maps and perceptions.[12] This illusion starts by hiding one arm behind a blinding screen and placing a life-sized rubber arm where the arm normally would be seen. Then the participant is asked to focus his or her vision on this "alien limb." For about ten minutes, experimenters then simultaneously brush the alien hand (fully in view) and the real hand (hidden out of view behind the screen). Then they brush only the rubber hand.

After the conditioning period in which both the alien hand and the real hand are brushed simultaneously, seeing the alien limb get brushed produces the sensation of touch on the real hand! This rubber hand illusion works in amputees,[13] too, and also would work on Darth Vader. This would be great news for Darth Vader—he learns to use his neuroprosthetics much as if they were his original limbs—but maybe doesn't turn out to be such great news for the rest of the galaxy.

References

Allston, A. (2010). *Outcast (Star Wars: Fate of the Jedi)*. New York, NY: Del Rey.

Botvinick, M., & Cohen, J. (1998). Rubber hands "feel" touch that eyes see. *Nature, 391*, 756–760.

Cardinali, L., Frassinetti, F., Brozzoli, C., Roy, A. C., Urquizar, C., & Farnè A (2009). Tool-use induces morphological updating of the body schema. *Current Biology, 19*(12), R478–479.

Ehrsson, H. H., Rosén, B., Stockselius, A., Ragnö, C., Köhler, P., & Lundborg, G. (2008). Upper limb amputees can be induced to experience a rubber hand as their own. *Brain, 131*, 3443–3452.

Ganguly, K., & Carmena, J. M. (2009). Emergence of a stable cortical map for neuroprosthetic control. *PLoS Biology, 7*(7), e1000153.

Gentleman, A. (2012, August 31). *US Paralympic coverage disappointing, says chef de mission*. The Guardian: http://www.theguardian.com/sport/2012/aug/31/us-paralympics-tv-coverage-disappointing.

Lewis, J. W. (2006). Cortical networks related to human use of tools. *The Neuroscientist, 12*(3), 211–231.

Penfield, W., & Rasmussen, T. (1950). *The cerebral cortex of man: A clinical study of localization of function*. New York, NY: Macmillan.

Ramachandran, V. S., & Altschuler, E. L. (2009). The use of visual feedback, in particular mirror visual feedback, in restoring brain function. *Brain, 132*, 1693–1710.

Ramachandran, V. S., & Hirstein, W. (1998). The perception of phantom limbs: The D.O. Hebb lecture. *Brain, 121*, 1603–1630.

Stover, M. (2005). *Star Wars Episode III: Revenge of the Sith*. New York: Del Rey.

Suminski, A. J., Tkach, D. C., Fagg, A. H., & Hatsopoulos, N. G. (2010). Incorporating feedback from multiple sensory modalities enhances brain-machine interface control. *Journal of Neuroscience, 30*(50), 16777–16787.

Notes

1. Stover (2005).
2. Gentleman (2012).
3. *Star Wars: Episode III Revenge of the Sith* (2005 motion picture).
4. Penfield & Rasmussen (1950).
5. Ramachandran & Hirstein (1998).
6. Ramachandran & Altschuler (2009).
7. Cardinali et al. (2009).
8. Allston (2010).
9. Suminski et al. (2010).
10. Lewis (2006).
11. Ganguly & Carmena (2009).
12. Botvinick & Cohen (1998).
13. Ehrsson et al. (2008).

A Discussion with Darth Maul: Sam Witwer Interview on the Antithesis of Self-Actualization

JENNA BUSCH AND TRAVIS LANGLEY

"What a man can be, he must be. This need
we may call self-actualization."
—founder of humanistic psychology Abraham Maslow[1]

The Jedi and the Sith, attuned as they are to the Force that binds every living thing in the Star Wars stories, all strive to become something more than they already are. Yet how they individually pursue enlightenment, power, or the greater good for all people varies widely. Even though the Jedi Order's *communal value system* prioritizes selfless devotion to all life, not all Jedi have incorporated the Jedi values into their own *personal value system*.[2] They can keep working and growing. They may spend their whole lives on the journey and make the best of it along the way. They may fail. Star Wars stories often depict the Jedi's journey as an extreme, seemingly black-and-white allegory of the struggle any person might undergo while making progress as a human being.

Self-Absorption versus Self-Actualization

Those who adhere to the selfless way of the Jedi could conceivably reach their potential through *self-actualization*, turning possibilities into realities. What progress might the *self-absorbed* Sith make?

Actualizing Potential: Yearning to be Greater

Although humanistic psychologist Abraham Maslow popularized *self-actualization* as the peak of personality growth,[3] neurologist and psychiatrist Kurt Goldstein was the theorist who first proposed the concept.[4] Goldstein believed that an innate *actualizing potential* motivated humans and other organisms to actualize as much as possible. In his view, that innate drive would be what makes Anakin Skywalker and, later, his son Luke each yearn to do so much more in life than they can on Tattooine.

Building on Goldstein's ideas about self-actualization and the earlier assertion by individual psychology founder Alfred Adler that people naturally strive to become greater,[5] Abraham Maslow developed his own theory of motivation. Maslow argued that deficiencies in more basic physical and psychological needs keep people from becoming self-actualized. Maslow said that people who cannot meet basic physiological and safety needs will have great difficulty progressing through a *hierarchy of needs* to feel love and belongingness, nurture self-esteem, and fulfill their potential.[6] Anyone driven by *deficiency needs*, dwelling on the things they do not have (e.g., Palpatine lusting for greater power) or worry about losing whatever they do have (e.g.,

Anakin obsessing over dreams about losing Padmé), whether real or imagined, will experience limited personal growth compared to those who feel motivated instead to appreciate and enhance the world that exists for everyone (*being needs*, a.k.a. *growth needs*). A person motivated mainly by deficiency (*D-motivation*) would be more possessive, envious, or jealous, whereas someone motivated for the betterment of society as a whole (*B-motivation*) would be more generous, appreciative, and trusting.[7]

Sith's Progress: Motivation among the Self-Absorbed

Darth Maul, with his red-and-black face and his double-bladed lightsaber, is one of the most visually recognizable characters in the Star Wars universe. Although Ray Park first brought Darth Maul to life when he played the role in *Star Wars: Episode I The Phantom Menace*, actor Sam Witmer has portrayed this character many more times in the animated series *Star Wars: The Clone Wars*. In addition to his many live-action roles, including the vampire Aidan in the American version of *Being Human* and the supervillain Doomsday on *Smallville*, Witwer has also voiced characters in video games and cartoons. His many Star Wars roles include several villains on the dark side: Emperor Palpatine,[8] Darth Vader's secret apprentice Starkiller,[9] and the mysterious Darth Maul.[10]

Witwer talked to us about Darth Maul's progression through the series, his self-obsession, and why the Sith are so driven.

> **Busch:** Sam, can you talk to us a bit about Darth Maul's progression from his first appearance in the prequels to where he goes later?
>
> **Witwer:** In the film [*Star Wars: Episode I The Phantom Menace*], he's a well-trained apprentice who had all this potential. He was anxious. He was confident.

He was in control and eager to prove himself to
his master. Things didn't really go as well as he'd
hoped. He got cut in half and sent down a bottom-
less pit and that's not really good for anyone. But
he survived. He survived because of the absolute
self-obsession that fuels the Sith. They don't necessarily believe in any sort of afterlife that is bigger
than them, so they kind of keep themselves around
at all costs. Look at Darth Vader, the Emperor—there
are a lot of examples of this. So he's this guy who
really had potential and then really blew it.

He survived and started trying to put his life back
together and put himself back together, but the
problem was that he couldn't get over what had
happened to him. He couldn't take responsibility for
his part in it. All he wanted to do was shame, embar-
rass, and destroy the person who cut him in half. He
certainly wasn't smart enough to realize that his own
master was far more responsible for what happened
to him, and that *he* was more responsible for what
happened to him than Obi-Wan Kenobi. He wasn't
that self-reflective. He needed that revenge and,
eventually, got it. But it certainly didn't make him
feel better. He painted a huge target on his back and
he put himself right back into the place he began
with the Emperor.

Progress toward self-actualization, as Maslow saw it, requires
self-reflection. Narcissistic individuals may think a lot of themselves without thinking carefully about themselves. Maslow felt
that people who are struggling daily to survive, deprived of
basic physical needs, might have trouble feeling good enough
about themselves (or have the time) to grow arrogant. Those

who do not have to worry about such things might begin to focus on needs higher up the hierarchy: love and belonging-ness, self-esteem, and eventually self-actualization. However, with basic needs met, a person might grow too conceited to advance far.[11]

> **Busch:** What do you think is Darth Maul's driving force? What keeps him going despite the odds?
>
> **Witwer:** His level of self-obsession requires a lot of someone to prove themselves, to themselves. It's the antithesis of being self-actualized, happy with where you are and content. There is always a need to prove yourself to others and a real insecurity, a hole that can never be filled.

The "antithesis of being self-actualized" would thwart one's potential and leave possibilities unfulfilled. Self-absorbed Maul cannot step outside himself. He cannot achieve the self-transcendence necessary to self-actualize.[12] If Darth Maul cannot feel love or develop healthy self-esteem, he will never be able to progress upward through Maslow's hierarchy of needs. Although the Jedi may limit themselves by discouraging their knights from falling in love with any specific individual, they do value feeling love toward all life. They also develop a strong sense of belong-ingness by building up an entire Jedi Order to support one another. Sith, on the other hand, restrict themselves to master and apprentice. Even that relationship is tenuous at best because many SithMasters and apprentices betray each other. While Darth Maul might feel more secure with his master than Darth Sidious deserves, Maul's insecurities and self-absorption never-theless keep him from developing the self-esteem necessary to achieve self-actualization.

Bias on the Light Side?

Is there Jedi bias? Among themselves, Jedi recognize the variety of characteristics shown by their fellow Jedi, demonstrating *ingroup differentiation*. Some of them make generalizations about Sith as if they think Sith Lords are all similar to each other (*outgroup homogeneity*). Such biases, however, can limit the growth of any Jedi who adhere to those narrow perspectives. According to Maslow, self-actualizers view their world, other people, and even themselves, with objectivity and without preconceptions.[13]

Busch: A lot of actors say they admire their characters, even the bad ones. Do you admire anything in Darth Maul?

Witwer: No, no. He's a little bit of a coward. He needs to let go of a lot of stuff if he ever hopes to move beyond where he is now. I don't think that will necessarily happen for him. I think he's too far gone. He's not a role model for kids and we needed to make a hard-core villain for that show. He's not just a warrior, he's a murderer. It's not a great thing to aspire to!

The whole thing with Star Wars, with the blue Force ghosts that keep showing up, the meaning behind that as I understand it is who's lived a life worth remembering. As we discovered through *The Clone Wars*, the Sith don't have the ability to live beyond death. What they get in life is only what they acquire from *this* life.

The Jedi are selfless. They try to inspire others and do great deeds and help other people and teach. That is the only path to immortality that is available to us. To live a life worth remembering. As I understand it, that's one of the main themes of Star Wars.

Based on his research on emotionally healthy people, Maslow concluded that self-actualizers shared characteristics that we might say Jedi value more than Sith: an unbiased view of reality, acceptance of themselves and others, simplicity, social interest, self-reliance for their own needs, focus on problems outside themselves, profound personal relations, creativity, and great tolerance. When they "try to inspire others," they do so for the sake of those others, not for their own aggrandizement.[14]

Power Betrays Promise

Sith Lords have the potential to transcend and become more, but selfishness and preoccupation with deficiencies keep them from growing beyond their existing internal achievements to become greater people. Although most Jedi have not yet achieved self-actualization, many are self-actualizing. More so than any Sith, the Jedi progress and grow in ways that Maslow considered ideal.

References

Adler, A. (1908/1959). *Understanding human nature.* New York, NY: Fawcett.

Adler, A. (1924). *The practice and theory of individual psychology.* London, UK: K. Paul, Trench, Trubner & Company.

Goldstein, K. (1939/1995). *The organism: A holistic approach to biology derived from pathological data in man.* New York, NY: Zone.

Koltko-Rivera (2006). Rediscovering the later version of Maslow's hierarchy of needs: Self-transcendence and opportunities for theory, research, and unification. *Review of General Psychology, 10*(4), 302–3317.

Kornhauser, R. R. (1978). *Social sources of delinquency.* Chicago, IL: University of Chicago Press.

Maslow, A. (1943). A theory of human motivation. *Psychological Review, 50*(4), 370–396.

Maslow, A. (1954). *Motivation and personality.* New York, NY: Harper.

Maslow, A. (1966). *The psychology of science: A reconnaissance.* New York, NY: Harper & Row.

Maslow, A. (1970). Motivation and personality (2nd ed.). New York, NY: Harper & Row.

Maslow, A. (1971). The farther reaches of human nature. New York, NY: Viking.

Millon, T., Davis, R., Millon, C., Escovar, L., & Meagher, S. (2004). Personality disorders in modern life. New York, NY: Wiley.

Schacter, D. L., Gilbert, D. T., & Wegner, D. M. (2011). Human needs and self-actualization. Psychology (2nd ed.). New York, NY: Worth.

Notes

1. Maslow (1943), p. 382.
2. Kornhauser (1978).
3. Maslow (1943).
4. Goldstein (1939/1995).
5. Adler (1908/1959; 1924).
6. Maslow (1954; 1966).
7. Schacter et al. (2011).
8. *Star Wars: The Force Unleashed* (2008 video game); *Star Wars: The Force Unleashed II* (2010 video game); *Kinect Star Wars* (2012 video game); *Lego Star Wars: The Empire Strikes Out* (2012 television movie).
9. *The Force Unleashed; The Force Unleashed II.*
10. *Star Wars: The Clone Wars* (2011–2013 television series); *Lego Star Wars: The Empire Strikes Out.*
11. Millon et al. (2004).
12. Kolkto-Rivera (2006).
13. Maslow (1971).
14. Maslow (1970).

An OCEAN Far Away

I. Openness versus Closedness

TRAVIS LANGLEY

Every individual personality has more characteristics than the visible sky has stars. These characteristics, or *personality traits*, are interrelated. They overlap and influence each other. Some form constellations that look related, even though they really are not; they're *illusory correlations*. Others, though, do gravitate together to form their own clusters.

A *trait cluster* is a group of traits that tend to go together, better known as *personality factors* because of how they are identified through a process of factor analysis. Many personality psychologists have looked for the smallest number of factors that sum up most of personality while being fairly distinct from each other. Popular estimates of that number range from two[1] or three[2] (which left out too many traits to offer a comprehensive understanding of any person) to sixteen[3] (which turned out to be too many when groups of those factors were correlated with each other and therefore belonged together in a smaller set of bigger clusters). The most consistently measured number has been five, the so-called "Big Five" personality factors.[4] While other theorists assign these factors different names, depending on how they interpret them, these have become popularly known by the acronym OCEAN: openness, conscientiousness, extraversion, agreeableness, neuroticism.[5]

Openness to Experience

Luke Skywalker stands on the sand, gazing out at the binary sunset of Tatooine's twin suns.[6] Curious about the universe, eager to explore, and aching for more than home could ever offer, Luke wonders what experiences might await him elsewhere and all that he might be missing. He's curious. He's open to new experience.

Openness involves an appreciation of things others might consider impractical and a readiness for new and unusual experiences. The traits that make up this factor tend to be more esoteric than those in the other factors, less based on *overt behavior* (observable actions) and more on *covert behavior* (the things we do that others cannot directly observe—thoughts, feelings, attitudes, beliefs). The highly open individual has a greater appreciation for subjective or abstract reality.[7]

Examples of Openness Traits

Abstract Thinking
Acceptance of Change
Active Imagination
Aesthetics
Appreciation of Culture
Appreciation of Intelligence
Challenging Norms
Curiosity
Desire for Adventure
Fantasy
Independent Thinking
Ingenuity
Intellectual Flexibility

Novelty
Open-mindedness
Originality
Preference for Variety
Rich Vocabulary
Symbolic Thinking
Valuing Emotions
Unconventional Beliefs

Luke may not show every trait in this list. For example, we know little about his aesthetic side; that is, how he feels about music, art, and poetry. A person can be generally high in a factor without showing every single trait, just as the Big Dipper constellation still forms a dipper shape even when clouds obscure a few of its stars. Luke has enough practicality in him that he does not immediately rush off with Ben Kenobi. Nevertheless, after Luke tells Ben that he cannot get involved because he has work to do on the farm, Obi-Wan knows Luke well enough to see where the young man's heart really lies. "That's your uncle talking," Ben says.[8] Greater spirituality correlates with greater openness, which is consistent with Luke's receptivity to the ways of the Force, whereas religious fundamentalism correlates with lower openness.[9]

Uncle Owen Lars demonstrates characteristics consistent with low openness, a.k.a. high *closedness*. Long before Owen has good reason to fear that his nephew might one day follow in Luke's father's dark footsteps, he is already a no-nonsense realist, described by his stepmother Shmi as "pragmatic and certain of his ways, grateful for simple joys and for his life on the moisture farm."[10] Features of closedness include concrete thinking, conventional interests, and shallowness. Preferring routine, the person who is closed to experience generally dislikes change, uncertainty, and ambiguity. This individual is more likely to be shallow, unimaginative, conforming, prone to anti-intellectual attitudes, and disdainful toward aesthetics.

Owen is no coward. He helps organize a group of over thirty other local settlers to try to rescue his stepmother from Tusken Raiders.[11] The fact that their mission fails and only four of them make it back alive, however, may contribute to his later aversion to adventure. While Owen and Beru love his nephew like their own child and raise him as best they can, the boy's desire for such adventure gives them, especially Owen, more than one reason for concern.

References

Cattell, R. B. (1946). *The description and measurement of personality*. New York, NY: World Book.

Cattell, R. B., Cattell, A. K., & Cattell, H. E. P. (1993). *16PF questionnaire* (5th ed.). Champaign, IL: Institute for Personality and Ability Testing.

Denning, T. (2003). *Tatooine ghost (Star Wars)*. New York, NY: LucasBooks, Random House.

Eysenck, H. J. (1947). *Dimensions of personality*. London, UK: Routledge & Kegan Paul.

Eysenck, H. J., & Eysenck, S. B. G. (1976). *Psychoticism as a dimension of personality*. London, UK: Hodder and Stoughton.

Goldberg, L. R. (1981). Language and individual differences: The search for universals in personality lexicons. In L. Wheeler (Ed.) *Review of Personality and Social Psychology* (Vol. 1, pp. 141–165). Beverly Hill, CA: Sage.

McCrae, R. R., & Costa, P. T. (1985). Updating Norman's "adequate taxonomy": Intelligence and personality dimensions in natural language and in questionnaires. *Journal of Personality and Social Psychology, 49*, 710–721.

McCrae, R. R., & Costa, P. T. (1987). Validation of the five-factor model of personality across instruments and observers. *Journal of Personality and Social Psychology, 52*(1), 81–90.

McCrae, R. R. & Costa, P. T. (1990). *Personality in adulthood*. New York, NY: Guilford.

McCrae, R. R., & John, O. P. (1992). An introduction to the Five-Factor Model and its applications. *Journal of Personality, 60*(2), 175–215.

Norman, W. T. (1963). Toward an adequate taxonomy of personality attributes: Replicated factor structure in peer nomination personality ratings. *Journal of Abnormal and Social Psychology, 66*(6), 574–583.

Saraglou, V. (2002). Religion and the five factors of personality: A meta-analytic review. *Personality and Individual Differences, 32*(1), 15–25.

Tupes, E. C., & Christal, R. E. (1961). Recurrent personality factors based on trait ratings. *USAF ASD Technical Report No. 61-97*. Lackland Airforce Base, TX: U.S. Air Force.

Notes

1. Eysenck (1947).
2. Eysenck & Eysenck (1976).
3. Cattell (1946); Cattell et al. (1993).
4. Goldberg (1981); Norman (1963); Tupes & Christal (1961).
5. McCrae & Costa (1985; 1987; 1990).
6. *Star Wars: Episode I A New Hope* (1977/1981 motion picture).
7. McCrae & John (1992).
8. *A New Hope.*
9. Saraglou (2002).
10. Denning (2003), p. 277.
11. *Star Wars: Episode II Attack of the Clones* (2002 motion picture).

2 »

Kinds

"We don't serve their kind here," says the cantina bartender, pointing to the droids while surrounded by beings of many different species from many different worlds. In the diverse universe of Star Wars, varied life-forms interact and work together as equals. Even though characters often seem oblivious to species, biases creep in. Some who seem wise in many ways make casual generalizations about Jawas, Tuskens, and Wookiees. Societies depicted are egalitarian in certain lights, and yet sexism also looms large throughout the stories. Biological beings often discriminate against sentient, mechanical beings. Audiences alert to these biases may also notice that characters contradict their groups' stereotypes all the time.

Everyone's an alien somewhere.

» 5 »

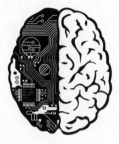

Droids, Minds, and Why We Care

JIM DAVIES

"Well, if droids could think, there'd be none of us here,
would there?"
—Obi-Wan Kenobi[1]

"The key issue as to whether or not a non-biological
entity deserves rights really comes down to whether
or not it's conscious. Does it have feelings?"
—futurist Ray Kurzweil[2]

Droids are the artificial intelligences (AIs) of the Star Wars universe. They are all embodied as robots, from the tiny mouse droids of the Death Star to the gigantic space-faring vulture droids of the Separatist Army. They can move and talk, but what do we know about their mental states? Are they intelligent? Are they conscious?

Artificial Brains Can be Pretty Smart

In Star Wars, it seems clear that no matter what the cognitive task, some droids can do it. There are medical droids who diagnose, protocol droids who translate, and battle droids who fight. All can think and make decisions and even strategize and manipulate, like the T-Series tactical droids from *Star Wars: The Clone Wars*, who can be formidable strategic commanders.

In spite of the fact that droids seem to be able to do just about any intelligent task, Obi-Wan Kenobi—just like many people on Earth—denies that machines can think at all.[3] Kenobi also shows very little compassion for the droids around him, in contrast to Anakin and Luke. Although most droids seem to be able to speak, many speak "binary," the whistling and beeping language of R2-D2. Kenobi doesn't appear to understand it. Anakin and Luke, on the other hand, can understand binary and also seem to care about droids' well-being much more. Is this a coincidence? Likely not. Auditory cues may be even more important than visual ones for judgments of intelligence in other people. In particular, the use of more words, less halting speech, and more easily understood speech makes someone appear more intelligent.[4] Therefore, it's easy to think people are stupid if you can't understand what they are saying. The same goes for machines.

From a young age, Obi-Wan has trained to be been in tune with the Force, which only connects with living things; perhaps droids just aren't on his radar. By contrast, Anakin and Luke have a great deal of exposure to droids before being introduced to the Force. In our world, studies indicate that frequent exposure to a person or group can increase empathy.[5]

Equally important is the question of whether droids feel empathy for us.

Emotions in Organic and Artificial Systems

Beyond their intelligence, another important question to ask of droids is whether or not they can feel emotions, suffering, and pain. In our culture, it's certainly easy to imagine something that thinks but has no emotion. In our everyday understanding of psychology, we typically think of reason and emotion as separate kinds of things. That's easy when we're contemplating emotions like sadness and joy, but it gets dicier when we look at borderline mental states. Is motivation an emotion? What about desire? Suspicion? Interest? Intuitions about the best course of action? Once we consider these kinds of mental states, we start to wonder about the feasibility of intelligence *without* emotion, which is why the famous AI scientist Marvin Minsky suggested, "The question is not whether machines can have any emotions, but whether machines can be intelligent without any emotions."[6]

The droids certainly *act* as though they have a wide range of feelings. C-3PO, especially, expresses happiness, sadness, and a tremendous amount of stress and worry. Even though we cannot understand R2-D2's language, the nature of the little droid's tones reflects the prosody of human speech, and we can easily infer emotion when R2 speaks.[7] Of course, there is a difference between actually feeling happiness and merely behaving as though one is happy. Only about 2 percent of people believe current robots have the capacity for feelings.[8] Unfortunately, cognitive scientists and psychologists do not have enough knowledge about how emotions work to judge whether a droid is *actually* feeling anything or merely acting like it. The same goes for consciousness.

Computer scientist Alan Turing suggested that asking whether machines could think was a troublesome question, because it depended so much on the definitions of "machine" and "think." Instead, he offered the Imitation Game, in which a computer chats with a person over a text-based chat interface and tries to imitate a human being. Cognitive scientists now call it the "Turing Test."[9] The good thing about the test is that it is very hard to pass (to fool a qualified human judge, anyway), meaning any machine that could pass it would certainly be impressive. The downside is that we're not sure what it would mean for a machine to pass it. Would it mean the machine was conscious? Although psychologists are learning more and more about the nature of consciousness, we may not be not learning the kinds of things that would help us understand whether droids—or any other artificial creatures, for that matter—have genuinely conscious experiences.

The problem is particularly important when it comes to pain and suffering.

Pain among the Inorganic

Can droids feel pain and suffering? In reality, the science is not definitive, but in Star Wars the answer appears to be yes. One hint appears in *Star Wars: Episode VI Return of the Jedi*, when a power droid is apparently being tortured by another droid in Jabba's palace.[10] When hot metal is lowered onto its feet, the power droid appears to squeal in pain. In *Star Wars: Episode IV A New Hope*, C-3PO bangs R2-D2 on the head, presumably as punishment. At other times, however, droids appear to feel no pain, such as when C-3PO's head is severed in *Star Wars: Episode II Attack of the Clones*.

Some people used to cut open live animals and marvel at how well they *imitated* the sensation of pain, when (according to those particular people) as beings without souls and rationality they could not actually feel any pain.[11] Most people believe that dogs and cats *can* feel pain, perhaps with the same certainty that they feel that robots *could never* feel pain. The point is that people's convictions as to whether or not an agent can feel any pain are culturally contingent. And, for most, assuming that a being cannot suffer means that one need not give that creature any consideration when it comes to how that being is treated.

If one is wrong, however, a great deal of suffering can be inflicted.

Computer Minds and Autonomous Action

Most droids are owned by people, and the owners are referred to as "masters," at least by C-3PO. Droids follow their masters' orders, most of the time. But it is left unclear how the ownership of droids is transferred, particularly in the minds of the droids themselves. For example, at the end of *Star Wars: Episode III Revenge of the Sith*, C-3PO and R2-D2 are given to Bail Organa. Why did R2-D2 suddenly stop serving Anakin, who was his loving master throughout Episodes II and III and the Clone Wars in between? When Jawas sell the captured droids to the Skywalkers, C-3PO announces that Luke is their new master. One might think that the droids would still be loyal to their previous master. Indeed, such loyalty is expressed by R2-D2, who tricks Luke into removing the restraining bolt so that the droid can search for Obi-Wan Kenobi.[12]

Some droids are masterless—the *ronin* of the droid world. The droid bounty hunters IG-88 and 4-LOM from *Star Wars: Episode V The Empire Strikes Back* are examples of these. An Expanded Universe story about IG-88 reveals that he is conscious and executes part of a plan to take over the galaxy in two ways.[13] First, IG-88 creates many droids and spreads them around the galaxy with a special code embedded in them so that when IG-88 commands it, the droids will kill all "biologicals."

This is reminiscent of Palpatine's infamous Order 66 implanted in the clones.[14] Second, IG-88 copies its vicious intelligence into the second Death Star, but the rebels destroy it before IG-88 uses it for its own desires.

The existence of these masterless droids suggests that droids (sometimes) have goals that are independent of their masters' goals. In trying to foment a droid revolution, IG-88 shows shame; amusement; feelings of superiority, annoyance, ambition; and aims of self-preservation and increasing power. Droids appear capable of intelligence, goals, emotions, and pain. And like Earth people, biological characters in Star Wars also care about droids.

How We Feel about Artificial Entities

In all the Star Wars movies, nobody cares as much about droids as Anakin, Luke, and Chewbacca. Anakin shows enormous care and loyalty to R2-D2.[15] A generation later, Luke expresses dismay at losing R2-D2 in the swamps of Dagobah right before Chewbacca desperately looks for C-3PO and puts him back together again.[16]

We understand this. It's very easy for us to anthropomorphize nonhuman things and feel compassion for them. A study showed people videos of a robot toy (the Pleo, which looks like a dinosaur) being "tortured." Not surprisingly, many people agreed that this video was disturbing, shocking, nerve-racking, repugnant, and depressing. And a Pleo toy is far less complex than a droid. Watching someone punch, strangle, and hit the Pleo's head on a table triggered deep psychological reactions in the participants that made them think of the toy as a living, feeling thing.[17]

Although it is a bit of an oversimplification, our minds have roughly two functioning parts—the old brain and the new brain.

The *old brain*, which tends to be at the back of the head and atop the spinal cord, largely runs the behaviors and responses we either evolved or have learned very well. It is fast. By contrast, the *new brain*, near the front of the head, thinks more slowly and deliberatively. This is why, when we watch a scary movie, we can only partially attenuate our fear by telling ourselves that "It's just a movie." Our old brain doesn't know that, and it reacts to the stimuli the same way it would if the events were actually happening in front of us.[18] We are literally of two minds about many things. This explains why we care about droids as characters.[19] We especially love R2-D2. At the end of *Star Wars: Episode III Revenge of the Sith*, Bail Organa orders C-3PO's memory wiped,* perhaps because he had witnessed the birth of Anakin and Padmé's children and knew that they had survived.

But why did he fail to erase R2-D2's memory? It could be that he didn't think R2-D2 could communicate anything important. It could also be because the audience might get upset by a violation of R2-D2. The audience thinks of droids, basically, as people. We attribute to them minds that can have experiences.[20] Audiences adored R2-D2 and would have been horrified to see the character's memory destroyed. R2-D2 is like Dorothy Gale's dog Toto in the novel *The Wonderful Wizard of Oz*[21]—a nonspeaking, lovable sidekick. One of the reasons the Star Wars stories are so compelling is that many of the creatures inhabiting that world—be they human, droid, or alien—are recognizable as *people* in how they act and think. However strange the aliens might look, they are always *psychologically* humanoid.

People tend to react to computers and software the same way they do to other people. Social psychology experiments replicated with computers showed that people responded to a spellchecker, for example, much as they did to an actual person.[22]

---

* R2-D2 makes a "chuckling" sound at this command (according to the subtitles), which seems pretty callous to me.

Why Our Moral Reasoning Allows
the Slaughter of a Robot Army

That said, we still tend to keep robots (and aliens) at some distance. As much as we personify them, a part of us holds back, knowing that they are not human. In the Clone Wars, the bulk of the Separatist Army is made up of droids.[23] Why?

Jedi and other good guys have to fight a war. Audiences might find it disturbing to watch Jedi slaughtering humans or other living aliens with the casual abandon we see in the Clone Wars. Although the battle droids exhibit some worry and fear, the audience never gets to know any of them. And when the Republic Army destroys enemy droids, the viewer's psychological response is one of joy or even laughter, not the horror of death. Killing enemy droids we don't care about is okay with us.

Making a character masked or mechanical effectively "dehumanizes" him or her. For example, when a person is standing on top of a building, considering suicide, crowds are more likely to bait the person when the person is harder to see as an individual human being—for example, when it is dark or when bystanders are far away.[24]

This is especially true for droids, who are all clearly machines, usually with no facial expressions. There appear to be no droids in the Star Wars universe who are indistinguishable from living creatures, unlike some androids in other franchises. This is in contrast to, for example, the replicants of *Blade Runner*[25] and the androids of the Alien franchise, in which human and android are visually indistinguishable from one another. When the Alien Queen tears the android Bishop in half, viewers emotionally react as if they were witnessing a human getting murdered.[26]

The Uncanny Valley

Masahiro Mori introduced a popular theory of the "uncanny valley."[27] It holds that as something looks more humanlike, we will like it more, with an exception—a valley in the graph where beings look realistic enough to trigger our person-detection but look just off enough to creep us out. Rocks don't interest us much and we like R2-D2, but characters in video games and many early computer-generated animated movies often look like walking corpses. The corpselike characters fall into that valley, the dip in the curve, so viewers like them less. Normal, healthy people at the top of the curve—these are the ones viewers like most of all.

Although the theory is popular, empirical evidence to support it has been spotty.[28] One study found that people liked toy robots and pictures of humanoids even more than they liked real people![29] Further studies show that realistic-looking robots are not liked less than real people, and that a robot moving realistically does not make it less likable.[30]

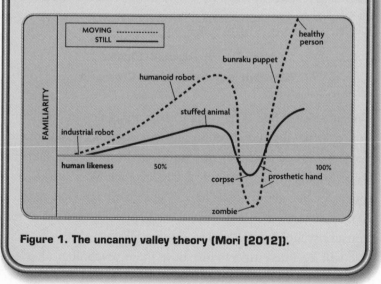

Figure 1. The uncanny valley theory (Mori [2012]).

Soldiers and Masks

Clone Troopers and Stormtroopers wear masks. This makes them look like droids,* dehumanizing them. Indeed, masks are known to have psychological effects. For instance, feeling more anonymous (either being in the dark or wearing sunglasses) makes people more aggressive, less generous, and more likely to cheat.[31] The anonymous Stormtroopers, like the droids in the Separatist Army, are psychologically easier to kill and easier to watch being killed.

This is likely due, in part, to the fact that we have trouble reading emotion and facial expression from faces that are even partially covered.[32] If we can't tell by looking at people that they are suffering, it's easy to miss that they are suffering. This goes for droids, too, which have few or no facial expressions. When machines *have* facial expressions, people respond to them emotionally, including extending feelings of empathy when the robot looks sad.[33]

We Care about Some Machines and Not Others

The creators of Star Wars faced a challenging design problem—how to make the audience like and care about some droids (and people) and see others as machines (or dehumanized soldiers). By manipulating psychological triggers, Star Wars affects how much we care about a character. If characters are alien, masked, or machines, we care about them less. When they exhibit a more human psychology, we tend to care more.

It will be interesting to see how these psychological effects play out in decades to come.

* In fact, when I watched *A New Hope* at age five, I thought the Stormtroopers *were* droids.

Phobias toward Mechanical Entities: Fear the Machines!

Why mistreat the machines? Few characters in Star Wars treat droids like fellow sentient entities. *Prejudice* (negative attitudes toward members of a group) and *discrimination* (negative actions toward members of a group)[34] rise for many reasons, one of which is fear. A *phobia* is a fear so extreme that it interferes with the phobic individual's ability to function.[35] A number of specific phobias could make characters biased toward droids.[36]

- Arithmophobia—fear of numbers. ("Never tell me the odds!"[37])
- Automatonophobia—fear of automatons or objects that represent human beings (e.g., toys, wax figures, mannequins, mechanical figures).
- Cyberphobia or Logizmomechanophobia—fear of computers.
- Electrophobia—fear of electricity.
- Hellenologophobia—fear of complex scientific terms.
- Gnosiophobia—fear of knowledge or information.
- Kinetophobia—fear of movement.
- Mechanophobia—fear of machines.
- Metallophobia—fear of metal.
- Prosophobia—fear of progress.
- Pupaphobia—fear of puppets.
- Robophobia—fear of robots or androids.
- Technophobia—fear of technology.

—T. L.

References

American Psychiatric Association (2013). *Diagnostic and statistical manual of mental disorders* (DSM-5) (5th ed.) Washington, DC: American Psychiatric Association.

Anderson, K.J. (1996). Therefore I am: The tale of IG-88. In K. J. Anderson (Ed.), *Tales of the bounty hunters*. New York, NY: Spectra.

Arras, K. O., & Cerqui, D. (2005). *Do we want to share our lives and bodies with robots? A 2000-people survey. Technical Report Nr. 0605V001.* Lausanne, Switzerland: Swiss Federal Institute of Technology, EPFL.

Barra-Chicote, R., Montero, J. M., Macias-Guarasa, J., D'Haro, L. F., Rubén, S. S., & de

Córdoba, R. (2006). Prosodic and segmental rubrics in emotion identification. In N. Thomas (Ed.), *2006 IEEE International Conference on Acoustics, Speech and Signal Processing, ICASSP 2006*. (pp. 1085–1088). Toulouse, France: IEEE.

Bartneck, C., Kanda, T., Ishiguro, H., & Hagita, N. (2007). Is the uncanny valley an uncanny cliff? In D. S. Kwon (Ed.), *The 16th IEEE International Symposium on Robot and Human Interactive Communication, 2007. RO-MAN 2007*, pp. 368–373.

Bartneck, C., Kanda, T., Ishiguro, H., & Nagita, N. (2009). My robotic doppelgänger: A critical look at the uncanny valley. In T. Matsumara (Ed.), *The 18th IEEE International Symposium on Robot and Human Interactive Communication, Japan, 2009* (pp. 269–276). Keju, Korea: IEEE.

Baum, F. L. (1900). *The Wonderful Wizard of Oz*. New York, NY: George M. Hill.

Borenstein, S. (2007, August 8). *Scientists struggle to define life*. USA Today: http://usatoday30.usatoday.com/tech/science/2007-08-19-life_N.htm.

Bourne, E. (2015). *The anxiety and phobia workbook* (6th ed., revised). Oakland, CA: New Harbinger.

Breazeal, C. (2003). Emotion and sociable humanoid robots. *International Journal of Human-Computer Studies, 59*(1), 119–155.

Brewer, M. B., & Brown, R. J. (1998). Intergroup relations. In D. T. Gilbert, S. T. Fiske, & G. Lindzey (Eds.), *The handbook of social psychology* (4th ed.). New York, NY: McGraw-Hill.

Burleigh, T. J., Schoenherr, J. R., & Lacroix, G. L. (2013). Does the uncanny valley exist? An empirical test of the relationship between eeriness and the human likeness of digitally created faces. *Computers in Human Behavior, 29*(3), 759–771.

Culbertson, F. (2010). *The phobia list*. http://phobialist.com.

Davies, J. (2014). *Riveted: The science of why jokes make us laugh, movies make us cry, and religion makes us feel one with the universe*. London, UK: Palgrave Macmillan.

Dovidio, J. F., Johnson, J. D., Gaertner, S. L., Pearson, A. R., Saguy, T., & Ashburn-Nardo, L. (2010). Empathy and intergroup relations. In M. Mikulincer & P. Shaver (Eds.), *Prosocial motives, emotion, and behavior: The better angels of our nature* (pp. 393–408). Washington, DC: American Psychological Association.

Gombay, A. (2007). *Descartes*. Oxford, UK: Blackwell.

Gray, K., & Wegner, D. M. (2012). Feeling robots and human zombies: Mind perception and the uncanny valley. *Cognition, 125*(1), 125–130.

Kahneman, D. (2011). *Thinking, fast and slow*. New York, NY: Farrar, Straus & Giroux.

Kret, M. E., & de Gelder, B. (2012). Islamic headdress influences how emotion is recognized from the eyes. *Frontiers in Psychology, 3*, 110.

Mann, L. (1981). The baiting crowd in episodes of threatened suicide. *Journal of Personality and Social Psychology, 41*(4), 703–709.

Minsky, M. (1986). *The society of mind*. New York, NY: Simon & Schuster.

Mori, M. (1970). Bukimi no tani [The Uncanny Valley]. *Energy, 7*(4), 33–35.

Mori, M., MacDorman, K. F., & Kageki, N. (2012). The uncanny valley [from the field]. *Robotics and Automation Magazine, IEEE, 19*(2), 98–100.

Page, R. A., & Moss, M. K. (1976). Environmental influences on aggression: The effects of darkness and proximity of victim. *Journal of Applied Social Psychology, 6*(2), 126–133.

Reeves, B., & Nass, C. (1996). *How people treat computers, television, and new media like real people and places*. Cambridge, MA: Cambridge University Press.

Reynolds, D. J., & Gifford, R. (2001). The sounds and sights of intelligence: A lens model channel analysis. *Personality and Social Psychology Bulletin, 27*(187), 187–200.

Rosenthal-von der Pütten, A. M., Krämer, N. C., Hoffmann, L., Sobieraj, S., & Eimler, S. C. (2013). An experimental study on emotional reactions towards a robot. *International Journal of Social Robotics, 5*(1), 17–34.

Turing, A.M. (1950). Computing machinery and intelligence. *Mind, 49*(236), 433–460.

Waytz, A., Gray, K., Epley, N., & Wegner, D.M. (2010). Causes and consequences of mind perception. *Trends in Cognitive Science, 14*(8), 383–388.

Zhong, C.B., Bohns, V.K., & Gino, F. (2010). Good lamps are the best police: Darkness increases dishonesty and self-interested behavior. *Psychological Science, 21*(3), 311–314.

Notes

1. *Star Wars: Episode II Attack of the Clones* (2002 motion picture).
2. Borenstein (2007).
3. Only 27 percent of people in 2005 thought robots were capable of intelligence. Strangely, the same study found only 72 percent of people thought humans in general were capable of intelligence (Arras & Cerqui, 2005).
4. Reynolds & Gifford (2001).
5. For example, Dovidio et al. (2010).
6. Minsky (1986).
7. Barra-Chicote et al. (2006).
8. Arras & Cerqui (2005), p. 10.
9. Turing (1950).
10. *Star Wars: Episode VI Return of the Jedi* (1983 motion picture).
11. Gombay (2007), p. ix.
12. *Star Wars: Episode IV A New Hope* (1977/1981).
13. Anderson (1996).
14. *Attack of the Clones.*
15. *Star Wars: The Clone Wars* (2008–2014 television series).
16. *Star Wars: Episode V The Empire Strikes Back* (1980 motion picture).
17. Rosenthal-von der Pütten et al. (2013).
18. Kahneman (2011).
19. This also explains why we care about fictional human characters. See Davies (2014).
20. Waytz et al. (2010).
21. Baum (1900).
22. Reeves & Nass (1996).
23. *Star Wars: Episode III Revenge of the Sith* (2005 motion picture).
24. Mann (1981).
25. *Blade Runner* (1982 motion picture).
26. *Aliens* (1986 motion picture).
27. Mori (1970); Mori et al. (2012).
28. Burleigh et al. (2013); Gray & Wegner (2012).
29. Bartneck et al. (2007).
30. Bartneck et al. (2009).
31. Page & Moss(1976); Zhong et al. (2010).
32. Kret & de Gelder (2012).
33. Braezeal (2003), p. 147.
34. Brewer & Brown (1998).
35. American Psychiatric Association (2013).
36. Bourne (2015); Culbertson (2010).
37. Han Solo to C-3PO in *Star Wars: Episode V The Empire Strikes Back* (1980 motion picture).

Grief and Masculinity: Anakin the Man

BILLY SAN JUAN

"Those who learned to know death, rather than to
fear and fight it, become our teachers about life."
—psychiatrist Elisabeth Kübler-Ross[1]

Grief. One word encompasses an entire spectrum of emotions over losing a loved one. For most people, the feelings of loss and sadness fade with time and support. Some people, though, experience grief on a deeper level. When the situations surrounding their loss are unusual, we may lose sight of the fact that, as Master Yoda says, "Death is a natural part of life."[2] The grief does not go away. Instead, it may lead to fear or anger.

Anakin Skywalker experiences immense grief because he experiences immense loss. Understanding the way grief and modern views of masculinity interact may help explain how the "chosen one" ultimately becomes Darth Vader, a feared and ruthless Sith. The same psychological underpinnings of grief and masculinity may also shed light on why Darth Vader eventually sacrifices himself to save his son Luke's life.

Grief and Loss

Grief is deep emotional distress caused by the loss of a close friend or family member. The emotional distress, also known as *bereavement*,[3] may involve a variety of symptoms. There may be intense sadness or longing, and thoughts surrounding the circumstances of death or loss may be difficult to control.

Psychologists who study grief have created models to understand the process by which human beings cope with the sudden and unexpected loss of a loved one.

Stages of Grief

Psychiatrist Elisabeth Kübler-Ross observed that people often deal with grief when coping with death and other losses in five stages: denial, bargaining, anger, depression, and acceptance.[4] Even though Kübler-Ross herself recognized that these were not the only responses people experience, her model became so influential that many people describe these stages as if they occurred in a universally fixed sequence.[5] Though each person experiences grief differently, this famous five-stage model sets a framework for understanding the emotional processes of loss.

1. *Denial* is the immediate reaction that helps to buffer the intense shock of a death or loss. The person may speak or act as if the lost loved one were still alive.
2. *Anger* may also be felt by the person experiencing a loss. The anger may be directed toward the circumstances of loss, self, others, or even the person who died.
3. *Bargaining* refers to trying to make deals with others or a higher power. The person begins to dwell on how the death could have been avoided. If the

bereaved person is religious, he or she may make
offerings to a higher power.

4. *Depression* involves immense feelings of sadness.
   During the depression stage, the bereaved person
   may also exhibit depressive symptoms, such as with-
   drawal from interpersonal contact, under- or over-
   eating, or bouts of crying.

5. *Acceptance* is the calm recognition of the loss and the
   ability to carry on. Not everyone who suffers a loss
   reaches this stage.

Anakin Skywalker experiences these five stages when his mother
is kidnapped and killed by Tusken Raiders,[6] and we can trace his
actions through each stage. He is in denial as he pleads for his dying
mother to "stay with me, Mom."[7] He quickly moves into the anger
stage and slaughters everyone in the Tusken Raider camp. Later,
when Padmé brings him food, Anakin declares, "Someday, I will
be the most powerful Jedi ever," able to protect those he loves.[8]
Unfortunately for Anakin and everyone in his path, he does not
reach the stages of depression or acceptance. Instead, he remains
in the bargaining stage, which eventually leads him to side with
Emperor Palpatine to prevent the death of Padmé.[9]

Grief Trajectories

Other grief research has indicated four "trajectories" that people
who experience a death or other intense situation might follow.[10]
The basis for these trajectories is the concept of psychological
resilience, the ordinary process by which human beings adapt to
adversity.[11]

• *Resilience*: People who follow this pattern of grief
  are resilient, meaning they are able to cope well

and remain emotionally stable through the process.

- *Recovery:* Some people who experience psycho-pathological conditions, such as depressive symptoms, will return to their normal level of functioning after a period of healing.
- *Chronic Dysfunction:* Others with psychological symptoms, however, may not heal as quickly as those following the recovery trajectory. Chronic dysfunction in their everyday life can be traced to the grief and troubles with resiliency.
- *Delayed Grief or Trauma:* In people who do not initially show signs of distress, symptoms may appear months later. Regarding trauma, posttraumatic stress disorder may not manifest full diagnostic criteria until six months or more after the traumatic event.[12]

Anakin Skywalker's trajectory is that of chronic dysfunction. His losses affect him throughout his lifespan and guide his choices. His lack of resilience prompts him to act out his anger and hurt. The pain he experiences eventually leads him to embrace the dark side and become Darth Vader.

Although research has been conducted on the emotional mechanisms of loss, ongoing research is proceeding apace. A disorder currently being researched for inclusion in the diagnostic manual used by psychologists is called *persistent complex bereavement disorder* (PCBD).[13] In PCBD, the feelings associated with grief last longer than expected for the bereavement process. Though the time frame is longer, PCBD involves the same symptoms as bereavement. PCBD may also be diagnosed when the loss is traumatic in nature. If the trauma leads to post-traumatic stress disorder (PTSD), a person might exhibit symptoms of both PTSD and PCBD. In that case, PTSD is a reaction to avoid reminders of the trauma and PCBD is a preoccupation with the loss.

Masculinity

Grief, for men, can be complicated by a phenomenon known as *normative male alexithymia*, a mild condition wherein men are unable to put feelings into words. This stems from the socialization of men to eschew emotions for fear of appearing weak or vulnerable.[14] Instead, vulnerable feelings are channeled into "acceptable" male emotions, such as anger.[15]

Normative male alexithymia is simply a small facet of the larger construct of masculinity. There are four main parts of the traditional masculine construct.[16] This list of *gender role norms* refers to traditional, culturally determined expectations, and it is *not* an assessment of how men necessarily are or ought to be. Men are commonly perceived as more masculine if they do the following:

- Avoid all things considered feminine. The traditional masculine construct suggests that a strict dichotomy exists between men and women, and that anything feminine is inherently unmasculine.
- Appear as pillars of strength and power, and thrive on competition.
- Show no emotion. Emotion is a sign of weakness, and weakness stands in direct contradiction to strength and power.
- Take risks. The more dangerous the risk, the more masculine the individual.

Men's inability to voice their feelings and societal pressure to act in a masculine fashion directly interfere with the processing of grief. During grief, a time of intense sadness and loss, men who have learned to avoid these very feelings may suffer difficulty coping or recovering.[17] Out of fear of these feelings, some men seek to avoid experiencing them at all by engaging in behaviors such as substance use or by channeling those feelings into the more "appropriate" emotion of anger, which may lead to hate, suffering, and the dark side.[18]

Through the Darkness

Anakin Skywalker's turn to the dark side is the result of many factors. Two of the major influences are the intense amount of loss he experiences and his inability to cope with the grief that stems from these events. Anakin leaves his mother as a young child. He loses a potential father figure when Qui-Gon Jinn dies. He loses his mother a second and final time when she dies in his arms. He loses a brother in Obi-Wan. And he loses both a wife and two children. Pain suffuses Anakin Skywalker's life.

By applying the concepts of normative male alexithymia and traditional construct of masculinity to Anakin's life, we can see how his grief intensifies over time. Anakin attempts to be strong, but only to his detriment. His sorrow and grief morph into anger and rage. But he doesn't know how to express his feelings. He only knows action. A prime example occurs when Amidala Padmé attempts to speak to him after he slaughtered everyone in the Tusken Raider camp.[19] He cannot speak about his despair, but only about "fixing things" and saving his mother. His grief is transformed into anger and he blames Obi-Wan while simultaneously throwing something at a wall. He cries and collapses and yells, "I hate them!"

The traditional construct of masculinity does not serve men well when it comes to grief. The core values with which men are inculcated do not neatly mesh with the natural emotional process of grieving. Men are instructed, from a young age, that seeking help is a sign of weakness. Instead, men will attempt to handle their emotions through a variety of methods that dovetail with stereotypical male values, such as changing careers, changing partners, drinking, drugs, sex, or even attempting to surpass their emotions through willpower.[20] Anakin's method involves acquiring power. He is unable to cope with the idea that death, especially the death of those he loves, is beyond his control. In seeking to control life and death, he paradoxically loses more of his loved ones. Anakin's maladaptive behaviors for coping with grief do not involve alcohol, drugs, or promiscuity. Rather, he seeks to exert control over his world and his fate and those of his loved ones.

Acceptance and Recovery

The anger and grief that consume Anakin Skywalker lead to his rebirth as Darth Vader. Later, though, while Emperor Palpatine is killing Luke with Force lightning during the final battle on the Death Star, Vader moves to save his son. In this act, Vader finally comes to accept all the deaths from his past. His acceptance of those losses is revealed when he asks Luke to remove his mask. Luke, in surprise, points out that Vader will die if the mask is taken off. Vader simply replies, "Nothing can stop that now."[21]

Anakin's decision to rescue Luke indicates immense personal growth. He has been able to resolve the grief surrounding the death of his mother, his mentors, and his wife. He also shows a newfound ability to sacrifice himself for the sake of his son. For the first time with Luke, Anakin does not work as an agent for the dark side. Instead, he acts as a father.

Absolution and Fatherhood

Fatherhood is a complicated thing—as is parenthood itself, of course—but the father has a different role to play in the child's life than the mother does. A strong father-child bond correlates with that child being able to regulate his or her emotional states in a healthy way, exhibit social competence, make friends, have meaningful relationships, and have few psychological and behavioral difficulties.[22] Most definitions of fatherhood and expectations about it, though, involve several common features, such as economic support of the family, psychosocial/emotional support of mothers and mates, and care for children.[23] These features parallel the previously mentioned social expectation that men be "pillars of strength." Men are expected to approach fatherhood from a provider perspective.

Anakin Skywalker is no exception. He experiences a phenomenon called *gender role strain* while fighting Luke on the Death Star.[24] A gender role strain occurs when there is incongruity between how a person is acting and how that person believes he or she should act, based on internalized gender values.[25] In this case, Anakin experiences two contradictory gender values. He is socialized to protect his own children, but he is also socialized to obey orders. A good man protects his child. A good man follows orders. The dichotomy creates internal stress (*cognitive dissonance*) and causes hesitation in the Sith Lord until, under the duress of witnessing his son's torture, he chooses the gender role that is consistent with protecting his child.

The following chart shows how the natural reaction to a death or loss contradicts many of the values that men are taught by their families, their peers, or in the media. The dichotomies of the first two columns highlight how powerfully the distress from gender role strain can affect a man. The third column posits possible negative consequences stemming from the discrepancy.

Event of Death or Loss	Socialized Masculine Values	Possible Negative Effects of the Gender Role Strain
Intense feelings of helplessness due to the irreversibility of death.	Power and control of situations are key to ensure survival of self and others.	An attempt to assert power or control in other situations.
Intense feelings of sadness.	Stoicism is paramount. Emotions are exploitable weaknesses.	Emotions are coped with by other means, such as alcohol or drugs.
Crying.	Crying is traditionally viewed as feminine, and anything feminine must be avoided.	Emotion is physically expressed in another way, such as muscle tension.
Reliance on social support.	Asking for help is a sign of weakness. A man must be a hero, and a hero must go it alone.	Isolation or depression.
Uncertainty about the future.	Uncertainty is unacceptable. Plans must be made and followed.	Confusion, anger, or depression.
"Heartache."	The only acceptable pain is physical, because physical pain can be witnessed and may serve as proof of toughness.	Self-destructive behaviors.
Realization of mortality.	A man must be indestructible.	All of the above.

Life and Death

Grief fills Anakin Skywalker's life. The losses he endures—and the brutality by which these losses turn him into a fearsome monster. Still, Anakin redeems himself through the faith and love of his son. At his own death, when Anakin looks into Luke's eyes with his own for the very first time, he smiles, possibly for the first time in years. A life of sadness ends with a smile of peace.

The loss of loved ones is a painful event in life. Our reaction to those losses, our willingness to accept the losses, and our personal resilience allow us to channel our grief in appropriate ways. For though death, as Yoda says, may be a part of life, life is also a part of death.

Coping with Clones

*Big Shiny Robot editor-in-chief Bryan Young shares an exam-
ple of how worrying about danger and loss creates strain in
a classically masculine situation: new fatherhood.*

May 22, 2002, six days after *Episode II*'s release, was
the most terrifying day of my life.

My wife went through hours of difficult labor until our
would-be newborn's heart stopped. Doctors performed an
emergency C-section. My wife lay unconscious on a table,
bleeding. My baby wasn't breathing.

In tears, I heard doctors behind a curtain performing
CPR. A nurse stopped to reassure me, "We're doing everything we can for your son."

"It's a boy?"

"Yes. You didn't know?"

"No . . . But his name's Anakin."

As they ushered me from the OR, I finally heard him cry.
He was alive, but they'd collapsed his lung. He needed to be
transferred to another hospital.

The next four days were spent stressfully dividing my
time between my wife and son. Once she was discharged
she kept a vigil over our little Padawan, who would spend
another week under constant care.

I needed a break.

"It's okay," she told me. "You deserve it. We'll be fine."

She was right.

Stress relief came in the form of a matinee of *Attack of
the Clones*. Since childhood, *Star Wars* had been my coping
mechanism and, as the bright yellow logo and theme song
burst forth, I knew everything was going to be okay.

Bryan Young

References

American Psychiatric Association (2013). *Diagnostic and statistical manual of mental disorders* (5th ed.). Arlington, VA: American Psychiatric Publishing.

Bonanno, G.A. (2009). *The other side of sadness: What the new science of bereavement tells us about life after loss.* New York, NY: Basics.

Brannon, R. (1976). The male sex role: Our culture's blueprint for manhood and what it's done for us lately. In D. David & R. Brannon (Eds.), *The forty-nine percent majority: The male sex role* (pp. 1–48). Reading, MA: Addison-Wesley.

Comeas-Diaz, L., Luthar, S., Maddi, S., O'Neill, H., Saakvitne, K., & Tedeschi, R. (n.d.). *The road to resilience.* American Psychological Association: http://www.apa.org/helpcenter/road-resilience.aspx.

Englar-Carlson, M., & M.A. Stevens (Eds.), *In the room with men: A casebook of therapeutic change* (pp. 91–107). Washington, DC: American Psychological Association.

Englar-Carlson, M. (2006). Masculine norms and the therapy process. In M. Englar-Carlson & M. A. Stevens (Eds.), *In the room with men: A casebook of therapeutic change* (pp. 13–47). Washington, DC: American Psychological Association.

Geary, D.C. (2010). *Male, female: The evolution of human sex differences* (2nd ed.). Washington, DC: American Psychological Association.

Kübler-Ross, E. (1985). *On children and death.* New York, NY: Touchstone.

Kübler-Ross, E. (1969). *On death and dying: What the dying have to teach doctors, nurses, clergy, and their own families.* New York, NY: Scribner.

Kübler-Ross, E. (2005). *On grief and grieving: Finding the meaning of grief through the five stages of loss.* New York, NY: Simon & Schuster.

Lamb, M. E. (2000). Fathering. In A. E. Kazdin (Ed.), *Encyclopedia of psychology* (vol. 3, pp. 338–341). New York, NY: Oxford University Press.

Levant, R. F. (1998). Treating male alexithymia. In L. B. Silverstein & T. Jean (Eds.), *Feminist family therapy: Empowerment in social context* (pp. 177–188). Washington, DC: American Psychological Association.

Pleck, J. H. (1995). The gender role strain paradigm: An update. In R. F. Levant & W. S. Pollack (Eds.), *A new psychology of men* (pp. 11–32). New York, NY: Basic.

Rabinowitz, F.E. (2006). Thawing the ice man: Coping with grief and loss. In M. Englar-Carlson & M. A. Stevens (Eds.), *In the room with men: A casebook of therapeutic change* (pp. 109–127). Washington, DC: American Psychological Association.

Notes

1. Kübler-Ross (1985), p. xii.
2. *Star Wars: Episode III Revenge of the Sith* (2005 motion picture).
3. American Psychiatric Association (2013).
4. Kübler-Ross (1969).
5. Kübler-Ross (2005).
6. *Star Wars: Episode II Attack of the Clones* (2002 motion picture).
7. *Attack of the Clones.*
8. *Attack of the Clones.*
9. *Revenge of the Sith.*
10. Bonanno (2009).

11. Comeas-Diaz et al. (n.d.).
12. American Psychiatric Association (2013).
13. American Psychiatric Association (2013).
14. Levant (1998).
15. Levant (1998).
16. Brannon (1976).
17. Cochran (2006).
18. *Star Wars: Episode I The Phantom Menace* (1999 motion picture).
19. *Attack of the Clones.*
20. Rabinowitz (2006)
21. *Star Wars: Episode VI Return of the Jedi* (1983 motion picture).
22. Geary (2010).
23. Lamb (2000).
24. *Return of the Jedi.*
25. Pleck (1995).

» 7 »

The Intergalactic Guide to Girls and Gender Psychology

. ELIZABETH A. KUS AND JANINA SCARLET

"Well, I guess you don't know everything
about women yet."
—Princess Leia[1]

> "What is happening at the time you come
> of age becomes a stamp of who you
> are, and you carry it forward."
> —psychologist Jeanne Marecek[2]

People's behaviors are more easily influenced by the actions of role models, fictional and nonfictional, who are of their own gender. Many children growing up in the 1970s and '80s were fascinated with Star Wars—play-fighting with flashlight lightsabers, waving their hands pretending that they had Jedi powers, and reciting famous lines from the original trilogy.[3] From Princess Leia to Padmé Amidala, the Star Wars universe features female role models whom children are likely to imitate. What kind of role models does Star Wars provide? How does it portray women and how does that relate to the viewers' psychosocial development?

Gender Psychology and Popular Culture

Gender-related behaviors are largely learned by observation,[4] and whether it is television shows or G-rated cartoons, they can all influence how young viewers develop their gender identity.[5] Once children form *gender identity*, a sense of oneself as belonging to a particular gender (typically by age four), children usually mimic the behavior of those perceived as the same sex as themselves. In addition to affecting how people act, same-sex role models can affect how people feel about themselves.[6] This is especially true when men and women take on stereotypical roles, where women are seen as inferior to men and the men are presented as being in control. However, when women are portrayed as being in control, *both* boys and girls seem to imitate the women's behavior,[7] which suggests that stereotypical depiction of women sends negative messages to both girls and boys while nonstereotypical role models can positively influence everyone.

The portrayals of strong female characters, such as Princess Leia, promote healthy psychological and social development. When girls identify with a positive role model, they tend to have improved self-confidence about their schoolwork and are more likely to do well in math.[8] Positive role models also seem to alleviate anxiety and boost overall confidence in women, and reduce sexist attitudes in men.[9] Princess Leia appears as a senator, as a warrior, and overall as a nonstereotypical representation of a woman. Even after getting shot in the arm during the battle of Endor, Leia still manages to push down a Stormtrooper with her foot and shoot two others who nearly capture her and Han Solo.[10]

Self-Fulfilling Prophecy

Because media portrayals of gender roles can be as influential on a person's own gender identity formation as people in their lives,[11] the availability of adequate role models of both sexes is essential. Men often appear in popular culture as adventure-seeking, pursuing or attaining high-powered careers, such as becoming doctors, while women assume domestic roles, caregiving positions, and lower-status jobs.[12] This potentially sends messages to both men and women that women are not valuable, that they are weak, and that men are more likely to achieve higher academic and professional status than women.[13] Such messages may, in turn, create self-fulfilling prophecies.

A *self-fulfilling prophecy* is a prediction (often an incorrect one) that causes people to act in ways that would make that prediction come true.[14] When researchers trick schoolteachers into expecting random students to perform well in school, the teachers treat those students in ways that actually lead to better academic performance.[15] On the other hand, children perform more poorly when working with teachers and other adults who have been led to expect the worst of them.[16] In *Star Wars: Episode III Revenge of the Sith*, Anakin Skywalker tries so hard to avert Padmé's death, a prediction he has seen in his nightmares, that he ultimately causes it to happen[17]

Some people's belief that men are smarter than women results in girls underestimating their academic abilities whereas boys are more likely to overestimate their abilities—an effect that seems to start in middle school and increase with age. Anxiety and depression apparently make both boys and girls perceive their academic ability less accurately.[18] Once children learn specific gender rules (stereotypical or not), they become more likely to apply them in their own lives. Many girls who initially find science compelling may therefore lose interest in that subject in middle school, around the same time that they start paying greater attention to their appearance and romantic relationships.[19] This is consistent with the cultural message they receive that boys are good at science, technology, engineering, and mathematics (STEM), while girls are not. Parents might reinforce that notion. Parents have been found to be three times more likely to explain a scientific concept to a boy than to a girl.[20] The other side of that message is that girls are supposed to be submissive to men—both obedient and sexually submissive.[21] *Revenge of the Sith* may give young girls a similar idea. Unlike previous portrayals, in which Padmé is an elected queen, a warrior, and a fierce protector of her people,[22] she has dropped out of politics and other Republic-related events since marrying Anakin. When she loses him to the dark side, she loses the will to continue living without him and dies shortly after giving birth to their twin children.

While many female characters, such as Princess Leia and Ahsoka Tano,[23] serve as examples of powerful women, the number of females portrayed in the series still represents only a small proportion of the total characters. Having too few identifiable role models can potentially have a negative impact on viewers' psychological development.[24] Specifically, the underrepresentation of women in media can potentially send negative messages to both men and women, undermining the importance of women, reducing women's self-esteem, bringing on depression or anxiety, and re-creating stereotypical attitudes toward women.[25]

A social movement with the central goal of gender equality

is commonly referred to as *feminism*.[26] *Feminist psychology* seeks to empower women and other stigmatized groups, to help them implement social change and self-care. *Feminist therapy* then applies these principles in order to help all clients, regardless of gender, develop a sense of equality, recognize their own abilities, and become agents of social change.[27]

One of the tools sometimes used to assess the parity of gender representation in the media is the *Bechdel Test*. This test looks at whether a film or a television show (1) has at least two women in it (2) who talk to each other (3) about something besides a man.[28] Many popular science-fiction and fantasy works, such as *Lord of the Rings*,[29] do not pass the Bechdel Test.[30] In the original Star Wars trilogy, only three women appear on the screen and have spoken lines: Princess Leia, Luke's aunt Beru, and a Rebel Alliance leader named Mon Mothma.[31] These women never speak to one another onscreen, so the trilogy does not pass the Bechdel Test.

On the other hand, the Star Wars prequels[32] feature more female characters, compared to the original films—Queen Padmé, Shmi (Anakin's mother), Sabé (Padmé's double), Zam Wesell (the assassin who tries to kill Padmé), and several others. In *Star Wars: Episode I The Phantom Menace* and *Star Wars: Episode II Attack of the Clones*,[33] Padmé speaks to other women about politics and the safety of their people, hence passing the Bechdel Test. However, in the theatrical release of *Revenge of the Sith*,[34] Padmé is only seen speaking to men and usually about Anakin. Hence, only two out of the first six live action Star Wars films pass the Bechdel test.

On the other hand, the animated series *Star Wars: The Clone Wars* features many strong female characters, even some notorious female villains, including an assassin and a bounty hunter.[35] Expanded Universe books, comics, and video games also feature a great number of powerful female characters as Jedi, Sith, and non-Force users.[36] These elements of the Star Wars universe do pass the Bechdel Test, having a larger number of female characters compared to the initial trilogy.

Harassment and Violence

Stereotypical portrayal of male and female characters in popular culture can affect the way both sexes respond to sexual harassment.[37] A large number of films portray women as submissive, and most fit women into one of the stereotypical roles, such as smart and dangerous ("femme fatale"), good ("the girl next door"), or nothing but beautiful ("bimbo").[38] Oftentimes, women are also depicted as sexual objects, as Princess Leia is when Jabba the Hutt takes her prisoner.[39]

Overall, Star Wars does a great job of steering clear of the stereotyped tropes, and yet there are some depictions of violence toward women—notably when Anakin Force-chokes and nearly kills Padmé.[40] Media depictions can affect the way men and women feel and behave. Among research participants who watched sexually violent films in which women were submissive, female viewers became more anxious and male viewers demonstrated increased negative attitudes toward women. Films with sexual violence in which female characters were dominant, on the other hand, did not affect viewers' attitudes.[41] In another study, men who watched films in which women were sexually abused became more likely to display harassing or violent behaviors toward women.[42]

Because pop culture depictions of men as violent and women as submissive can potentially increase these behaviors,[43] they might also affect women's *locus of control*, the degree to which they believe that they control situations in life. People who are harassed or abused often report feeling depressed, hopeless, and sometimes also suicidal, and they are more likely to develop an

Role Models

Albert Bandura, a famous psychologist who studied social learning, found that preschool boys and girls are likely to become aggressive after seeing researchers act aggressively toward an inflated Bobo doll, either in real life or on film.[44] The amount of aggression that the children displayed depended on the experimenter's gender and their own. Overall, boys displayed more aggression than girls did. When they witnessed real-life aggression, both boys and girls tended to be more aggressive after witnessing aggressors of the same sex as themselves. This indicates that people are more strongly influenced by role models of the same sex and that in order to promote gender equality, the media should include role models who are diverse in gender. *The Clone Wars*, for example, includes diverse role models, including a female Jedi Master named Luminara,[45] as well as male Jedi Masters, such as Obi-Wan Kenobi.

external locus of control (feeling that one is not in control of one's own life) than an *internal locus of control* (feeling in control).[46] Padmé appears to feel this way when she gives up her will to live after Anakin physically abuses her, leaving her hurt and heartbroken.[47]

Harassment, prejudice, and hostility toward women and other stigmatized groups, such as the LGBTQ population, can lead to a number of physical and mental health problems. People who experience stigma and harassment often feel alienated, depressed, and self-critical.[48] Getting to know someone from a marginalized group, however, allows people to become more empathetic toward that person and possibly treat him or her more kindly. This reduction in prejudice toward typically stigmatized groups can even be achieved through fiction.[49] By learning about characters from underrepresented groups (such as the LGBTQ character Moff Mors from the novel *Lords of the Sith: Star Wars*),[50] readers are likely to become more empathetic toward the members of the LGBTQ community in real life.

A Quest toward Gender Equality

Because audience members (children and adults alike) can be influenced by real people or fictional heroes, storytellers may want to consider carefully how they depict their characters.[51] Specifically, presenting viewers with influential role models like Princess Leia, Ahsoka, and Padmé (as she was depicted in *The Phantom Menace* and *Clone Wars*), as opposed to characters that adhere to stereotypical gender roles, can provide both female and male viewers with empowering messages about equality. This, in turn, can lead to better psychological health, less anxiety and depression, fewer instances of eating disorders in order to achieve unrealistic standards of beauty, and an internal locus of control.[52] As science-fiction sagas, such as the Star Wars epic, continue to proliferate, further creating more inspiring female characters (such as Princess Leia) and other minority characters, they can potentially enhance the lives of audiences of all cultural backgrounds.

References

Bandura, A., Ross, D., & Ross, S. A. (1963). Imitation of film-mediated aggressive models. *Journal of Abnormal and Social Psychology, 66*(1), 3–11.

Baumgardner, J., & Richards, A. (2000). *Manifesta: Young women, feminism, and the future.* New York, NY: Farrar, Straus and Giroux.

Bechdel, A. (1986). *Dykes to watch out for.* Ann Arbor, MI: Firebrand.

Burger, J. M. (1984). Desire for control, locus of control, and proneness to depression. *Journal of Personality, 52*(1), 71–89.

Bussey, K., & Bandura, A. (1984). Influence of gender constancy and social power on sex-linked modeling. *Journal of Personality and Social Psychology, 47*(6), 1292–1302.

Bussey, K., & Bandura, A. (1999). Social cognitive theory of gender development and differentiation. *Psychological Review, 106*(4), 676–713.

Cantrell, A. (2013, November 11). *10 famous films that surprisingly fail the Bechdel Test*. Film School Rejects: http://filmschoolrejects.com/features/10-famous-films-that-surprisingly-fail-the-bechdel-test.php/5.

Cole, D. A., Martin, J. M., Peeke, L. A., Seroczynski, A. D., & Fier, J. (1999). Children's over and underestimation of academic competence: A longitudinal study of gender differences, depression, and anxiety. *Child Development, 70*(2), 459–473.

Crowley, K., Callanan, M. A., Tenenbaum, H. R., & Allen, E. (2001). Parents explain more often to boys than to girls during shared scientific thinking. *Psychological Science, 12*(3), 258–261.

Erchull, M. J., & Liss, M. (2013). Feminists who flaunt it: Exploring the enjoyment of sexualization among young feminist women. *Journal of Applied Social Psychology, 43*(12), 2341–2349.

Ferguson, C. J. (2012). Positive female role-models eliminate negative effects of sexually violent media. *Journal of Communication, 62*(5), 888–899.

Ferguson, C. J. (2014). One smaugy day. *PsycCritiques, 59*(13): http://dx.doi.org/10.1037/a0036535

Galdi, S., Maass, A., & Cadinu, M. (2014). Objectifying media: Their effect on gender role norms and sexual harassment of women. *Psychology of Women Quarterly, 38*(3), 398–413.

Gerding, A., & Signorielli, N. (2014). Gender roles in tween television programming: A content analysis of two genres. *Sex Roles, 70*(1), 43–56.

Gilbert, P., & Procter, S. (2006). Compassionate mind training for people with high shame and self-criticism: Overview and pilot study of a group therapy approach. *Clinical Psychology and Psychotherapy, 13*(6), 353–379.

Harris, M. J., Milich, R., Corbitt, E. M., Hoover, D. W., & Brady, M. (1992). Self-fulfilling effects of stigmatizing information on children's social interactions. *Journal of Personality and Social Psychology, 63*(1), 41–50.

Hearne, K. (2015). *Star Wars: Heir to the Jedi*. New York, NY: Del Rey.

Herlihy, B., & Corey, G. (2013). Feminist therapy. In G. Corey (Ed.), *Theory and practice of counseling and psychotherapy* (pp. 360–394). Belmont, CA: Brooks/Cole.

Kemp, P. S. (2015). *Star Wars: Lords of the Sith*. New York, NY: Del Rey.

Launius, M. H., & Lindquist, C. U. (1988). Learned helplessness, external locus of control, and passivity in battered women. *Journal of Interpersonal Violence, 3*(3), 307–318.

LucasArts. (2006). *Star Wars: Knights of the old Republic* [Xbox video game]. San Francisco, CA: LucasFilm.

MacKay, J. (2010). Profile of Jeanne Marecek. In A. Rutherford (Ed.), *Psychology's feminist voices multimedia Internet archive*. Feminist Voices: http://www.feministvoices.com/jeanne-marecek/.

Marx, D. M., & Roman, J. S. (2002). Female role models: Protecting women's math test performance. *Personality and Social Psychology Bulletin, 28*(9), 1183–1193.

Merton, R. K. (1948). The self-fulfilling prophecy. *The Antioch Review, 8*(2), 193–210.

Rosenthal, R., & Jacobsen, L., (1968). *Pygmalion in the classroom*. New York, NY: Holt, Rinehart & Winston.

Salvatore, R. A. (1999). *The New Jedi Order: Vector prime*. New York, NY: Ballantine.

Sanchez, D. T., Kiefer, A. K., & Ybarra, O. (2006). Sexual submissiveness in women: Costs for sexual autonomy and arousal. *Personality and Social Psychology Bulletin, 32*(4), 512–524.

Smith, S. L., Pieper, K. M., Granados, A., & Choueiti, M. (2010). Assessing gender-related portrayals in top-grossing G-rated films. *Sex Roles, 62*(11–12), 774–786.

Steinke, J. (2005). Cultural representations of gender and science portrayals of female scientists and engineers in popular films. *Science Communication, 27*(1), 27–63.

Vezzali, L., Stathi, S., Giovannini, D., Capozza, D., & Trifiletti, E. (2014). The greatest magic of Harry Potter: Reducing prejudice. *Journal of Applied Social Psychology, 45*(2), 105–121.

Notes

1. *Star Wars: Episode V The Empire Strikes Back* (1980 motion picture).
2. MacKay (2010).
3. *Star Wars: Episode IV A New Hope* (1977/1981 motion picture); *The Empire Strikes Back*; *Star Wars: Episode VI: Return of the Jedi* (1983 motion picture).
4. Bussey & Bandura (1984).
5. Galdi et al. (2014); Gerding & Signorielli (2013); Smith et al. (2010).
6. Ferguson (2012).
7. Bussey & Bandura (1984).
8. Marx & Roman (2002).
9. Ferguson (2012); Herlihy & Corey (2013).
10. *Return of the Jedi.*
11. Bandura et al. (1963).
12. Bussey & Bandura (1999).
13. Bussey & Bandura (1999); Cole et al. (1999); Ferguson (2012); Galdi et al. (2014).
14. Merton (1948).
15. Rosenthal & Jacobsen (1968).
16. Harris et al. (1992).
17. *Star Wars: Episode III Revenge of the Sith* (2005 motion picture).
18. Cole et al. (1999).
19. Steinke (2005).
20. Crowley et al. (2001).
21. Sanchez et al. (2006).
22. For example, *Star Wars: The Clone Wars*, episodes 1–8, "Bombad Jedi" (November 21, 2008).
23. For example, *Star Wars: The Clone Wars*, episodes 3–6, "The Academy" (October 15, 2010).
24. Smith et al. (2010).
25. Smith et al. (2010).
26. Baumgardner & Richards (2000); Erchull & Liss (2013).
27. Herlihy & Corey (2013).
28. Bechdel (1986).
29. Cantrell (2013).
30. Ferguson (2014).
31. *A New Hope; The Empire Strikes Back; Return of the Jedi.*
32. *Star Wars: Episode I The Phantom Menace* (1999 motion picture); *Star Wars: Episode II Attack of the Clones* (2002 motion picture); *Revenge of the Sith.*
33. *The Phantom Menace; Attack of the Clones.*
34. *Revenge of the Sith.*
35. *The Clone Wars* (2008–2014 television series).
36. Hearne (2015); LucasArts (2006); Salvatore (1999).
37. Ferguson (2012); Galdi et al. (2014).
38. Smith et al. (2010).
39. *Return of the Jedi.*
40. *Revenge of the Sith.*
41. Ferguson (2012).
42. Galdi et al. (2014).
43. Galdi et al. (2014).
44. Bandura et al. (1963).

45. *The Clone Wars*, episodes 2–6, "Weapons Factory" (November 13, 2009).
46. Burger (1984); Launius & Lindquist (1988).
47. *Revenge of the Sith*.
48. Gilbert & Procter (2006).
49. Vezzali et al. (2014).
50. Kemp (2015).
51. Bandura et al. (1963); Bussey & Bandura (1999); Galdi et al. (2014).
52. Ferguson (2012); Galdi et al. (2014); Herlihy & Corey (2013); Launius & Lindquist (1988).

The Force of Relationships: Tie Strength in Star Wars

JENNIFER GOLBECK

"Love comes . . . When you dare to reveal yourself
fully. When you dare to be vulnerable."
—media psychologist Dr. Joyce Brothers[1]

We all have a range of relationships, from passing acquaintances to those with whom we've forged deep, trusted bonds. These relationships develop over time and, as they strengthen, they can have a profound impact on the choices we make in life. *Tie strength* is a way to describe the strength of these social connections. Though there is a full spectrum of tie strength, we tend to think most often about two categories: *strong ties* (close, intimate, trusted relations) and *weak ties* (casual acquaintances).

The early scenes in *Star Wars: Episode IV A New Hope* reveal character information that can help viewers judge the strength of the characters' relationships. Luke Skywalker obviously has strong, if sometimes tense, relationships with Uncle Owen and Aunt Beru. However, at this point he has a weak tie to Obi-Wan

Kenobi. Luke knows him—as Ben Kenobi—but only as an older man who lives nearby. Kenobi, on the other hand, feels stronger ties to Luke, having witnessed Luke's birth[2] and kept an eye, albeit distantly, on Luke's development throughout his life. All the relationships develop and change over time, and we can see why the characters *grow closer* by applying tie strength theories. Relationships evolve in known ways.[3] These dynamics play out in clear ways in the Star Wars universe.

How to Strengthen a Tie

One of the first formal analyses of tie strength as a formal concept came from Stanford University professor Mark Granovetter[4] in the 1960s and 1970s. He postulated that there were four major factors that played into the strength of the relationship between two people: time, emotional intensity, intimacy, and reciprocal services. While Granovetter is a sociologist, the psychological community has, in many ways, looked at these attributes in the development and maintenance of relationships.[5]

Time

The time that people put into a relationship impacts its strength. This includes how long they have known one another, how often they see each other, and how much time they spend together. More time tends to lead to stronger relationships. Relationships that are relatively new can grow strong very quickly if the people involved spend a lot of time together. Time is a foundational element of relationship strength, so much so that it makes up a major component of the Relationship Closeness Inventory, a questionnaire designed to measure relationship strength.[6]

Obi-Wan's relationship with Yoda shows that a long-term relationship can be quite strong, even when the two people do not see each other often. On the other hand, Luke forms strong bonds with Obi-Wan, Han Solo, and Princess Leia over a relatively short amount of time. Within their first film alone, they go through a lot together. The other factors related to tie strength also play in to this relationship development.

Emotional Intensity

When two people share an intense emotional experience, it strengthens the relationship between them.[7] The characters in Star Wars often go through intense, dangerous events together; these experiences promote this emotional intensity.

One of the best examples of this is in the garbage compactor scene on the Death Star.[8] When R2-D2 finally stops the compactor, the characters' relief and celebration turn into a moment of bonding among the four trapped inside, even if C-3PO misinterprets their joyous noises as suffering.

Intimacy

Intimacy can take many forms. While physical and sexual intimacy certainly counts, any instance where one person makes him- or herself vulnerable to another is an intimate moment. Successful moments of intimacy build trust and tie strength.[9]

As Leia and Han develop their romantic relationship, physical intimacy plays into their strengthening connection. The most notable of these moments is their kiss aboard the *Millennium Falcon* in *Star Wars: Episode V The Empire Strikes Back*. Much later, Han makes himself surprisingly vulnerable to Leia at the end of

*Star Wars: Episode VI Return of the Jedi,*when he offers to back off because he misunderstands her affection for Luke.

He drops the tough–guy demeanor he has maintained through-out the trilogy, and he reveals his caring and his love for Leia, and his willingness to sacrifice his own happiness for hers.When Leia reveals that Luke is her brother and Han, after a moment's confusion, rejoices in her love and availability, the relationship between them feels more intimate as a result of his moment of vulnerability.

Reciprocal Services

The favors or help that people give one another is measured as *reciprocal services*, also known as benevolence.Asking someone for a favor can make that person readier to like the person who asks, Benjamin Franklin noted long ago.[10] As Nelson Mandela put it, "If you want to make peace with your enemy, you have to work with your enemy.Then he becomes your partner."[11] This effect arises from this component of tie strength. When one person does something for another, both parties feel closer.[12]

Because of the risky, covert, and military-style situations that the Star Wars characters typically find themselves in, they demonstrate many dramatic examples of reciprocal services. One of the most heroic of these is when Han risks his own life to save Luke and is lost in a Hothice storm in *Return of the Jedi.*

Case Study: Han Solo and Lando Calrissian

Han and Lando's relationship is established before Han appears in the StarWars films. Though Lando's betrayal of Han could be bad for their relationship, he and Han clearly have a long-standing strong tie. Han mentions that he received the *Millennium Falcon* from Lando long ago, and Han trusts Lando enough to head to Cloud City for help in the first place.[13]

How does this strong tie develop, and do the four attributes of tie strength play into it?

Time is clearly on the side of Han and Lando's relationship. Lando and Han first meet years before. Chronicled in Star Wars novels, Han serves as a mentor to Lando, teaching him to be a pilot and smuggler. In this process, they know each other for quite a while.[14]

This relationship is one that deals with *reciprocal services*, the favors and work people do for one another. Han teaches Lando to be a pilot. They work together in *Rebel Dawn*, where Lando joins Han, Chewbacca, and others in a raid on the planet Ylesia.[15]

Emotional intensity arises from the dangerous situations they face together. Similarly, because they often engage in illegal or risky behavior and must trust one another, there is a lot of *intimacy* (the ability to be close and vulnerable) through vulnerability between the two men. Viewers see the strength of that bond even after Lando's betrayal in Cloud City. For instance, Lando's role in Han's rescue in *Return of the Jedi* is one example of that. Not only does Lando risk his life to help save Han and others, but Han saves Lando from the Sarlacc pit when they are on Jabba's barge. Reciprocal services, intimacy, and emotional intensity are all at play again.

The trust that flows from a strong tie is revealed toward the end of *Return of the Jedi*. Han helps Lando become a general in the Rebel Alliance. The best indicator of their strong relationship comes when Han warmly gives Lando the *Millennium Falcon* for the raid.[16]

That exchange reflects trust, warmth, intimacy, reciprocal services, emotional intensity, and the long history of the two men (i.e., time). Clearly, the bond between Han and Lando is

Rating Relationship Closeness

The Relationship Closeness Inventory[17] is a survey to measure how close two people are. It asks questions about how much time you have spent with a person and the kinds of things you have done together in the past week as a snapshot of your relationship. It's a checklist of activities people do together, plus a set of rankings about how much one person influences the other.

If we examine Obi-Wan and Luke's relationship when they are aboard the *Millennium Falcon*, we know the answers to many questions on the survey. They spend most of their waking hours together. For activities that appear in the Relationship Closeness Inventory, we can check off that they "discussed things of a personal nature," "went on a trip," and "went to a bar" (the Mos Eisley Cantina), among many others.

From Luke's perspective, we can give high ratings regarding how much Obi-Wan "influences the extent to which I accept responsibilities in our relationship" and "influences the way I feel about the future," among others.

After completing the inventory, we observe that the closeness of their relationship scores an 8.35/10—a very strong tie.

still strong indeed after all the ups and downs they go through in *The Empire Strikes Back* and *Return of the Jedi*.

The Forbidden Triad

The theories of tie strength lead to higher-level theories of relationships. One of these is the *forbidden triad*. A triad is any group of three people. For example, in Figure 1, the people are represented as A, B, and C. A has relationships with both B and C, but B and C have no relationship with one another.

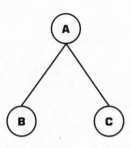

Figure 1. A triad. In this case, B and C both have ties to A but not to each other.

There are three possible ties in a triad (A to B, B to C, and A to C). Each of those ties has a strength. For example, there could be a strong tie between A and B, a weak tie from A to C, and no tie between B and C.

The forbidden triad deals with the situation where one person has strong ties with the other two, but they have no relationship with each other. For example, if the relationships in Figure 1 are strong ties, this would be a forbidden triad.

Imagine two people who you are very close to people with whom you spend a lot of time, have intense emotional experiences, share intimacy, and for whom you do favors. It is very unlikely that those two people don't have at least a passing acquaintance. They do not need to have a strong relationship, but we would expect them to have *some* connection to one another. It is so unlikely that this situation occurs, that Granovetter termed it *forbidden*.[18]

Of course, forbidden triads do occur in real life, but many will eventually resolve themselves when a tie forms between the two previous strangers. In Star Wars, this happens many times.

When Obi-Wan sends Luke to study under Yoda, Obi-Wan Kenobi has a strong tie with Yoda, even though they have not spent time together for a long while. Obi-Wan also has a strong connection with Luke. At that point, we have a classic situation in which a forbidden triad forms. There simply has been no opportunity for the two previous strangers, Luke and Yoda, to have met before this. Over the course of the film, Yoda develops a strong relationship with Luke as well, and the forbidden triad disappears.

A Binding Force

The theory of tie strength specifies a way to think about our relationships to others, how strong they are, and what that implies about our larger social network. People develop stronger relationships by spending time together, sharing intense emotional experiences and intimacies, and doing things for one another. In Star Wars, we see many of the features of strong ties at work. Higher-level lessons that follow from tie strength insights, like the forbidden triad, also help to predict the dynamics between characters, explaining why the relationships that develop are destined to be.

References

Ben-Ari, A., & Lavee, Y. (2007). Dyadic closeness in marriage: From the inside story to a conceptual model. *Journal of Social and Personal Relationships, 24*(5), 627–644.

Berscheid, E., Snyder, M., & Omoto, A. M. (1989). The Relationship Closeness Inventory: Assessing the closeness of interpersonal relationships. *Journal of Personality and Social Psychology, 57*(5), 792–807.

Bradbury, T. N., & Karney, B. R. (2014). *Intimate relationships* (2nd ed.). New York, NY: Norton.

Brothers, J. (1992). *Widowed*. New York, NY: Ballantine.

Bouzereau, L. (1997). *Star Wars: The annotated screenplays*. New York, NY: Del Rey.

Crispin, A. C. (1998). *Rebel dawn*. New York, NY: Bantam Spectra.

Franklin, B. (1791). *The autobiography of Benjamin Franklin*. Paris, France: Buisson.

Granovetter, M. S. (1973). The strength of weak ties. *American Journal of Sociology, 78*(6), 1360–1380.

Larzelere, R., & Ted, L., & Huston, T. L. (1980). The dyadic trust scale: Toward understanding interpersonal trust in close relationships. *Journal of Marriage and the Family, 42*(3), 595–604.

Levine, A., & Heller, R. S. F. (2010). *Attached: The new science of adult attachment and how it can help you find—and keep—love*. New York, NY: Tarcher/Penguin.

Levinger, G. (1980). Toward the analysis of close relationships. *Journal of Experimental Social Psychology, 16*(6), 510–544.

NewsOne Staff (2011, July 18). *The top 10 Nelson Mandela quotes of all time.* NewsOne: http://newsone.com/1397375/nelson-mandela-quotes-93rd-birthday/.

Palmatier, R. W., Houston, M. B., Dant, R. P., & Grewal, D. (2013). Relationship velocity: Toward a theory of relationship dynamics. *Journal of Marketing, 77*(1), 13–30.

Prager, K. J. (1997). *The psychology of intimacy.* New York, NY: Guilford.

Reis, H. T., Clark. M. S., & Holmes, J. G. (2004). Perceived partner responsiveness as an organizing construct in the study of intimacy and closeness. In D. J. Mashek & A. P. Arons (Eds.), *Handbook of closeness and intimacy* (pp. 201–225). New York, NY: Psychology Press.

Smith, L. N. (1983a). *Lando Calrissian and the Mindharp of Sharu.* New York, NY: Del Rey.

Smith, L. N. (1983b). *Lando Calrissian and the Flamewind of Oseon.* New York, NY: Del Rey.

Smith, L. N. (1983c). *Lando Calrissian and the Starcave of ThonBoka.* New York, NY: Del Rey.

Notes

1. Brothers (1992).
2. *Star Wars: Episode III Revenge of the Sith* (2005 motion picture).
3. Bradbury & Karney (2014); Granovetter (1973); Levine & Heller (2010); Palmatier et al. (2013).
4. Granovetter (1973).
5. Levinger (1980).
6. Berscheid et al. (1989).
7. Ben-Ari & Lavee (2007).
8. *Star Wars: Episode IV A New Hope* (1977/1981 motion picture).
9. Prager (1997); Reis et al. (2004).
10. Franklin (1791), p. 48.
11. NewsOne (2011).
12. Larzelere & Houston (1980).
13. *Star Wars: Episode V The Empire Strikes Back* (1980 motion picture).
14. Smith (1983a, 1983b, 1983c).
15. Crispin (1998).
16. Bouzereau (1997).
17. Berscheid et al. (1989)
18. Granovetter (1973).

An OCEAN Far Away

II. Conscientiousness versus Recklessness

TRAVIS LANGLEY

C-3PO chastises R2-D2 and Chewbacca over details when they're each trying to help. Threepio, in turn, offers so many details when trying to help that others snap at him. "Never tell me the odds!" Han Solo growls.[1] Han's so attentive to details that he sometimes misses the big picture. *Conscientiousness* involves thoroughness, caution, and vigilance. Conscientious individuals strive to be orderly, organized, and efficient.

Examples of Conscientiousness Traits

Achievement Motivation
Attention to Detail
Carefulness
Competitiveness
Controlling Nature
Deliberation
Disciplined
Dutifulness
Lack of Spontaneity
Meticulousness
Neatness
Organization

Perfectionism
Perseverance
Productivity
Punctuality
Reliability
Self-Control
Self-Direction
Systematic
Thoroughness
Time Awareness
Vigilance

By addressing problems before they can grow larger, conscientious individuals maintain better health overall and, on average, live longer with better quality of life.[2] Conscientious individuals perform better at some jobs than others. The relationship between conscientiousness and job performance generally curves: Although reliable, conscientious people who meet deadlines and attend to details tend to do better work than those who are less reliable; the excessively meticulous person may, however, be less efficient.[3] Spending all morning trying to get paper in the printer to line up right is unproductive for someone who needs to type and print a report by noon. Adhering to procedure while trying to frame Tusken Raiders for killing Jawas makes the Stormtroopers who really killed them leave footsteps and blaster marks in patterns that Ben Kenobi recognizes easily. At the less conscientious end of the scale, though, failing to get details right quickly reveals that Han Solo is not the Stormtrooper he pretends to be while infiltrating the Death Star to rescue Princess Leia. The more effective princess has to take charge of her own rescue.[4]

The anxiety disorder known as obsessive-compulsive disorder (OCD) does not usually accompany conscientiousness,[5] but obsessive-compulsive personality disorder (OCPD) may.[6] In fact, a lack of trait conscientiousness could make the anxiety disorder sufferer worry that he or she has not done everything necessary to feel safe and secure. The individual with the personality disorder—preoccupied with orderliness, perfectionism, and control—is less likely than the anxiety disorder sufferer to see anything wrong with his or her own behavior. The one with the personality disorder is overconscientious, scrupulous, rigid, and inflexible, suffering stress but without the severe obsessions or compulsive, ritualistic behavior.[7] The value of therapy for people with such deeply ingrained personality patterns is uncertain, although clients with OCPD show greater progress than those with most other personality disorders.[8] Though they lack insight into how they differ from other people, they are even conscientious in how they approach treatment. A droid can be reprogrammed more easily than a human, of course, but changing particular characteristics of C-3PO's identity could make him C-3PO no more. The droid has quirks, to be sure, but quirks confer character. There are things he does very well. As with a human being, his meticulousness gets the job done when it's the right job under the right circumstances, and he has proven himself worthy of retaining the pattern of personality that makes him who he is.

References

American Psychiatric Association (2013). *Diagnostic and statistical manual of mental disorders* (DSM-5) (5th ed.). Washington, DC: American Psychiatric Publishing.

Carson, N. T., Dalal, D. K., Boyce, A. S., O'Connell, M. S., Kung, M., & Delgado, K. M (2014). Uncovering curvilinear relationships between conscientiousness and job performance: How theoretically appropriate measurement makes an empirical difference. *Journal of Applied Psychology, 99*(4), 564–586.

Hwang, J. Y., Shin, Y., Li, S., Park, H. Y., Shin, N. Y., Jang, J. H., Park, H., & Kwon, J. S. (2012). Multidimensional comparison of personality characteristics of the big five model, and affect in pathological gambling and obsessive-compulsive disorder. *Journal of Gambling Studies, 28*(3), 351–362.

Kallestad, H., et al. (2010). The relationship between insight gained during therapy and long-term outcome in short-term dynamic psychotherapy and cognitive therapy for cluster C personality disorders. *Psychotherapy Research, 20*(5), 526–534.

Roberts, B. W., et al. (2014). What is conscientiousness and how can it be assessed? *Developmental, 50*(5), 1315–1330.

Samuel, D. B., & Gore, W. L. (2012). Maladaptive variants of conscientiousness and agreeableness. *Journal of Personality, 80*(6), 1669–1696.

Samuel, D. B., & Widiger, T. A. (2011). Conscientiousness and obsessive-compulsive personality disorder. *Personality disorders: Theory, research, and treatment, 2*(3), 161–174.

Simon, W. (2009). Follow-up psychotherapy outcome of patients with dependent, avoidant and obsessive-compulsive personality disorders: A meta-analytic review. *International Journal of Psychiatry in Clinical Practice, 13*(2), 153–165.

Wilson, R. S., Boyle, P. A., Yu, L., Segawa, E., Sytsma, J., & Bennett, D. A. (2015). Conscientiousness, dementia related pathology, and trajectories of cognitive aging. *Psychology and Aging, 30*(1), 74–82.

Notes

1. *Star Wars: Episode V The Empire Strikes Back* (1980 motion picture).
2. Roberts et al. (2014); Wilson et al. (2015).
3. Carter et al. (2014).
4. *Star Wars: Episode IV A New Hope* (1977/1981 motion picture).
5. Hwang et al. (2012).
6. Samuel & Gore (2012); Samuel & Widiger (2011).
7. American Psychiatric Association (2013).
8. Kallestad et al. (2010); Simon (2009).

3 »

Journeys

The Star Wars saga went through its own journey to creation, and psychology gave that journey some direction. The writings of Carl Jung and Joseph Campbell helped George Lucas find his way when he was lost in a creative wilderness. He discovered that his characters' journeys echoed those undertaken by heroic characters in tales told throughout history and across the world. Heroes grow. In addition to gaining skills and performing heroic deeds, their journeys are spiritual as well.

These Archetypes You're Looking For

ALEX LANGLEY

"Knowing your own darkness is the best method for
countering the darkness of other people."

—psychiatrist Carl Jung[1]

C arl Jung was a storyteller. He just didn't know it.

It's no secret that the original *Star Wars* trilogy draws heavily from the story patterns of the *monomyth* ("one myth"), Campbell & Moyers (1991). Joseph Campbell's term for the basic three-act story structure found in heroic narratives around the world and across time. The monomyth utilizes character and story tropes, many of which are neatly categorized into the Jungian *archetypes*, distinctive elements of the unconscious that manifest as images, motifs, and behaviors, Campbell (1949); Campbell & Jung (1976). Jung often referred to archetypes as manifestations of evolution and predestination (more later in support of nature in the "nature versus nurture" debate), and believed that human behavior was based on the varying archetypes comprising their psychological landscape.[2] While the idea of personal archetypes is debatable, Jung's archetypal ideology does resonate in the realm of fiction, particularly in the original *Star Wars* trilogy.

Luke Skywalker's base archetype is easy to identify—he's the *Hero*, a rescuer, defender, and champion; he's also much more. The young, fresh-faced Luke we see on Tattooine embodies elements of the *Child* through his naive desire for adventure. Luke wants so desperately to break away from the banal safety of his aunt and uncle's moisture farm that he never considers the dangers elsewhere. He has romanticized the idea of growing up and exploring the larger universe, focusing only on the excitement and not on the pain of potential loss or difficult moral quandaries. Luke's no Jungian Child for long, though; once Ben Kenobi becomes one with the Force, we see a different Luke through the rest of the trilogy. After losing Ben, Luke realizes that more freedom leads to less security, and Luke takes personal responsibility for helping others out of altruistic motives, rather than a hunger for youthful adventure. Henceforth Luke is, above all else, a Hero.

Bravery through Empathy

Star Wars may be well-known for its thrilling depictions of heroism through daring acts of bravery, like flying spaceships, dueling Sith Lords, or drinking that blue milk, and for most of its protagonists, heroism means taking valiant but ultimately aggressive, actions. Luke's greatest heroism, however, stems from his compassion. In both *Star Wars: Episode V The Empire Strikes Back* and *Star Wars: Episode VI Return of the Jedi*, Luke's journey of growth centers around themes of his *Anima*, the Jungian archetype of femininity primarily focusing on empathy, sensitivity, intuition, and spirituality.*

---

* It's worth mentioning that these references to masculinity/femininity are based on Jungian ideas that may not entirely correspond to modern ideas regarding the concepts.

From the very beginning, Luke is more attuned to the emotions of others than any non-Jedi character in the series; he's a people person. Luke learns his many fellow fighter pilots' names and gives them words of encouragement when others don't. When pilot Wedge Antilles fears that the Death Star's two-meter-wide weak point is impossible to target, Luke encourages him by saying, "I used to bulls-eye womp rats in my T-16 back home. They're not much bigger than two meters."[3] Basically, he's saying that if a silly kid on Tatooine can do it, a seasoned pilot like Wedge can definitely do it.

Luke is also the only human to treat droids with any semblance of decency. Han and Leia constantly ignore C-3PO, yell at him frequently, and even deactivate him midsentence, which is the human equivalent of chloroforming someone when you're tired of hearing that person talk. Droids are sentient beings who have real fears (which C-3PO often expresses, *loudly*), can feel pain (as indicated by the droid being tortured in Jabba's palace and R2-D2's many squeals), and have thoughts and ideas, yet they're treated like second-class citizens at best and slaves at worst. Luke, on the other hand, treats droids like friends and equals. When he emerges from his medical treatment on Hoth, he genuinely thanks the medical droid who has overseen his recovery. He converses with R2-D2 as he would with anyone else. When Jabba's sail barge is exploding in the deserts of Tatooine, Luke's the first one *to remember* to rescue the droids. Droids are metal life-forms, and yet Luke's the only organic who consistently sees them as more than tools because he understands the value of life and empathy, even when those lives aren't carbon-based and their emotions are electronic, rather than biochemical.

The Jedi Knights of Star Wars prequels play up their powers as being mostly flashy lightsaber swinging and telekinesis, forgetting that a Jedi's greatest weapon is sensitivity. When facing off against Darth Vader and Emperor Palpatine aboard the new

Death Star in *Return of the Jedi*, Luke doesn't triumph through superior lightsaber skills, more powerful Force abilities, or flashy dance moves. Luke triumphs through an act of compassion. After a lengthy battle with Vader and repeated emotionally manipulative jabs from the Emperor, Luke throws aside his lightsaber and proclaims that he is a Jedi Knight, like his father before him. Had he given in to his anger and struck down Palpatine as the cackling crone wanted, he might have been temporarily victorious, but ultimately he would have fallen to the dark side. With this act, Luke stays firmly in the light and reignites the long-dormant good that lay within his father. The ability to destroy a planet may be insignificant compared to the power of the Force, but the power of the Force is insignificant compared to the power of human empathy.

The Princess, the Scoundrel, and the Other Scoundrel

It's fortunate that Princess Leia, as the lone lady of the trilogy's ridiculously gender-imbalanced cast, shows such a strong character arc. In *Star Wars: Episode IV A New Hope*, she represents the archetypal *Maiden*, a being of purity and youthful innocence as indicated by her white garb and youthful naiveté during interrogation. However, unlike most damsels in distress, Leia's a wisecracker and a thinker. During *A New Hope*, Leia spends most of her time bossing people around, though she does take the occasional crackshot with a blaster, but by the time *Return of the Jedi* rolls around, Leia's a changed woman. Whether she's disguised as the Boushh bounty hunter, choking Jabba to death, or helping destroy the Death Star's shield generator, *Return of the Jedi*'s Leia shows herself to be a woman of action in touch with her *Animus*, her masculine side emphasizing action and initiative. She's also the only character to deal extensively with the concept of a *Persona*, the social face presented to the world. During the medal ceremony at the end of *A New Hope*, we see Leia the diplomat, handing out the medals instead of receiving them and serving as a figurehead above her friends rather than standing beside them. In *The Empire Strikes Back*, she's a crucial behind-the-scenes figure in the rebellion. In *Return of the Jedi*, audiences get Leia the Bounty Hunter (a Persona manifestation that wears qualities of the Animus), Leia the Slave (a Persona emphasizing males' early Anima development oriented around women as objects of desire), and, finally, Leia the *Adventurer* and *Romancer*. This Leia's no longer a Persona. As an active force in both leading the rebellion and showing her love for Han Solo, this is no social self; it's Leia's *true* self.

Han is a *Shapeshifter*, changing from acting as a Jungian *Father* to Luke before becoming a hero alongside him. In *A New Hope*, Luke dislikes Han's greed and apparent laziness, and Han tries to discourage Luke from getting involved, even going as far as to encourage him to become a passive nonentity in the Rebellion, as Han himself is. However, the young Skywalker's natural heroism rubs off on Han, and Han the scoundrel becomes Han the Hero (who's still a bit of a scoundrel). When Leia's upset in the Ewok Village but won't tell Han why, Han starts to leave out of frustration but returns to comfort her. The Han Solo of *A New Hope* would likely have left her to her tears, but by now he has learned from Luke's example: No longer is he a man strictly bound by the Animus with all its masculine expectations, only able to take action and ignore emotions. Here, Han has gotten more in touch with what Jung might call his feminine side, his Anima, and he's a more complete human being as a result.

Lando Calrissian's journey is a smaller, more compact version of Han's arc from Shapeshifter to Hero. Lando seems charismatic and friendly at first, but then betrays Han, Leia, Chewie, and

C-3PO to the Empire in exchange for Bespin's safety. Lando is a man married to his city, a loner who stumbled into the oversize responsibility of taking care of a city and who now does whatever he can to ensure its survival. After dealing with weighty moral dilemmas in *The Empire Strikes Back*, the Lando of *Return of the Jedi* is less of a Shapeshifting Scoundrel and more of a Hero who's just along for the ride.

Misleading Masters

Few characters so clearly embody their archetypal origin as Ben Kenobi does as the *Wise Old Man*. Ben's wise, he's old, and he's a man; he offers Luke advice, guidance, and encouragement throughout the trilogy. Jung indicated that the Wise Old Man represents a state of individuation achieved by those who have successfully triumphed in their struggles over the Anima; a Wise Old Man is a protector and a problem-solver, offering advice and being highly attuned to the emotions of those around him.[4] As a master of the Force, Ben has great insight into both his own emotions and the emotions of those around him, and his self-actualized approach can offer Luke greater perspective.

Ben's also a bit of a *Trickster*, misleading Luke as a catalyst for change. He lies to Luke about his father's death, telling him Darth Vader killed him, then, when confronted with the truth, spinning a yarn about how Darth Vader *did* kind of kill Anakin Skywalker from a "certain point of view." He also encourages Luke to believe Leia to be his twin sister while neither confirming nor denying that it's true ("Your insight serves you well" is as much as he says on the matter), leading to the possibility that Leia may well *not* be Luke's sister. So why is Ben such a fibber? In the case of Darth Vader's identity, it is probably to keep Luke away from him, fearing he might be drawn to his father's

Yub Nub: The Archetypes of Star Wars' Many Secondary Characters

The Emperor: The **Shadow**, a representation of one's own hidden qualities. Emperor Palpatine represents Darth Vader's own dark side. He beckons Vader, trying to keep him swathed in darkness. He recognizes the glimmer of light still present in Vader's subconscious and tries to snuff it out before he's aware of it.

Jabba the Hutt: The **Ruler**, one for whom attaining and flaunting power is the greatest achievement. Jabba's fat and sedentary but clearly powerful, and his physical presence both disgusts and intimidates, marking him as an Influencer and a Ruler (albeit a spectacularly ugly one).

Boba Fett: The **Warrior**, a subclass of the Hero with emphasis on proving his mastery to the world. Boba Fett proves his worth through guile and skill. Unfortunately, if you surmise his value based on what we see of him in the original trilogy, he's not worth very much, since he mostly just wears a backpack and falls in a hole.

The Ewoks: The **Child**, a being of innocent simplicity. Ewoks have a simple approach to everything, whether it's hunting or warfare. They're a primitive people, unfettered by the moral ambiguities and complexities of higher thought.

Malakili the Rancor Guard: The **Mother**, a nurturer and caregiver, as indicated by his tears when he believes his beloved Rancor is dead.

Willrow Hood, the escaping Bespin inhabitant holding what seems to be an ice cream maker: The **Lover**, one whose focus is passion and fears being alone. Willrow hanging onto an ice cream maker in the face of impending disaster shows that he will pursue, above all else, hedonistic pleasures, like the lusciousness of ice cream.

darkness and therefore to the Force's dark side. For a viewer who takes the "head canon" interpretation that Ben could be misleading Luke about Leia being his sister, perhaps he does so because he senses Han and Leia's children would be of great importance in the future, maybe he thinks Luke's destiny will be better served with someone else, maybe he is protecting Luke's real sister in case Vader detects her in Luke's thoughts (which does happen), or perhaps Ben is just having a bit of mischief with the boy.

Yoda, the wild, linguistically-challenged Jedi master, is a much sterner guide for Luke than Ben is. While Ben was a voice of support, Yoda's words are much harsher, more cynical, and more realistic. Whereas Luke the Child initially needs someone to guide him gently, Luke the Hero needs to face harsh truths about himself and the galaxy at large. Yoda does not take the initiative that Ben did in most situations, but he still counsels and trains Luke in ways that are typical of the Wise Old Man (albeit with a much harder attitude). Of course, Yoda is a bit of a Trickster, too. He knows who Luke is the second the young man lands on Dagobah, and yet Yoda plays coy, partly to test Luke and partly because it's fun for Yoda.

Shadows and Rage

The *Shadow* embodies unconscious aspects of the personality—desires we wish to suppress, base instincts we refuse to recognize. Darth Vader acts as a Shadow to Luke throughout the trilogy, representing the allure of the dark side and the rage and frustration brewing within the young Skywalker. Once he realizes Luke is out there, Vader becomes obsessed with finding him and turning him to the dark side for some father-and-son villainy. Perhaps beneath the body that's more machine than man, Vader still feels guilt for the part he played in destroying the Jedi Knights, and as long as Luke stays on the light side he's a constant reminder of Vader's biggest regret.

Whatever his reason, the Sith Lord obsessively pursues Luke throughout *The Empire Strikes Back* and *Return of the Jedi*. Vader frequently channels his rage toward Luke, something typical of a character locked in the first stage of Animus development as a being of mere power, "the wholly physical man" like "the fictional jungle hero Tarzan."[5]

Jung described the Anima and Animus as paired opposites, the divine couple or *Syzygy* representing completeness or wholeness. Combined, they bring great power. Stories that best symbolize their archetypal relationship often depict a Heroine whose compassion and support bring out the Hero's better qualities and who, herself, grows in the process—*Beauty and the Beast* being a classic example.[6] Although Darth Vader initially appears as a Shadow figure, his role evolves when he takes a fatherly interest in Luke. That, in turn, changes how Luke relates to him. Luke's compassion and other qualities that Jung perceived in the Anima, the man's feminine side, lead Luke to try to bring out the best in Darth Vader, to find the light in his dark father.

Vader's rage is one of his defining characteristics. He's constantly Force-choking subordinates, accidentally killing interrogatees before he can elicit information from them, even dueling with Luke with such ferocity that he slices off his son's hand and nearly kills him. At times, however, he's not content merely to rage at whatever he encounters. He takes active measures to channel his anger productively, tracking down Luke by expending immeasurable Imperial resources and even going so far as to hire bounty hunters to find him. This is Darth Vader symbolically reaching Animus development stage two, where he becomes a man of action.

His interactions with Luke during *Return of the Jedi* are different; by this point he's no longer fueled by rage, but by what seems to be sadness and a need for connection. He desperately wants Luke by his side, to act as Luke's mentor, according to the third stage of the Animus. In the end, Darth Vader's ability for good surpasses his ever-present rage, and we see him exemplify the final level of Animus development, reaching a point of clarity and self-actualization that culminates in him silently* throwing the Emperor to his death (at the cost of his own life) to save his son.

Mothers and Fathers

In the brief time Uncle Owen and Aunt Beru are anything more than charred skeletons, they act as *Father* and *Mother* to Luke. Uncle Owen is a roadblock on Luke's path to adventure: As a Father figure, he is the strict authority meant to slow down Luke's accelerating movement toward adulthood. Owen grunts tersely, trying to keep Luke on the moisture farm, and discourages him from talking to Ben Kenobi. He wants Luke to stay young and safe. After Uncle Owen beats Luke down with his stern words, Aunt Beru cleans him up with a bit of comfort. Aunt Beru is domestic and nurturing, an exemplar of motherhood that resonates across time and culture.

C-3PO, the nagging, nervous protocol droid fluent in over three billion forms of communication, also acts as a Mother, although mostly to R2-D2, his brave compatriot whose purity of focus and black-and-white moral development put the smaller droid firmly in the role of the archetypal Child. C-3PO whines and worries while R2-D2 throws himself in harm's way

* Yes, he says, "No . . . No!" in the Special Edition of *Return of the Jedi*. Vader is silent in the original version and that's how I'm going to remember it.

in pursuit of the mission. R2-D2 is heroic, to be sure, but it's a youthful heroism that's oblivious to danger. R2-D2 is constantly acting but rarely *thinking* about the repercussions of his actions.

In spite of being a member of a species reportedly prone to pulling people's arms out of their sockets, Chewie has a nurturing streak bigger than a gundark. He, too, serves mostly as a comforting, maternal presence throughout the Star Wars trilogy. When Han emerges from carbonite freezing, Chewie's immediate response is to give him a giant, furry hug. When C-3PO goes missing in Bespin, not only is Chewbacca the first one to notice, he's the only one to take any action to search for the droid. Chewie does find the missing droid and reassembles him, again displaying highly maternal instincts for someone who barks and growls as his primary form of communication.

Carl Jung was a psychiatrist, but he was also a storyteller. These archetypes, which he believed existed within the human subconscious, aren't just terms in a psychology textbook. They're story elements that speak to all of us (or, at least, aspects of all of us). Nearly everyone can relate to young Luke's desire for greatness or Leia's journey from damsel in distress to active heroine, Han's growth from greedy and emotionally stunted to (somewhat) empathetic hero, or Darth Vader's journey for emotional control and redemption. Compassion and empathy—qualities Jung saw in the Anima—save the day. These characters' universal desires and deeds figure prominently in why this seemingly straightforward tale of good and evil became and remains such a resounding modern parable.

References

Campbell, J. (1949). *The hero with a thousand faces.* New York, NY: Pantheon.
Campbell, J., & Jung, C.G. (1976). *The portable Jung.* New York, NY: Penguin.
Campbell, J., & Moyers, B. (1991). *The power of myth.* New York, NY: Anchor.
Coward, H.G. (1991). *Jung and Eastern thought.* Albany, NY: Sri Satguru.
Henderson, J. L. (1964). Ancient myths and modern man. In C. G. Jung & M.-L. von Franz (Eds.), *Man and his symbols* (pp. 105–157). New York, NY: Windfall.

Jung, C. G. (1937, September 25). Letter to Kendig. In G. Adler & A. Jaffe (Eds.) (1973), *Letters of C. G. Jung, 1906–1950* (p. 237). London, UK: Routledge.

Jung, C. G. (1942/1961). *Alchemical studies.* CW 13. Princeton, NJ: Princeton University Press.

Jung, C. G. (1957/2006). *The undiscovered self.* New York, NY: Signet.

Jung, C. G. (1948/1969). *The archetypes and the collective unconscious.* CW 9. Princeton, NJ: Princeton University Press.

Von Franz, M.-L. (1964). The process of individuation. In C. G. Jung & M.-L. von Franz (Eds.), *Man and his symbols* (pp. 158–229). New York, NY: Windfall.

Notes

1. Jung (1937), p. 237.
2. Jung (1957/2006; 1969).
3. *Star Wars: Episode IV A New Hope* (1977/1981).
4. Jung (1948/1961).
5. Von Franz (1964), p. 194.
6. Henderson (1964).

10

Feel the Force: Jung's Theory of Individuation and the Jedi Path

LAURA VECCHIOLLA

Luke Skywalker: "You know, I did feel something! I could almost see the remote."
Obi-Wan Kenobi: "That's good. You've taken your first step into a larger world." [1]

"The growth of the mind is the widening of consciousness… each step forward has been a most painful and laborious achievement."
—psychiatrist Carl Jung [2]

Swiss psychiatrist Carl Jung founded *analytical psychology*, an approach to studying mental health and personality development by analyzing conscious and unconscious processes. He maintained that personal development involves a process of *individuation*, growth as an individual, in which each person can better understand both themselves and aspects of a universal level of the unconscious mind akin to the Jedi's path in growing attuned to the Force.

In the Star Wars universe, Jedi are stoic beings who walk a noble path. From Youngling to Master, Jedi spend each moment in focused and deep reflection. Tasked with protecting peace throughout the galaxy, the Jedi must remain unwavering. They are eternally composed and judicious, despite the chaos that surges around them. It is the Jedi's connection to the Force that permits such achievements. The Force opens the Jedi up, as Obi-Wan Kenobi puts it, to a "larger world."[3] In the Star Wars universe, Jedi are able to both sense and manipulate the Force. Much like the process of becoming a Jedi, becoming individuated is a challenging, yet transformative, process.

Individuation

Individuation refers to the effort to become a whole person and to grow into one's true and limitless self. Individuation involves choosing to become fully conscious of all that we are—the good and the bad, the light and the dark. This is by no means an easy or quick choice. Rather, individuation can be seen as a lifelong discipline of taking that which is unconscious and making it conscious—of casting light into the dark side of the psyche.[4]

Individuation begins in our early years. Early in life, the *ego* (as Jung called each person's conscious personality) forms[5] and is tasked with the challenge of adapting to an outer reality.[6] Part of this adaptation involves developing a suitable *Persona*, a mask each person unconsciously presents to the outside world. The Persona protects the fragility of an individual's true, authentic self. Han Solo's Persona protects his caring nature with cynicism and apathy, because exposing this genuine side of himself would trigger feelings of vulnerability or uncertainty. Han likely finds it easier to convince the world that he doesn't care than to risk disappointment and heartbreak. The Persona can act as a sort of façade, albeit

The Path of C.G. Jung

Born in 1875 in the pastoral village of Kesswil, Switzerland, Carl Gustav Jung recalled being a solitary boy with a quiet and spiritual soul. As a young student, Jung became an "omnivorous reader of philosophy" and devoted himself to his studies.[7] After schooling, Jung began working as a psychiatrist at Burghölzli Psychiatric Hospital in Zurich. His work soon led him to contact Sigmund Freud. The two psychiatrists began an immediate friendship. After six years and irreconcilably differing ideas, however, their friendship came to a painful end. At the loss of his friend and mentor, Jung retreated deep inside himself, exploring the deep recesses of his own personal unconscious and its connection to the collective unconscious. He would emerge with a new perspective on the forces at play in the psyche. Jung spent the remainder of his life, as he put it, attempting to understand the human spirit and how it might relate to the infinite mysteries of the universe.[8]

one that may be necessary to ensure positive and successful social interactions. Ego development inevitably entails the rejection of some parts of the person that are threatening to a relatively painless experience of living. These rejected contents form each person's *Shadow* self.[9] Anakin wrestles with his Shadow self as it continually threatens his way of life as a Jedi Knight. His conflicting craving for revenge bubbles at the threshold of his consciousness until it finally boils over and he attacks the Tusken Raiders in a vengeful rage.[10] Each person's Shadow, like Anakin's, represents the individual's discordant desires, instincts, or shortcomings. Because the conscious ego can only know itself, the contents of the Persona and the Shadow reside in the unconscious.[11]

Once one's ego has fully emerged and taken hold, Jung believed, the main task of development is no longer adapting to an outer reality, but rather to an inner reality. Later in life, one has the opportunity to turn his or her focus inward and create a dialogue with the unconscious—the personal and the collective. This turning inward is the individuation process, and it might only occur when the ego finally allows for a symbiotic dialogue between the conscious and the unconscious.[12]

The Personal and Collective Unconscious

The Jedi initiate soon learns to recognize the Force as a complex and dynamic energy composed of two parts: the Living Force (the "raw and close at hand"[13] manifestation most easily sensed by the Jedi) and the Unifying Force (a vast and willful cosmic power). Communing with the Unifying Force allows the Jedi to transcend death and to appear among the living as a spirit of the Force.[14] Jung similarly divided his "force," the unconscious, into the personal unconscious and the collective unconscious. The *personal unconscious*, like the Living Force, is close at hand, as it lies at the threshold of individual consciousness. Jung said that unique aspects of the individual, such as the Shadow and the Persona, reside in the personal unconscious, as do other elements that are forgotten, repressed, or ignored. Though not presently conscious, anything in the personal unconscious has the potential to become conscious. The *collective unconscious* that Jung posited supposedly encompasses content shared by all of humankind.

The Individuation Academy

In the Star Wars universe, it is a rare privilege to be recruited to the Jedi Order and trained in the secrets of the Force, but one need not be recruited to follow the path of individuation. Such growth, as Jung saw it, requires an individual to abide by several values and precepts that prepare the way for the journey ahead. The core principles that guide Jedi in training, the Three Pillars of the Jedi, parallel Jung's requirements for individuation.

Awareness

Awareness is paramount to the individuation process. According to Jung, one must surrender to the unconscious, first accepting that it has swayed, and always can sway, feelings and actions outside of one's immediate awareness. Like the Jedi, the individuating person must strike a balance in allowing the unconscious to permeate one's actions while also remaining cognizant of and vigilant regarding its grasp. To allow for individuation to occur, one must occasionally let the ego sit back and simply observe.[15] Without an observing ego, one cannot participate in a mutual rapport with the unconscious. Similar to the individuating person, the Jedi cannot tap into the Force without first having a deep, reverential awareness of its power. This awareness entails a sort of surrender, relinquishing part of one's own ego in order to be guided by the Force.

Knowledge

The individuating person must make a lifelong commitment to self-examination and knowledge of oneself, according to Jung. An evolving familiarity with the limits of one's consciousness is central to avoiding the ignorance of a life unexamined. This knowledge first begins with the understanding that the ego does not constitute the whole of one's self. Jedi initiates commit themselves to intense scholarship and to the attainment of knowledge throughout their training. On Dagobah, Yoda reminds Luke, "A Jedi uses the Force for knowledge and defense, never for attack."[16] A Jedi hopeful cannot continue on the path to Jedi Master without diligent study.

Self-Discipline

Jung held that the mind of the individuating person should remain contemplative as the spirit converses and assimilates with the unconscious. As one progresses through individuation, actions may change, as the body now acts in congruence with the mind and the spirit. As with a person's individuation, Jedi training becomes a lifelong commitment that begins at a young age. A Jungian analyst would try to provide guidance and supervision, much as a Jedi Master might. The pillar of self-discipline signifies that the bulk of the work must be self-initiated and self-sustained. Both the Jedi and the individuating person devote their life to a holistic and personal journey in which the mind, body, and spirit must be disciplined.

The Trials of Individuation

The first trial of individuation, as outlined by Jung,[17] is to venture outside the safe confines of known consciousness and into the unknown and unlimited unconscious. The same trial is required of the Jedi. Upon completion of the trials, the Padawan is expected to leave the safe confines of the Jedi Temple. Whether moving outside the limits of consciousness or outside the Jedi Temple, the move ensures growth and progression as a result of exposure to an expansive and limitless galaxy.

Becoming a Jedi Knight or a Jedi Master is analogous to individuation. Simply leaving the temple is not enough for one to become a Jedi, just as stepping into the unconscious is not enough for one to become individuated. Once out in the unknown, there is more work to be done.

Meeting with the Persona

The first experience of the personal unconscious often involves a meeting with the Persona, the part of the unconscious that connects one's consciousness to the outside world.[18] The Persona is a compromise one makes between the true self and the social self. The mask of the Persona can be beneficial, as it can make a favorable impression on others, although potentially at the cost of hiding fragments of one's true self.

Jungians see the recognition of incongruent or distressing feelings as the first step in acknowledging the Persona. The path to individuation involves a reconciliation between the conscious ego and the Persona. Luke Skywalker confronts his Persona early on in his journey, dutifully performing the moisture farmer's role. Aunt Beru, picking up on this falsehood, insists to Uncle Owen, "Luke's just not a farmer."[19] If Luke were later to deny the Jedi path, he might remain discontented and ignorant for the rest of his days. The same holds true for the individuating person.

Encountering the Shadow

Meeting our Shadow side can be a painful and frightening experience, according to Jung.[20] Our Shadows represent the unknown parts of ourselves that are too reprehensible, incongruent, or forbidding to incorporate into our conscious personality. Before examining our own hidden qualities, we may be in complete denial of our Shadow elements, yet what we deny in ourselves can often easily be spotted in others.[21] A person may despise another's quick temper while at the same time fervently suppressing a wish to respond with anger. The first step in making the acquaintance of a person's own Shadow is admitting that the scary, annoying, or irritating qualities found in others are often the qualities in that individual that evoke the very same responses. The blithe demeanor Princess Leia so despises in Han is certainly an aspect of herself that she needs to eradicate from her role as a senator.

While some of the Shadow should stay suppressed, complete disavowal of one's own characteristics may be dangerous. The more the Shadow remains unconscious, the more it might grow in strength and the greater the risk that it will commandeer the personality entirely. This appears to happen with Anakin's inevitable descent into the dark side as he embraces his Sith identity as Darth Vader. In individuation, the encounter with the Shadow is not combative in nature. The goal of this encounter is not to defeat or overcome the Shadow, but rather to develop a reciprocal relationship with it.[22] The Shadow holds messages that it may be wise for the person to heed. These messages may come in the form of dream content, particularly if the dream includes a character that is the same gender as the dreamer.[23] By paying attention to the message, or the dream, the encounter with the Shadow becomes collaborative, rather than hostile in nature. As paradoxical as it may seem, the Shadow is still part of our true and whole self. According to Jung, each person should accept it, attune to it, guide it, and control it. Jedi strive to stay mindful and aware of anger and other shadowy feelings, as when Obi-Wan Kenobi advises to "be mindful of your thoughts."[24]

Exploring the Collective Unconscious

The inborn collective unconscious becomes known to us through dreams, myths, and synchronistic events. Jung stressed the dream as one of the most important means of accessing the collective unconscious. Anakin encounters his *Anima* archetype (the male's unconscious representation of womanhood) in his dreams, represented by Padmé.[25]

Integral Journey

Whereas Carl Jung looked at how archetypes shape individual growth, *integral psychology* (which integrates knowledge from different areas of psychology) looks at many factors. Its *Integral Operating System,* a.k.a. AQAL ("all quadrants, all levels"), framework[26] can help explore why a hero might turn villainous and later heroic again

Quadrants (Ways of Knowing Our World)
- *Subjective perspective* ("I")—individual, interior experiences, like Anakin's thoughts, emotions, memories, perceptions, and dreams, even nightmares.
- *Intersubjective perspective* ("We")—collective, interior experience a person shares with others, including language, culture, and values. Anakin starts with one set on Tatooine, then is expected to adopt the Jedi way.
- *Objective perspective* ("It")—individual, exterior things. Anakin loses his legs and other body parts, which are replaced with mechanical or robotic parts.
- *Interobjective perspective* ("Its")—collective, exterior things such as our systems, networks, technology, government, and the natural environment. Important interobjective realities in Anakin's life are the Jedi Order and Galactic Republic.

Lines of Development (Areas of Growth)
- *Bodily-Kinesthetic*—control of body and motion. As a child, Anakin is a successful podracer and pilot. Grown, he uses his remarkable reflexes to fence, leap, and navigate his way through an elevator shaft.
- *Cognitive*—intellectual ability. Nine-year old Anakin builds a podracer, builds C-3PO, and masterminds the Jedis' escape from Tatooine.
- *Emotional*—emotional expression and control. Anakin's emotions become volatile over time and ultimately prove to be his greatest weakness.
- *Moral*—differentiating right from wrong. Instead of serving high moral principles, the adult Anakin bases his actions upon fear of loss and desire for recognition.
- *Spiritual*—access to altered states and experiences. Anakin cannot master the non-attachment that is central to the Jedi Code, thus the Council refuses to make him a Master.

—Dana Klisanin

We can also recognize messages from the collective uncon-scious when we experience the phenomenon Jung called *synchronicity*, making meaning out of sheer coincidence.[27] Qui-GonJinn speaks to the significance of synchronicity when he tells young Anakin, "Nothing happens by accident."[28] The Jedi find profound significance in what others may perceive as random, inconsequential coincidences. On the path to individ-uation, a person examines synchronistic events as meaningful expressions of the collective unconscious.

Mastering Individuation

Jung and other psychologists have held that we all have the innate capacity to walk a path that leads us to our true selves. The Jedi's journey does not differ greatly from our own. Just as the Jedi gather their strength from a connection to the Force, Jungians say we gather ours from communing with the forces of the personal and collective unconscious. The unconscious has wisdom to share—wisdom that brings with it peace, balance, and wholeness, but to benefit from this wisdom, we must first learn to feel the Force.

References

Dunne, C. (2012). *Carl Jung: Wounded healer of the soul*. New York, NY: Watkins.
Jacobi, J. (1983). *The way of individuation*. New York, NY: New American Library.
Jung, C. G., & Baynes, H. G. (1921). *The psychology of individuation*. London, UK: Kegan Paul.
Jung, C. G. (1928/2008). *Contributions to analytical psychology*. New York, NY: Harcourt Brace and Company.
Jung, C. G. (1938). *Psychology and religion*. New Haven, CT: Yale University Press.
Jung, C. G. (1959). *Aion: Researches into the phenomenology of the self* (2nd ed.). Princeton, NJ: Princeton University Press.
Jung, C. G. (1961). *Memories, dreams, reflections*. New York, NY: Random House.
Jung, C. G. (1962). *Symbols of transformation* (vol. 2). New York, NY: Harper.
Jung, C. G. (1966). *Two essays on analytical psychology* (3rd ed.). Princeton, NJ: Princeton University Press.
Jung, C. G. (1970). *The structure and dynamics of the psyche* (2nd ed.). Princeton, NJ: Princeton University Press.

McNeely, D. (2010). *Becoming: An introduction to Jung's concept of individuation.* Carmel, CA: Fisher King.

Stein, M. (2006). *The principle of individuation: Toward the development of human consciousness.* Wilmette, IL: Chiron.

Wallace, D. (2011). *The Jedi path: A manual for students of the Force.* London, UK: Titan.

Wilber, K. (2000). *Integral psychology: Consciousness, spirit, psychology, therapy.* Boston: Shambhala.

Zweig, C., & Abrams, J. (1991). Introduction: The shadow side of everyday life. In C. Zweig & J. Abrams (Eds.), *Meeting the shadow: The hidden power of the dark side of human nature* (pp. xvi–xxv). New York, NY: Tarcher/Putnam.

Notes

1. *Star Wars: Episode IV A New Hope* (1977/1981 motion picture).
2. Jung (1928/2008), p. 340.
3. Wallace (2011).
4. Stein (2006).
5. Jung (1966).
6. Jacobi (1983).
7. Dunne (2012).
8. Jung (1961), p.356.
9. Jung (1966).
10. *Star Wars: Episode II Attack of the Clones* (2002 motion picture).
11. Jung (1966).
12. Jung & Baynes (1921).
13. Wallace (2011), p. 23.
14. Wallace (2011).
15. McNeely (2010).
16. *Star Wars: Episode V The Empire Strikes Back* (1980 motion picture).
17. Jung (1962).
18. Jung (1966).
19. *A New Hope.*
20. Jung (1938).
21. Jung (1966).
22. Zweig & Abrams (1991).
23. Jung (1959).
24. *Attack of the Clones.*
25. *Star Wars: Episode III Revenge of the Sith* (2005 motion picture).
26. Wilber (2000).
27. Jung (1970).
28. *Star Wars: Episode I The Phantom Menace* (1999 motion picture).

11

A Distressing Damsel:
Leia's Heroic Journey

MARA WOOD

"Women are so much tougher than men underneath."
—psychiatrist Carl Jung[1]

Carl Jung and Joseph Campbell's observations about archetypal themes directly shaped the creation of Star Wars.[2] Writers discussing their influence tend to focus on the hero's journey as demonstrated by Anakin or Luke Skywalker,[3] yet these are not the only transformative journeys in the saga. Among others, Luke's twin sister Leia changes throughout the saga as she embarks on a journey of her own.

The Hero

No happy accident, Luke's storyline reflects centuries of myths and stories. Carl Jung, a Swiss psychiatrist, theorized that everyone in the world has the ability to recognize certain figures. For example, people from any culture would be able to recognize a hero when they saw one without any formal knowledge of what a hero was. Jung called these unconscious themes *archetypes*. They are the building blocks of his theory of the *collective unconscious*, a psychological phenomenon that permeates all cultures and explains shared features in stories. The collective unconscious is not a personal trait we cultivate, but one with which we are all born.[4] The contents and modes of behavior that stem from the collective unconscious are essentially the same for individuals everywhere. Through Jung's observations and research, he outlined many archetypes he considered influential in dreams and psychological processes.

While Jung concentrated on the establishment of archetypes as they influenced individual growth and psychosis, other academics applied his ideas to different fields. Mythologist Joseph Campbell, in his book *The Hero with a Thousand Faces*, explored the hero archetype and the journey on which the hero embarks (Campbell 1999). As Lucas prepared his drafts of *Star Wars*, he was heavily guided by the traditional hero myth without even realizing it, unconsciously influenced by archetypes in the way Jung predicted. Only after rereading Campbell's definitive book did Lucas consciously rework his original story for *Star Wars* to reflect more of the heroic aspects Campbell described.[5] As a result, Lucas deliberately introduced audiences to the classic hero's journey. What is less evident, but arguably just as important, is the heroine's journey through Star Wars.

The Heroine

While attending a workshop hosted by Campbell, therapist Maureen Murdock attempted to map out the Hero's Journey from the feminine perspective. During this exercise, Murdock realized something: A woman's experience does not necessarily mirror the arc of the hero's journey. After she presented this idea to Campbell, he stated that women don't need to make the journey; "all she needs to do is to realize that she's the place that people are trying to get to."[6] This notion did not ring true for Murdock who knew, from experience with women in therapy, that women take their own journeys throughout life. Murdock's interaction with Campbell prompted her to reflect on her therapeutic and writing experience to write *The Heroine's Journey: Women's Quest for Wholeness* in 1990. Much as Campbell's work influenced the development of Star Wars, it also inspired Maureen Murdock to describe the heroic journey more common to women.

While the hero's journey involves going outward into the vast world, Murdock describes the heroine's as one of introspection and the exploration of one's soul. The hero supposedly concentrates on doing whereas the woman must learn how to be. Like Campbell, Murdock found heroic descriptions in mythology and literature from different cultures over centuries and throughout the world.

Even before Luke embarks on his hero's journey, Leia starts on her own heroine's journey. Her role in the Star Wars saga closely follows Murdock's outline of the heroine's journey and serves as an explicit example of the journey many women undertake, much as Luke's journey follows Campbell's description of the hero's journey. For women of all walks of life, there is a need to embrace the feminine nature, value the self as a woman, and heal the deep wounds of the feminine.[7] As Leia moves through each stage of the journey, she battles her own personal demons while simultaneously growing into the leader the new Republic needs.

Separation from the Feminine

In a male-dominated society, women who identify with the feminine may be punished for doing so, whether they are overlooked for promotions or are simply not taken seriously. It becomes advantageous to a woman to set aside her femininity to make progress in a traditionally male world. The woman sheds culturally feminine characteristics, like inferiority, passivity, dependence, seduction, manipulation, and powerlessness.[8]

One of Leia's most notable attributes is demonstrating qualities often considered masculine in terms of traditional gender roles.[9] Her first appearance onboard the *Tantive IV* shows her stubborn, insistent nature as well as her fearless response to the ominous Darth Vader. Leia endures torture, sees her home planet destroyed without shedding a tear, commands the Rebel fleet, and assumes a position of authority upon meeting the hero. Leia's seemingly masculine nature is a reflection of the first step of her heroine's journey.

Leia's adoptive parents, Breha and Bail Organa of Alderaan, are thoughtful, loving parents. Breha's history of miscarriages leaves her wanting a child, and adopting Leia becomes the answer to the couple's prayers.[10] Leia grows up in the presence of a respected queen of Alderaan, yet she finds power and prestige in her adoptive father's career. Many cultures are patriarchal, and people who engage in patriarchal careers and thinking are rewarded.[11] In patriarchal cultures, girls internalize the idea of female inferiority, leading to a greater need than boys for approval and validation.[12]

Seeing her adoptive mother as a restrictive ruler, Leia rejects the cultural lessons of her mother in favor of the more aggressive and physically demanding lessons her father provides.[13] Murdock's model states that women often create an inner mother archetype that is vengeful, possessive, and devouring.[14] Women associate this archetype with mothers in order to facilitate a separation, even if one's own mother does not possess these characteristics. Fiction often reflects this separation by making the mother figure absent (*Veronica Mars*), dead (*The Little Mermaid*), or villainous (many versions of stepmothers, including the fairy tale *Cinderella*). In other cases, the separation is a result of the mother being too perfect and supportive, prompting the woman to step out of her shadow. Leia ends up symbolically rejecting the femininity her adoptive, supportive mother represents and following in her father's footsteps. Leia, like others who know him, idolizes Bail and his work for the Republic.

Identification with the Masculine and the Gathering of Allies

Many successful women in male-dominated professions embody traits common to men and identify with masculinity.[15] Greek mythology provides an example of a woman adopting and identifying with the masculine in Athena, who is the sole daughter of Zeus, his ally, and his favorite child.[16] Athena is a warrior goddess, the pinnacle of a masculine-defined woman.

Leia and her adoptive father work together to gather allies from around the galaxy to oppose the Empire's rule. Admiral Dodonna respects Leia and her leadership, despite being a liability after the destruction of Alderaan, and Leia is established as an influential leader of the Rebel Alliance, prior to the beginning of *Star Wars: Episode IV A New Hope*.[17] The male allies who surround her validate her position and further reinforce her decision to embrace masculine traits.

Road of Trials

The bulk of Leia's trials during her heroine's journey occur onscreen throughout the original trilogy. Murdock writes that

many women's trials relate to the impact of society's expectations. The trials women face center on one line: "Yes dear, you
can do anything you want to do as long as you do what *we* want
you to do."[18] A dissonance grows in women who are told to act
one way when they're expected to act another. Oftentimes, the
threat of dependency faces women on their personal road of
trials.[19] After separating from the characteristics of the mother
and adopting masculine traits, dependency acts as a threat to the
woman's autonomy and power. As a result, she denies her own
needs in favor of what is expected of her by those around her.
Leia asserts her independence and self-reliance in the face of the
death of her planet, Alderaan.

Leia's reaction to the destruction of her planet is notable.
Tarkin destroys Alderaan, and yet Leia does not give him the
satisfaction of seeing her break down. After the rebels destroy
the Death Star, Leia works with fellow Alderaanian Evaan to
find and protect Alderaanians living across the galaxy. She exhib-
its guilt over her role in Alderaan's death, but never fully and
openly grieves the loss.[20]

Much like other women portrayed in cultures around the
world, Leia is a princess trapped by her antagonist. Her initial
encounter with the hero, Luke, is from a position of powerlessness. Leia, in her virginal white dress, appears to Luke to be an
unobtainable goddess. She is repeatedly typecast as the damsel
in distress, not only by Luke but also by Han, who constantly
calls her "princess" and "your worship," reminding her that they
saved her life. Unaccustomed to people outright devaluing her
status, Leia faces the challenge of asserting her power in front of
these men. It is at this juncture that we see Leia deal with expectations of her sex and position as women in real life do.

Boon of Success

In identifying with and adapting to a masculine world, women may find temporary success, especially in their chosen careers.[21] On the surface, these women exude power, yet feel something is missing from their lives. The male-dominated culture is not accommodating to their needs. Through her leadership, Leia strengthens the Rebellion and helps bring about the destruction of the Death Star. However, this boon is short-lived. The destruction deals a substantial blow to the Empire, but the Empire responds by doubling down on breaking up the Rebellion now that the rebels pose a real threat.

Leia's all-business approach is much like Murdock's description of the *illusory boon of success*. Just beyond reach, success keeps pulling the woman forward without allowing time for her to fully address her holistic needs. The illusory boon of success is subtler in everyday life. Women may feel as if they finally have it all—a career, a family, power, and recognition. It is usually at this time, however, that they start to feel worn down and empty. The success they enjoy in their outer life stands in stark contrast to the emptiness they feel inside.[22]

Awakening to Feelings of Spiritual Aridity

As Murdock theorized, the journey of the heroine is not an outward adventure but one that delves deeper into the soul. There is a desire to rediscover the feminine and mesh the masculine and feminine together into a complete, whole person. Without attending to her inner needs, the woman feels incomplete. For Leia, this part of her heroine's journey begins with the opening of *Star Wars: Episode V The Empire Strikes Back*.

The hard-won battle gives the Rebellion more legitimacy, and Leia gains more power as one of their leaders. However, without the growth of the inner self, boons of success, such as the brief security of the Rebellion, are empty. Denial of the feminine, over time, might drive a woman to seek out femininity in her world. In Leia's case, she slowly begins her romance with Han Solo. Even the feelings she develops for Luke never match the passion that sparks between Han and Leia. Jung's theory of the Anima and Animus may best describe their relationship. Jung believed that every man has an inner feminine entity, a being that is in essence an opposite force to him.[23] In every burly, pig-headed man's collective unconscious lies the archetypal concept of a woman who carries all the qualities he lacks; this is called the *Anima*. Jung claimed that the Anima directs men in their interactions with the world. Additionally, when a man meets a woman who possesses the qualities of the Anima, he experiences a completion of himself. The same is true of women and the *Animus*, the masculine being within them.

With Jung's theory in mind, it becomes easy to see how these two fall in love. Responsible and logical Leia falls for the dashing smuggler who lives day to day. By falling in love, Leia realizes the aridity in her inner soul and her need for Han. This portion of the heroine's journey does not always mean falling in love; rather, it is the recognition that outward success does not necessarily equate with true happiness. Despite the brief (and often interrupted interactions) between Han and Leia in *The Empire Strikes Back*, fans see that their bond brings genuine happiness and joy to both characters.

Initiation and Descent into the Goddess

One of the most gut-wrenching moments of the Star Wars saga is the moment when Han and Leia confess their love to each other. In the presence of their enemies, Leia bares her heart to Han while he acknowledges that he has known her true feelings all this time. He locks eyes with her and descends into the carbon-freezing chamber. For all intents and purposes, Leia loses her true love.

Murdock explains this feeling as universal to the female experience. Whereas many would call it a descent into depression, Murdock describes this moment as crucial to the woman's development. At one of the lowest points in her life, she gains the knowledge and strength needed to pull herself out of despair. The experience is unique to each woman in terms of the cause, the symptoms, and the strength required to navigate through it. It often begins at a time of loss or transition. Murdock describes this "underworld" as outside of time and pervasive.[24] The woman may enter a period of voluntary isolation. She emerges from this period by going deeper into herself.

Reclaiming of the Feminine

A woman's descent triggers her need to seek out and reclaim her femininity.[25] The descent helps release the woman from society's patriarchal demands through the natural introspection that accompanies it. As a result, the woman who emerges is stronger because she now accepts the femininity she once rejected. She can focus on being rather than doing.[26] Leia, now fully in charge of her deep feelings for Han and the agency she's discovered in her personal life, reclaims her femininity through finding him and reaffirming her love.

It is interesting to note that at this point in the saga Leia is portrayed in her most traditionally sexual role: the infamous metal bikini. This image of raw femininity would not carry the same meaning without the journey thus far. It is simultaneously a recognition of her return to her feminine nature while also an attempt to trivialize the power of the feminine. One of the outcomes of emerging from the descent is reclaiming the feminine body. The symbolism extends to the moment when she kills Jabba using the chains of her costume, thus overcoming Star Wars' most prominent example of sexism. This reconnection to the feminine has not diminished the power Leia possesses, but rather enhances it.

Healing the Mother/Daughter Split

The major result of a woman reclaiming her femininity is the healing of the initial split that has driven her to the masculine. It is a return to the mother figure, the act of accepting nurturing from others and acting as a nurturer herself. Women in this stage of the heroine's journey are revitalized by performing ordinary acts that reflect both their femininity and their grounding in everyday life.[27] Both Leia's biological and adoptive mothers have died, and the healing comes more in the form of acknowledging the lives of her mothers and subtly growing into the roles they played. Luke helps to initiate this stage by directly asking Leia to share any memories of her mother.

This reclaiming of her femininity primes Leia for the journey to find her biological roots. Leia has followed in her adoptive father's footsteps for most of her life. In learning of her parentage, she has the opportunity to reconnect with her biological mother and discover the parallels between their two lives. It is through this revelation that Leia begins to recognize the presence of the Force in her life, a power that requires a connection to wisdom.[28]

Healing the Wounded Masculine

In the process of healing the masculine, the heroine recognizes the benefits of masculinity as well as its limitations. Through this process, she develops a healthy masculine identity that dovetails with her newly reclaimed femininity. Murdock describes this step as the woman's ability to let go of ego, financial gain, and passivity.[29] Murdock speaks of a positive inner masculine, a piece of the woman representing masculine compassion and strength to support her full integration. Leia's healing of the masculine is demonstrated in *Return of the Jedi* through Han, who represents Leia's relationship with her own inner masculine. Leia grows to trust Han more and more, especially with the mission on Endor.

Integration of the Masculine and Feminine

The integration of the masculine and the feminine in the heroine's journey occurs as she accepts and recognizes both parts of her psyche and restores the balance in her life. It hinges on the woman's ability to process the inherent feminine qualities she possesses while also learning to be successful in a male-dominated world.[30] She moves beyond the duality of gender and embraces a more fluid perspective. This change, though it may be almost imperceptible, becomes evident through Leia's further acceptance of Han as her lover, Luke as her brother, and herself as a female leader in the Rebellion against the Galactic Empire. Onscreen, audiences see a brief glimpse of this integration as Leia accepts Han's worry over a blaster injury while simultaneously saving his life from a Stormtrooper. Gaining this duality is important not only to Leia's personal heroine's journey, but for the good of the Republic. By possessing both the masculine and the feminine, Leia becomes the natural choice for leading the new Republic.

Sexist Journey?

When Joseph Campbell outlined the hero's journey, he did so based largely on tales of male characters. Women specifically figure into that journey twice, each time in terms of how she affects the male.[31]

- **Meeting with the Goddess:** The hero discovers the "good girl," a love interest or a mother (maybe a sister) figure who helps him on his way. In Star Wars, this happens when Luke meets Leia.
- **Woman as Temptress:** A feminine distraction, maybe a "bad girl," threatens to divert the hero from his journey. Padmé becomes Anakin's distraction, and his fear of losing her diverts him from the heroic path.

Some writers try to reconcile this by treating gender as interchangeable when looking at Campbell's sequence, while others, like Murdock, question the whole thing.

—T. L.

More Than Just Saving the Galaxy

Lucas tailored Star Wars to follow Campbell's formula for a hero's journey in regard to Luke, but Leia serves as more than a prop in the hero's journey. She represents the divine within his journey while simultaneously completing her own. Murdock's analysis of the heroine's journey, created in response to Campbell's hero's journey, universalizes the experience to all women across cultures, helping to explain how women interact with and understand their environments differently than men. The heroine's journey that Leia completes primes her for loving Han, leading the Republic, and becoming a Jedi.

References

Athens, O. (2014, May 4). *Star Wars: Luke Skywalker and the Hero's Journey.* Geeks of Doom: http://www.geeksofdoom.com/2014/05/04/luke-skywalker-heros-journey.

Bem, S. L. (1974). The measurement of psychological androgyny. *Journal of Consulting and Clinical Psychology, 42*(2), 155–162.

Bem, S. L. (1981). Gender schema theory: A cognitive account of sex typing source. *Psychological Review, 88*(4), 354.

Campbell, J. (1949). *The hero with a thousand faces.* Princeton, NJ: Princeton University Press.

Jung, C. G. (1949/1969). *The archetypes and the collective unconscious.* CW 9. Princeton, NJ: Princeton University Press.

Jung, C. G. (1951/1983). *The essential Jung.* A. Storr (Ed.). Princeton, NJ: Princeton University Press.

Larsen, S., & Larsen, R. (2002). *Joseph Campbell: A fire in the mind.* Rochester, VT: Inner Traditions.

Murdock, M. (1990). *The Heroine's Journey: Women's quest for wholeness.* Boston, MA: Shambhala.

Sands, F. (1961, September 10). The trouble with women. *The Pittsburgh Post-Gazette, 35*(41), 7.

Waid, M., & Dodson, T. (2015). *Star Wars: Princess Leia, 1*(1–5). New York, NY: Marvel Worldwide, LLC.

Notes

1. Sands (1961).
2. Larsen & Larsen (2002).
3. For example, Athens (2014).
4. Jung (1948/1969).
5. Larsen & Larsen (2002).
6. Murdock (1990).
7. Murdock (1990).
8. Murdock (1990).
9. Bem (1974; 1981).
10. *Star Wars: Episode III Revenge of the Sith* (2005 motion picture).
11. Murdock (1990).
12. Murdock (1990).
13. Waid & Dodson (2015).
14. Murdock (1990).
15. Murdock (1990).
16. Hamilton (1942)
17. Waid & Dodson (2015).
18. Murdock (1990).
19. Murdock (1990).
20. Waid & Dodson (2015).
21. Murdock (1990).
22. Murdock (1990).
23. Jung (1951/1983).
24. Murdock (1990).
25. Murdock (1990).

26. Murdock (1990).
27. Murdock (1990).
28. Jung (1948/1969).
29. Murdock (1990).
30. Murdock (1990).
31. Campbell (1949).

12

Faith and the Force: Star Wars and the Psychology of Religion

CLAY ROUTLEDGE

"Don't be too proud of the technological terror you've constructed. The ability to destroy a planet is insignificant next to the power of the Force."
—Darth Vader[1]

"I am against all big organizations as such, national ones first and foremost; against all big successes and big results; and in favor of the eternal forces of truth which always work in the individual and immediately unsuccessful way, under-dogs always, till history comes, after they are long dead, and puts them on the top."
—psychologist William James[2]

Psychologists have always been fascinated by humanity's spiritual nature. Humans are apparently a unique species in that we possess the advanced neurological circuitry and cognitive architecture necessary to reflect on our own existence and ponder questions of a metaphysical nature: Why are we here? What happens when we die? Is there more to the world than what our senses can detect? Is there a grander meaning to our lives? Do we have an immaterial essence (that is, a soul) that transcends the material body?

One way humans grapple with these kinds of existential questions is by subscribing to and investing in religious faiths, or what psychologists refer to as *cultural worldviews*.[3] Religious pursuits are not exclusively tied to activities like attending church services, praying, or studying sacred texts. Our species also explores religion and spirituality through storytelling. Our ancestors told stories of mythical creatures, supernatural agents, and gods with different powers and motives. We are not so different. Our culture abounds in science-fiction/fantasy movies, books, and games. So how does Star Wars help us explore our spirituality and our religious proclivities?

Psychologists have posited that fiction serves important psychological functions. Fictional stories and characters, such as those in Star Wars, provide simulations of the social world[4] and give people a rich and compelling means of exploring basic psychological needs.[5]

The Search for Immortality

As humans, we are motivated by the goal of self-preservation, but we know that we are mortal. The prospect of death is unsettling so we endeavor to be more than mortal. For example, psychological studies reveal that giving people reasons to believe in life after death reduces the anxiety surrounding death.[6] Anxiety compromises mental health, so beliefs that help people cope with anxiety about death prove advantageous for psychological functioning.

Mortality

In *Star Wars: Episode IV A New Hope*, Obi-Wan allows Darth
Vader to deliver a kill strike. Providing the first clue that Jedi
may be immortal, Obi-Wan Kenobi's body disappears; only his
robe is left behind. Later in the film, Ben's voice, saying, "Use the
Force, Luke," and "Let go, Luke," offers a further glimpse into
Jedi immortality.[7] Trusting his mentor's guidance, Luke disen-
gages his targeting computer and uses the Force to deliver a critical strike to the Death Star. Other Jedi Masters appear in ghost
form throughout the saga,[8] further signaling that Jedi possess
some kind of immortality. Like us, these characters understand
their mortality and invest in a supernatural belief system that
paves the way for immortality.

Theory and research in social psychology shed light on
people's efforts to gain feelings of immortality through invest-
ment in religion. According to *terror management theory*, a prominent social-psychological theory, humans are religious, in part,
because religious faith helps alleviate the fear of death by offering a means to transcend mortality, to achieve some kind of
perception of immortality.[9] Studies show that people reminded
of their mortality subsequently report greater levels of religiosity
as well as belief in the afterlife.[10]

Immortality does not always come in the form of transcendence over literal death. According to terror management theory,
people can achieve a sense of immortality by believing that they
are connected to and thus part of something larger than themselves, something that will continue to exist after they die.[11] This
sentiment is echoed in Star Wars. When first describing the Force
to Luke, Ben says, "It is an energy field created by all living things.
It surrounds us and penetrates us. It binds the galaxy together"[12]—
something that connects all life but is also eternal. As the guardians
of peace in the galaxy, Jedi Knights are regularly thrust into situations that put them in mortal danger. Thus, they gain protection

from the anxiety surrounding death by investing in a religious-like belief system that makes them feel, in some way, immortal.

Supernatural Thinking

More generally, religious beliefs involve *supernatural thinking*: thoughts and attitudes that relate to entities, events, or actions that are at odds with our understanding of the laws of physics. Cognitive and developmental psychologists have argued that supernatural thinking is a normal part of human development, which can help children understand what they see around them.[13] Long before humans came up with scientific explanations for natural phenomena, supernatural thinking helped our ancestors make sense of the world.

Supernatural thinking is not confined to childhood or the ancestral world. Many twenty-first-century adults subscribe to supernatural beliefs derived from religious faith (e.g., belief in the power of prayer). Psychological research demonstrates that religious supernatural thinking serves psychological functions. For example, it increases people's sense of control when they feel uncertain or stressed out.[14] Because supernatural beliefs are at odds with a scientific understanding of the world, though, tension may arise between religious individuals who hold such beliefs and nonreligious people who reject such beliefs.

Star Wars provides many examples of supernatural thinking and the friction that often develops between religious and nonreligious people regarding the validity of supernatural thinking. Han Solo responds to Luke Skywalker's attempt to harness the power of the Force in his lightsaber training by commenting, "Hokey religions and ancient weapons are no match for a good blaster at your side, kid."[15] In this exchange, Han is essentially arguing that a religious belief in a supernatural force is antiquated and inferior to a more scientific, technological worldview. Likewise after Darth Vader proclaims that the power to

Extrinsic vs. Intrinsic Spirituality: Using Religion or Living It?

"The exintrinsically motivated person uses his religion, whereas the intrinsically motivated lives his religion."
—psychologist Gordon Allport[16]

Dozens of studies have observed that people who belong to organized religions show, on average, greater prejudice and intolerance of outgroups than people who do not.[17] Churchgoers' different motivations for joining religious organizations appear to explain much of this correlation. People with an *extrinsic* religious orientation, that is, those who participate as a self-serving way to gain social rewards, like meeting people or obeying their parents (*extrinsic motivation*), express more prejudice. They hate more. Extrinsically motivated, the Sith use the power of the Force to benefit themselves and manipulate or hurt others. To people with *intrinsic* religious orientation, on the other hand, spirituality itself is part of their self-concept and their religion's teachings give them guidance in life. They value religion for its own sake (*intrinsic motivation*). Intrinsically religious individuals show less prejudice and less self-serving biases, at least when their religious teachings encourage tolerance and do not directly promote discrimination.[18] Just as Jedi get in tune with the Force, those who are intrinsically spiritual come to appreciate the great variety of life and endeavor to serve others.

—T. L.

destroy planets is insignificant compared to the power of the Force, Admiral Mottisays, "Don't try to frighten us with your sorcerer's ways, Lord Vader. Your sad devotion to that ancient religion has not helped you conjure up the stolen data tapes or given you clairvoyance enough to find the rebels' hidden fort."[19] In these scenes, the friction between believers and nonbelievers takes center stage and is a source of animosity and derision.

Beyond dramatizing the debate between believers and nonbelievers, Star Wars echoes how many religious adherents mentally balance the natural (science) and the supernatural (religion).

Though science and religion are often portrayed as being at odds with each other, many people possess *cognitive schemas* (mental frameworks that help organize and make sense of information) that allow science and religion to co-exist peacefully. Many religious people do not reject science entirely, just specific ideas that challenge their religious worldviews. In fact, they very much rely on the technological advancements and medical interventions derived from science.[20] They simply believe that there are metaphysical forces beyond science at work in the world. In Star Wars, the Jedi and the Sith illustrate this kind of cognitive schema. Jedi are students of science and technology. For example, they construct their own lightsabers. In many ways, Jedi represent a scholarly social class that is very invested in the scientific world. At the same time, they also believe that science and technology have limits and they therefore embrace the supernatural, religious qualities of the Force.

Self-Control

Self-control is at the core of the Jedi lifestyle. Psychologists have proposed that religious-inspired practices can benefit mental and physical health by helping people exercise self-control.[21] Studies reveal that self-control promotes adaptive psychological functioning because it helps people regulate their emotions and behavior.[22] Religious doctrines typically include prescriptions for taking care of one's own body (e.g., your body is a temple), and support psychological traits that are associated with self-control, such as humility, patience, mindfulness, and compassion. In addition, religious doctrines offer behavioral techniques, including meditation and prayer, that can help people regulate their emotions and actions. When people are exposed to religious themes or call to mind their religious beliefs, they are better able to endure discomfort, delay gratification, and follow through on challenging tasks.[23]

The Jedi Knights illustrate the idea of self-control derived from religious doctrine. Jedi live by a strict moral code, rooted in the Force. They have few possessions. They learn through training to control their emotions, particularly the negative emotions of fear, anger, and hatred, as these can push a Jedi Knight toward the dark side of the Force. Jedi are mindful of their thoughts and intentions and meditate on their choices.

This theme of using the Jedi Code to control oneself is prominent throughout all Star Wars stories. For example, a major story arc running through *Star Wars: Episode V The Empire Strikes Back* and *Star Wars: Episode VI Return of the Jedi* is Luke Skywalker's Jedi training in which Yoda teaches him to face and, ultimately, control his fear and anger so he can avoid being seduced by the dark side of the Force when he confronts Darth Vader. Both Darth Vader and the Emperor try to push Luke to give in to his baser impulses, to relinquish control and indulge his anger. Luke does not give in. Through his training and faith in the Jedi Way, the light side of the Force, he is able to resist the temptation of the dark side of the Force.

Episodes I through III showcase what transpires when a Padawan fails to exercise the self-discipline taught by the Jedi Code and gives in to the dark side of the Force. Anakin Skywalker grows increasingly frustrated and angry. His mother's torture and death torment him. He believes the Jedi Council is holding him back from reaching his full potential and is not giving him the recognition and respect he deserves. His inability to control these negative emotions eventually leads him to act on them violently. This is consistent with psychological research linking self-control to aggression: Higher levels of self-control are associated with lower levels of aggression, and when people are angry and feel the urge to hurt others, their level of self-control determines whether or not they act on these urges.[24] In addition, studies show that self-control helps people empathize with and act sensitive toward others.[25] Anakin's lack of self-control and his inability to regulate his negative emotions propel him down a path of violence. Through escalating acts of anger-induced violence toward Sand People (Tusken Raiders), Younglings, and eventually his own wife, Padmé, Anakin transitions to the dark side of the Force.

Finding Meaning

The psychological benefits of religion extend beyond self-control. Religion also helps people find a sense of meaning in life, the feeling that one's existence has purpose and value. People can derive meaning from life without religion, but psychological studies indicate that, for many, religion is a major source of meaning in life.[26] Religion also helps people cope with life stressors that threaten meaning, such as the death of a loved one.[27] The meaning that religion inspires can be of great consequence because people who perceive their lives as meaningful tend to be healthier and live longer.[28]

The Jedi address the concept of meaning in life in a way that is very similar to religion. Religious worldviews often hold that people have a destiny, a predetermined purpose in life. Similarly, the Jedi advocate for a purpose predetermined by the Force. For example, in Episodes I through III, there is much discussion as to whether or not Anakin is the chosen one. Qui-Gon Jinn tells the Jedi Council, "Finding him was the will of the Force. I have no doubt of that."[29] Similarly, Jinn's dying request to Obi-Wan is to train Anakin because he believes him to be the chosen one.

The Psychological Function of Fantasy Fiction

It is easy to think of fantasy fiction and science fiction as silly entertainment or something people are interested in solely as a form of escapism, but when we engage these magical worlds as fans, we are not trying to escape or avoid our problems and responsibilities. Often, it is quite the opposite. We are using these worlds to probe basic questions about our own existence, our fears and desires—essential aspects of human sapience. Through storytelling, we explore our humanity and, among other things, our spiritual and psychological nature.

References

Allport, G. W., & Ross, J. M. (1967). Personal religious orientation and prejudice. *Journal of Personality and Social Psychology, 5*(4), 432–443.

Batson, C. D., Schoenrade, P., & Ventis, W. L. (1993). *Religion and the individual: A social psychological perspective.* New York, NY: Oxford University Press.

Baumeister, R. F., Vohs, K. D., & Tice, D. M. (2007). The strength model of self-control. *Current Directions in Psychological Science, 16*(6), 351–355.

DeWall, N. C., Baumeister, R. T., Stillman, T. F., & Gailliot, M. T. (2007). Violence restrained: Effects of self-regulation and its depletion on aggression. *Journal of Experimental Social Psychology, 43*(1), 62–76.

Ecklund, E. H., & Scheitle, C. (2014, February). *Religious communities, science, scientists, and perceptions: A comprehensive survey.* Paper presented at the annual meeting of the American Association for the Advancement of Science, Chicago, IL.

Heflick, N. A., & Goldenberg, J. L. (2012). No atheists in foxholes: Arguments for (but not against) life after death buffer mortality salience effects for atheists. *British Journal of Social Psychology, 51*(2), 385–392.

Hood, B. (2009). *Supersense: Why we believe in the unbelievable.* New York, NY: HarperCollins.

Hunsberger, B. (1995). Religion and prejudice: The role of religious fundamentalism, quest, and right-wing authoritarianism. *Journal of Social Issues, 51*(2), 113–129.

James, W. (1899, June 7). *Letter to Mrs. Henry Whitman.* Critical Animal: http://criticalanimal. blogspot.com/2014/04/the-invisible-moral-molecular-forces-of.html.

Kay, A. C., Whitson, J., Gaucher, D., & Galinski, A. D. (2009). Compensatory control: Achieving order through the mind, our institutions, and the heavens. *Current Directions in Psychological Science, 18*(5), 264–268.

Leak, G. K., & Finken, L. L. (2011). The relationship between the constructs of religiousness and prejudice: A structural equation model analysis. *International Journal for the Psychology of Religion, 21*(1), 43–63.

Mar, R. A., & Oatley, K. (2008). The function of fiction is the abstraction and simulation of social experience. *Perspectives on Psychological Science, 3*(3), 173–192.

McCullough, M. E., & Willoughby, B. (2009). Religion, self-regulation, and self-control: Associations, explanations, and implications. *Psychological Bulletin, 135*(1), 69–93.

Park, C. L. (2005). Religion as a meaning-making framework in coping with life stress. *Journal of Social Issues, 61*(4), 707–729.

Rounding, K., Lee, A., Jacobson, J. A., & Ji, L. (2012). Religion replenishes self-control. *Psychological Science, 23*(6), 635–642.

Routledge, C. (2014, November 3). *To feel meaningful is to feel immortal.* Scientific American: http://blogs.scientificamerican.com/mind-guest-blog/2014/11/03/to-feel-meaningful -is-to-feel-immortal/.

Solomon, S., Greenberg, J., & Pyszczynski, T. (2004). The cultural animal: Twenty years of terror management theory and research. In J. Greenberg, S. L. Koole, & T. Pyszczynski (Eds.), *Handbook of experimental existential psychology* (pp.13–34). New York, NY: Guilford.

Steger, M. F., & Frazier, P. (2005). Meaning in life: One link in the chain from religiousness to well-being. *Journal of Counseling Psychology, 52*(4), 574–582.

Sullivan, D., & Greenberg, J. (Eds.) (2013). *Death in classic and contemporary film: Fade to black.* London, UK: Palgrave Macmillan.

Tangney, J. P., Baumeister, R. F., & Boone, A. L. (2004). High self-control predicts good adjustment, less pathology, better grades, and interpersonal success. *Journal of Personality, 72*(2), 271–324.

Vail, K. E., Rothschild, Z. K., Weise, D., Solomon, S., Pyszczynski, T., & Greenberg, J. (2010). A terror management analysis of the psychological functions of religion. *Personality and Social Psychology Review, 14*(1), 84–94.

Notes

1. *Star Wars: Episode IV A New Hope* (1977/1981 motion picture).
2. James (1899).
3. Solomon et al. (2004).
4. Mar & Oatley (2008).
5. Sullivan & Greenberg (2013).
6. Heflick & Goldenberg (2012).
7. *A New Hope.*
8. *Star Wars: Episode V The Empire Strikes Back* (1980 motion picture) and *Star Wars: Episode VI Return of the Jedi* (1983 motion picture).
9. Solomon et al. (2004).
10. Vail et al. (2010).
11. Solomon et al. (2004).
12. *A New Hope.*
13. Hood (2009).
14. Kay et al. (2009).
15. *A New Hope.*
16. Allport & Ross (1967), p. 434.
17. For example, Batson et al. (1993); Leak & Finken (2011).
18. Hunsberger (1995).
19. *A New Hope.*
20. Ecklund & Scheitle (2014).
21. McCullough & Willoughby (2009).
22. Baumeister et al. (2007).
23. Rounding et al. (2012).
24. DeWall et al. (2007).
25. Tangney et al. (2004).
26. Steger & Frazier (2005).
27. Park (2005).
28. Routledge (2014).
29. *Star Wars: Episode I The Phantom Menace* (1999 motion picture).

An OCEAN Far Away

III. Extraversion versus Introversion

T R A V I S   L A N G L E Y

The dimension of extraversion-introversion was the earliest personality factor identified, originally described by psychiatrist Carl Jung.[1] Put simply, the extravert is outgoing; the introvert is not.

Examples of Extraversion Traits

Assertiveness
Boldness
Boredom If Alone
Enthusiasm
Excitement Seeking
External Focus
Gregariousness
Low Arousal
Need for People
Positive Emotion
Outgoing Nature
Risk-Taking
Social Interaction
Talkativeness

Extraversion is adventurous, although not in the same way the openness factor is: Extraverts seek excitement whereas open individuals seek new experience, which may involve quiet novelties. Getting to know the ways of the Force can be an inner adventure that might bore the extravert. Luke Skywalker's own eagerness, his desire to get to the exciting part, figures into his periodic impatience when Yoda trains him in the swamp.[2]

Star Wars characters exhibit many extraverted traits as they run around interacting with others. Heroes and villains are largely defined by their treatment of others. Introverted characteristics, inwardly focused as they are, can be harder to see. Unlike some personality factors, which are described in terms of individuals being high or low in them (e.g., the opposite of conscientiousness is essentially just low conscientiousness), extraversion and introversion each have their own distinct characteristics. The extravert, while scoring high in extravert traits, also scores low on specific introvert traits.

Examples of Introversion Traits

Calmness
Contemplation
Enjoyment of Solitude
Inward Focus
Lack of Social Interaction
Need for Privacy
Quiet Manner
Reflection
Risk Aversion

The Jedi value introverted qualities. Force-sensitive individuals come from many walks of life, and some tune out their surroundings to "use the Force" more easily than others. Extraverts may have more trouble adapting to the meditative Jedi lifestyle. That does not necessarily make them more likely to turn to the dark side, though, not unless they're also neurotic. Extraverts pursue more happiness-seeking activities and experience positive emotions more frequently and intensely than introverts do.[3] The negative emotions of fear, anger, and hate have more to do with neuroticism. Neurotic extraverts, who experience a roller coaster of positive and negative emotional states,[4] will more readily summon those emotions in the heat of battle and turn to the dark side. Emotionally stable extraverts report greater happiness and life satisfaction. They also make better leaders—at least among groups who, like the Jedi, value emotional stability.[5]

Few people are fully extraverted or fully introverted; these traits are distributed across humankind in a bell curve. The extraverted person usually has some introverted traits and vice versa, which suits both the social and the private aspects of Jedi training. Between extraversion and introversion lies a wide range of *ambiversion*, having traits from both, just as the ambidextrous person can write with both hands.[6] Even among the ambidextrous, though, one hand dominates more often, and so it is with ambiverts who tend toward either extraversion or introversion. Anakin's ambiverted potential for both outward and inward focus may be part of why Qui-Gon quickly sees Anakin Skywalker as the person with the ability to bring balance to the Force. If only the kid hadn't been so neurotic.

References

Cohen, D., & Schmidt, J. P. (1979). Ambiversion: Characteristics of midrange responders on the introversion-extraversion continuum. *Journal of Personality Assessment, 43*(5), 513–516.

Ensari, N., Riggio, R. E., Christian, J., & Carslaw, G. (2011). Who emerges as a leader? Meta-analyses of individual differences as predictors of leadership emergence. *Personality and Individual Differences, 51*(4), 532–536.

Jung, C. G. (1921). *Psychologische typen* [*Psychological Types*]. Zurich, Switzerland: Rascher Verlag.

Lucas, R. E., Le, K., & Dyrenforth, P. S. (2008). Explaining the extraversion/positive affect relation: Sociability cannot account for extraverts' greater happiness. *Journal of Personality, 76*(3), 385–414.

Pychyl, T. A. (2010, January 1). *An enemy of the good life: Happiness and personality*. Psychology Today: https://www.psychologytoday.com/blog/dont-delay/201001/enemy-the-good -life-happiness-and-personality.

Savelsbergh, M., & Staebler, B. (1995). Investigating leadership styles, personality preferences, and effective teacher consultation. *Journal of Educational and Psychological Consultation, 6*(3), 277–286.

Tamir, M. (2009). Differential preferences for happiness: Extraversion and trait-consistent emotion regulation. *Journal of Personality, 77*(2), 447–470.

Notes

1. Jung (1921).
2. *Star Wars: Episode V The Empire Strikes Back* (1980 motion picture).
3. Lucas et al. (2008); Tamir (2009).
4. Pychyl (2010).
5. Ensari et al. (2011); Savelsbergh & Staebler (1995).
6. Cohen & Schmidt (1979).

4 »

Paths

Light side or dark side, Jedi or Sith, good or evil.

Star Wars often dichotomizes right and wrong, especially among those who are sensitive to the Force. Morally complex characters will do both, yet the dichotomy remains. Why do good? Why do evil? What factors influence whether a person will make a choice that is selfless or one that is selfish? What *is* the path to the light side versus the path to the dark?

» 13 »

Explaining the Empire:
Why Good People Do Bad Things

C O L T   J .   B L U N T

"Throughout history, it has been the inaction of those
who could have acted, the indifference of those who
should have known better, the silence of the voice of
justice when it mattered most, that has made it possible
for evil to triumph."

—emperor of Ethiopia Haile Selassie[1]

A s a teenager from the middle of nowhere, you have limited prospects. You spend your free time watching reports about the war
effort and imagine a life more exciting. You decide to enlist against your
family's wishes. They tell you war isn't a game and things aren't always
as they seem. Training takes you far from home. You muster through
history lessons about the chancellor's rise and eventual assumption of
power for the good of the people. More important, you learn to pilot a
fighter and find out you're good at it. You're assigned to a fighter squadron after graduation.

Your earliest experiences during the war are little more than patrols
that seem more a matter of protocol than anything else. The enemy

continues to disrupt supply lines. Even some of the populace of liberated lands turns traitor and engages in cowardly sabotage missions. Your commander frequently reminds you the enemy is a blight that needs to be destroyed. You hear stories of pilots who fail to carry out their missions as ordered. They are rarely heard from again.

One night you're jarred from your sleep and told to man your fighter. Once away from the hangar, your squadron is informed an enemy ship is in the vicinity. Your squadron comes upon a civilian transport ship; your commander's voice fills your helmet, telling you to target the ship's crew quarters. The veteran at your right tells your squadron to maintain formation and fire when within range. Your thoughts turn momentarily to your family's warning, but you remember your training and everything you were taught about the enemy. You imagine your fellow pilots, all willing to do the bidding of your commander. You think about the consequences of failure. You arm your weapons, close your eyes, and squeeze the trigger, unleashing a barrage that pierces the unarmed transport. You tell yourself it's for the glory of your people.

Although the preceding scenario could have been torn from nearly any page of the fictional Empire's history, could it also be true in our own history? What about the Third Reich and its campaign to take over the world? Be warned! We're going to be talking about Nazis in the pages ahead.

There is no question that like the Third Reich, the Galactic Empire is evil. However, to assume that all soldiers, technicians, and others in the service of an evil regime or empire are evil is overly simplistic. In cases of oppressive regimes, we often ask why the populace does not speak up against atrocities. Surely the average just and moral human would not stand to be part of such a society, and so many people will think that those who do not act must be at best indifferent and at worst evil. However, things are rarely that simple. Normal people can do evil things.

The Empire and the Third Reich

Adolf Hitler and Emperor Palpatine both prove themselves adept at capitalizing on circumstances and using political maneuvering to assume power. Hitler jockeys for power in the wake of World War I and the 1929 stock market crash, whereas Palpatine creates his own crises, including the separatist movement. Both use subterfuge to make constitutional changes, transferring all of the government's power to themselves. Both blame specific groups, their *scapegoats*, for the downfall of their respective societies. Once in power, they rule with an iron fist, set their sights on expanding their empires, and push a doctrine of oppression and annihilation of those they deem undesirable and inferior.

The Stanford Prison Experiment

The Stanford Prison Experiment was a study that psychologist Philip Zimbardo[2] designed to study the psychological effects of being either a prisoner or a guard, though the implications can be generalized to other situations in which an extreme power differential exists, including the Galactic Empire and the people over whom it holds dominion. In Zimbardo's study, 24 volunteers deemed psychologically stable were assigned to be guards or prisoners. Those in the prisoner roles were transferred to a mock prison in the Stanford psychology building. Those in the guard or administrator roles referred to the prisoners only by their numbers. Each prisoner wore prison attire and a chain around one ankle. The guards wore military clothing, not unlike Imperial soldiers, although they were informed they could not physically harm the prisoners. Zimbardo served as the superintendent of the prison, providing oversight and direction throughout the study.

Much as in the birth of the Rebel Alliance, the prisoners staged a revolt on the second day. The guards used fire extinguishers to force the prisoners back from the doors, entered their cells, stripped them naked, removed their beds, and placed the organizers of the rebellion in solitary confinement cells. The guards then established a "privilege cell" in which the three prisoners least involved in the revolt were given their uniforms and beds back and received special meals. The Empire uses similar techniques by coercing and intimidating everyone while reinforcing those who show loyalty and complacency, often at the same time, as when they promise to leave Cloud City alone if Lando Calrissian cooperates with their plans.[3] Zimbardo's guards eventually cycled some of the other prisoners into the privilege cell, resulting in some inmates believing that their peers had become informants. The guards began to control every aspect of prison life. A prisoner began to present with emotional disturbance and was sent home. The prisoner was moved after the guards heard about a possible escape attempt, though it never happened. The guards then punished the prisoners by forcing them to do menial tasks.

Most of those in prisoner roles stated that they would forgo their pay if they were granted parole. They began to lose any semblance of group cohesion and solidarity. A replacement prisoner was brought in and promptly began a hunger strike. The guards placed him in solitary confinement, stating that he would be released only if the others relinquished their blankets; they all refused. The prisoners in the experiment lacked the sort of cohesion seen in the Rebel Alliance, or rather, they presented exactly as we might expect the remaining rebels to act if the *Death Star* succeeded in destroying Yavin. The organizers of the study eventually intervened and returned the prisoner to his cell. The study was discontinued after six days when Zimbardo learned that the guards had been escalating their abuse of the prisoners at night. A consultant brought in to conduct interviews was the only person who objected to the treatment of the prisoners.

Zimbardo found that three types of guards surfaced during the study: those who were tough but fair, those who were disinclined to punish prisoners, and those who were hostile and seemed to relish their power over the inmates. Zimbardo noted that no such patterns were predicted by preliminary personality testing. If the well-adjusted, intelligent college students in the Stanford Prison Experiment could engage in oppressive behavior, it's no surprise that the pawns in the Empire's game—individuals who could be assumed to be no different from the average galactic citizen—might be compelled to commit atrocities, engage in abuse, and generally treat the opposition as subhuman.

The Stanford Prison Experiment cannot be ethically replicated as the current field of psychology, unlike the Empire, expressly forbids psychological or physical abuse. Zimbardo has acknowledged that his taking on a role in a study of roles was a mistake[4] and that his role prevented the study from having a true experimental design.[5] The British Broadcasting Corporation (BBC) conducted a prison simulation study[6] that took a different, though not better, turn. In the BBC study, the guards were given no direction or oversight, although increased ethical controls were used. The guards failed to step into their roles, and the prisoners ended up controlling the prison. The same might have been true of an Empire without the Emperor. The BBC researchers concluded that it was the presence of a strong personality that led to the abuses seen in the Stanford Prison Experiment and the actions of those guards who went along with and followed the strong leadership's actions and commands, and even though Zimbardo ultimately discredited the results of the study,[7] the BBC study indicates that having no leader may not be better than having a tyrant. Strong leadership, in this case Emperor Palpatine and Darth Vader, provides the authority and oversight, instructing the ranks of the Empire's soldiers and giving them leave to carry out their tasks as necessary to achieve the Empire's goals.

Kitty Genovese: The Bystander Effect and Diffusion of Responsibility

Most first-year psychology students have heard about the murder of Kitty Genovese, a New York City resident who was sexually assaulted and stabbed to death outside her apartment in 1964. Several neighbors reportedly heard Genovese's cries or witnessed the assault but, like the crew of the Death Star who sit idly by as Alderaan is destroyed,[8] did not intervene. Original accounts of the incident have been called into question,[9] and it may be here that few people were aware she was in the process of being murdered. Regardless of its accuracy, the popular account of the murder inspired much research by social psychologists.

Some of the earliest research in the wake of the Kitty Genovese murder was conducted by John Darley and Bibb Latané, who researched *diffusion of responsibility* (the belief that individuals are unlikely to take responsibility for acting in a situation in which others are present because they believe the others are responsible) and the *bystander effect* (the theory that individuals are unlikely to come to the aid of a victim when others are present). An initial study[10] showed that individuals were quicker to report smoke in a room when they were alone than when they were with a group of people. A later study[11] showed that participants were more likely to call out or come to the aid of a confederate (a researcher's accomplice who pretends to be a fellow bystander or research participant) who fell when they were alone (70 percent) than when they were paired with a stranger (40 percent); when an unsuspecting participant was paired with a confederate who

Hidden in Helmets: The Influence of Anonymity

Most of us tend to dress similarly to (or at least not significantly different from) those we spend the most time with, but members of the Imperial Navy, like most military units, are required to wear uniforms. The Empire takes things a step further, though, referring to soldiers by their serial numbers. ("TK-421, why aren't you at your post?"[12])

Wearing a uniform produces a state of *deindividuation*— reduced consciousness of oneself as an individual—and anonymity deindividuates a person even more. This state can heighten conformity, diminish the influence of individual traits, heighten responsiveness to situational cues such as military trappings, and make a person's behavior and even personality more malleable.[13] Reduced self-awareness can create *disinhibition*, a lessening of inhibitions that may keep a person from, among other things, acting aggressively.[14]

The uniform makes it easier to get lost in a crowd and to act in unison with that crowd. Outnumbered by others who are doing the wrong thing, a person can find it more stressful to resist the crowd than simply to go along and do the wrong thing, too.[15] A helmet can hide any inner turmoil until it has passed.

—C. B. & T. L.

did not respond, the participant responded only 7 percent of the time. When Grand Moff Tarkin orders Alderaan's destruction, not one of the many people present speaks up to object. Even Darth Vader becomes a mere bystander.

The Milgram Menace

Many denizens of the Star Wars universe engage in harmful and atrocious acts toward others under orders from their superiors.

Is blind obedience merely a convenient trope in fiction, or does this hold true in real life? The work of Stanley Milgram can help answer this question. Milgram was a social psychologist of Jewish descent who became interested in the subject of obedience after the trial of Adolf Eichmann, a Nazi member of the *Schutzstaffel* (SS) who was a primary organizer of the Holocaust. In 1961, Milgram, then a psychologist with Yale University, set out to conduct his seminal work on obedience.[16] In the first of a series of 19 experiments that changed views on morality and free will,[17] Milgram gathered volunteers from the surrounding community to participate in a paid study that was ostensibly about memory. Once paired with a *confederate* (a research associate pretending to be a participant or bystander), each participant was told that he or she would be randomly assigned to be either a "teacher" or a "learner," though the assignment was rigged to ensure that the subject would always be assigned to be the teacher and the confederate would always be the learner. The participants were told they would be teaching a list of paired words and then would be testing the confederate's memory by reading the first word of each pairing followed by multiple choices for the second word. They were informed they would need to administer an electroshock after each incorrect answer. The researcher gave each teacher one real shock to provide a sample of a low-level electroshock in order to demonstrate the painful nature of the shocks the learner supposedly would receive. A researcher was present to ensure that instructions were followed and to issue directives; this relationship was not dissimilar to that of a soldier and his or her commander or even a Sith Master and his apprentice. The confederate went into a different room so that the participant would administer the shocks remotely. In actuality, the confederate received no shocks. The shocks were purported to begin at 15 volts and increase by 15-volt increments to a maximum shock of 450 volts, with shock labels ranging from "Slight Shock" to "Danger: Severe Shock" on the control panel.

A panel in front of the participants displayed the confederates' responses in a series of memory tasks. During the course of the experiment, the confederate provided predominately incorrect answers, thus requiring the subject to administer steadily increasing electric shocks after most responses despite the confederates' shouts of feigned pain. If the subjects expressed concern about proceeding at any point, the experimenter would provide up to four separate prompts to continue, ultimately informing the subject, "You have no other choice, you *must* go on," and though some pushed back, ultimately most gave in and followed the authority's direction despite knowing it would cause harm to the subjects. This finding harkens back to Star Wars and provides insight into the scene in which Chancellor Palpatine instructs Anakin Skywalker to kill Count Dooku:

Chancellor Palpatine: "Good, Anakin, good. Kill him. Kill him now."
Anakin Skywalker: "I shouldn't."
Chancellor Palpatine: "Do it!"[18]

Anakin pushes back but follows his future master nonetheless and knowingly causes harm, but this is fiction and a part of war, so what of the average subject in Milgram's study? Surely most would refrain from doing harm even in the face of a direct order, right? Professionals in the fields of psychology and psychiatry and Milgram's students estimated that about 1 percent would administer the maximum shock. In the initial 40-person study, however, no participant discontinued before the 300-volt shock. Five disobeyed when told to administer the 315-volt shock, and an additional four disobeyed when told to administer the 330-volt shock; five other subjects refused at various points before the administration of the maximum shock of 450 volts. In all, 26 (65 percent) administered the maximum shock, a finding replicated in other studies and by other researchers as well.[19] It is also important to point out that the participants did not believe the shocks they were doling out were minor; after the completion of the study, subjects rated the final few shocks as probably being "extremely painful." Each of those who administered the maximum voltage questioned the experiment during the administration, with some of them expressing concern for the health of the confederates and others even offering to forgo their pay if they could stop. Many participants demonstrated clear signs of distress, including nervous laughing, sweating, groaning, and digging their fingernails into their skin.

The fictional Anakin and Palpatine would later echo exchanges in which Milgram's participants resisted their direct instructions.

> **Volunteer:** No, I can't continue. I'm sorry.
> **Researcher:** The experiment requires that you go on. . . .
> **Volunteer:** Well, I won't—not with the man screaming
> to get out.
> **Researcher:** You have no other choice. [20]

Milgram's study demonstrated the power of authority in enabling normal people to engage in behavior that generally would be beyond their moral limits, explaining (but not justifying) responses from German soldiers after World War II who stated that they were just following orders. Zimbardo's findings supported these conclusions, especially in light of his role in establishing an environment in which psychological torture was permissible. Similarly, in the Star Wars universe, this study can help explain how an average Stormtrooper might not be inclined to shoot an unarmed civilian; however, when given direct orders, especially knowing that the authority was granted through the Emperor, that Stormtrooper probably would make the kill without hesitation. Relinquishing personal responsibility to an authority figure is a defining aspect of *authoritarian obedience*. Directives provided to soldiers during war, as when Imperial officers order the Stormtroopers or when the Emperor tells Anakin to kill, can be seen as substantively different from those provided by researchers to the subjects in Milgram's study because of a difference in the potential consequences to oneself. Unlike research participants who can quit at any time, soldiers who disobey direct orders could be cited for insubordination, dereliction of duty, or even treason and could face investigations, legal battles, protracted detention, or summary execution. Though research indicates that capital punishment is not an effective deterrent to criminal behavior, having the potential threat of an eventual death sentence is far different from having an executioner looking over one's shoulder at all times. The constant threat of immediate punishment creates subordinates who feel constant anxiety about their ability to perform adequately and reduces the likelihood of dissent; this is especially true in Star Wars because Darth Vader and Emperor Palpatine both have the reputation of being ruthless, unstoppable kill machines who often are shown harming soldiers who fail or question orders.

A Matter of Perspective

Even Josef Stalin and Adolf Hitler are unlikely to have considered themselves evil. It's even more unlikely for an entire civilization to band together with the expressed intent to be evil. Generations of children from Coruscant to Corellia didn't look up to the skies and say, "I want to go into space and serve as an oppressor of billions of people." Successful dictatorships have proved themselves adept at cultivating a culture of "us versus them," which is not difficult to spot in Star Wars, in which the Empire, though arising out of the multispecies Republic, seemingly is run only by humans. Alien species, such as the Wookiees, are subjugated and sometimes enslaved. This harkens back to the Nazi oppression and slaughter of peoples deemed racially inferior.

Palpatine argues that constitutional changes and consolidation of power were necessary to protect the Republic. The government insists the members of the opposition are traitors and a legitimate threat. Jedi are vilified and blamed for the troubles experienced by the Republic, and members of the Rebel Alliance are viewed with contempt. This sentiment comes from the top down, spun by propagandists or by the Emperor himself. Propaganda is a powerful tool as it distorts facts to support a regime's goals. Nazi Germany created elaborate films, posters, and auxiliary organizations to convince the people of its moral rightness. Hitler was adept at making the populace believe the war effort was just and necessary for the survival of the country, painting the opposition as morally wrong and diametrically opposed to the regime. Similarly, the average Imperial soldiers probably are conditioned from an early age to believe that their government's position is right, or at least that the opposition is in the wrong.

Why Good People Do Bad Things

Even today, we see entire nations under the rule of dictators whose sense of morality seems almost alien compared with our own. The Galactic Empire is no different. If we apply our knowledge of the theories and research of social psychology, the actions of the typical Imperial soldier might be explained:

1. From an early age, the Empire subjects its citizens to propaganda that glorifies the views of the government and vilifies those who seek to oppose it. Humans are taught they are superior to aliens, and the Jedi are labeled traitors.
2. Imperial leaders issue orders to eradicate traitors and opposing forces. This shifts the responsibility upward and legitimizes actions that otherwise would be seen as reprehensible (authoritarian obedience).
3. Not only does the administration demand a lack of dissent, but fellow soldiers are likely to chastise those who disagree or speak out. The average soldier conforms to expectations to avoid negative attention and to fit in (conformity).
4. A soldier on an Imperial ship is but one person among thousands, significantly increasing the likelihood that he will do nothing in the face of a faction bent on committing atrocities (diffusion of responsibility).
5. Imperial soldiers are under constant threat of imminent punishment. They live with the knowledge that their lives could be extinguished at any moment if they fail to follow orders (coercion).
6. Citizens who obey or simply remain complacent are offered rewards (reinforcement).

Like soldiers fighting for Germany in World War II, not every Imperial soldier embodies evil. Sure, some subscribe to the master plan of genocide and imperialism, but others are just citizens who were conscripted into service or who legitimately see themselves as defending their territory. The distinction between good and evil is almost always nuanced.

References

Asch, S. E. (1951). Effects of group pressure on the modification and distortion of judgments. In H. Guetzkow (Ed.), *Groups, leadership and men* (pp. 177–190). Pittsburgh, PA: Carnegie Press.

Blass, T. (2009). From New Haven to Santa Clara: A historical perspective on the Milgram obedience experiments. *American Psychologist, 64*(1), 37–45.

Burger, J. M. (2009). Replicating Milgram: Would people still obey today? *American Psychologist, 64*(1), 1–11.

Darley, J. M., & Latané, B. (1968). Bystander intervention in emergencies: Diffusion of responsibility. *Journal of Personality and Social Psychology, 8*(4), 377–383.

Fischer, P., Krueger, J. I., Greitemeyer, T., Vogrincic, C., Kastenmuller, A., Frey, D., Helene, M., Wicher, M., & Kainbacher, M. (2011). The bystander-effect: A meta-analytic review on bystander intervention in dangerous and non-dangerous emergencies. *Psychological Bulletin, 137*(4), 517–537.

Haney, C., Banks, C., & Zimbardo P. (1973). A study of prisoners and guards in a simulated prison. *Naval Research Reviews, 26*(9), 1–17.

Johnson, R. D., & Downing, I. L. (1979). Deindividuation and valence of cues: Effects on prosocial and antisocial behavior. *Journal of Personality and Social Psychology, 37*(9), 1532–1538.

Langley, T. (2012). *Batman and psychology: A dark and stormy knight.* New York, NY: Wiley.

Latané, B., & Rodin, J. (1969). A lady in distress: Inhibiting effects of friends and strangers on bystander intervention. *Journal of Experimental Social Psychology, 5*(2), 189–202.

Mann, L. (1981). The baiting crowd in episodes of threatened suicide. *Journal of Personality and Social Psychology, 41*(4), 703–709.

Manning, R., Levine, M., & Collins, A. (2007). The Kitty Genovese murder and the social psychology of helping: The parable of the 38 witnesses. *American Psychologist, 62*(6), 555–562.

Milgram, S. (1963). Behavioral study of obedience. *Journal of Abnormal and Social Psychology, 67*(4), 371–378.

Milgram, S. (1974/2009). *Obedience to authority.* New York, NY: Harper Perennial.

Postmes, T., & Spears, R. (1998). Deindividuation and antinormative behavior: A meta-analysis. *Psychological Bulletin, 123*(3), 238–259.

Reicher, S., & Haslam, S. A. (2006). Rethinking the psychology of tyranny: The BBC prison study. *British Journal of Social Psychology, 45*(1), 1–40.

Simpson, J. B. (1988). *Simpson's contemporary quotations.* Boston, MA: Houghton Mifflin.

Zimbardo, P. G. (1971, October 25). *The psychological power and pathology of imprisonment.* A statement prepared for the U.S. House of Representatives Committee on the Judiciary, Subcommittee No. 3: Hearings on Prison Reform, San Francisco, CA.

Zimbardo, P. G. (2006). On rethinking the psychology of tyranny: The BBC prison study. *British Journal of Social Psychology, 45*(1), 47–53.

Zimbardo, P. G. (2008). *The Lucifer effect.* New York, NY: Random House.

Zimbardo, P. G., Maslach, C., & Haney, C. (1999). Reflections on the Stanford Prison Experiment: Genesis, transformations, consequences. In T. Blass (Ed.), *Obedience to authority: Current perspectives on the Milgram paradigm* (pp. 193–237). Mahwah, NJ: Erlbaum.

Notes

1. Simpson (1988).
2. Haney, Banks, & Zimbardo (1973); Zimbardo (1971); Zimbardo (2008).
3. *Star Wars: Episode V The Empire Strikes Back* (1980 motion picture).
4. Quoted in Langley (2012), p. 65.
5. Zimbardo et al. (1999).
6. Reicher & Haslam (2006).
7. Zimbardo (2006).
8. *Star Wars: Episode IV A New Hope* (1977/1981 motion picture).
9. Manning et al. (2007).
10. Darley & Latané (1968).
11. Latané & Rodin (1969).
12. *A New Hope* (1977/1981 motion picture).
13. Johnson & Downing (1979); Postmes & Spears (1998).
14. Mann (1981); Zimbardo (1969).
15. Asch (1951).
16. Milgram (1963).
17. Milgram (1974/2009).
18. *Star Wars: Episode III Revenge of the Sith* (2005 motion picture).
19. Blass (2009); Burger (2009).
20. Milgram (1974/2009), p. 51.

Lando's Choice:
Anatomy of a Moral Dilemma

JAY SCARLET

"You fixed us all real good, didn't you? My friend!"
—Han Solo[1]

> "[I]f you think that decomposing chess into
> a set of cognitive operations is challenging,
> try decomposing our thinking about
> abortion or the Israeli-Palestinian conflict."
> —psychologist Joshua Greene[2]

Despite his later heroics, Lando Calrissian has for years incurred Star Wars fans' wrath for betraying his friend Han Solo in *Star Wars: Episode V The Empire Strikes Back*. Lando's moral decision to accept Darth Vader's deal and the aftermath of this choice may be considered critical moments in the Star Wars universe. At the same time that fans angrily ask, "How could he do that?" they may also wonder, "What would I do?"

Han Solo describes his old friend to Princess Leia as a card-player, a gambler, and a scoundrel, who has become administrator of the Cloud City of Bespin after he "won it in a game of sabacc, or so he claims."[3] Once Han and his companions arrive at Bespin, Lando seems to have become quite good at his job. Only later is it revealed that Darth Vader has arrived at Bespin shortly before Solo's ship, the *Millennium Falcon*, and immediately struck a deal with the administrator: The Empire will supposedly leave Bespin alone in exchange for Han. For Lando, this presents the moral dilemma of either betraying his friend or risking the lives of the Bespin inhabitants. People facing such choices may be influenced one way or the other by a number of factors, including rational thought, various emotional states, self-interest, and relationships with others.

Moral Dilemmas

The decision Lando faces is similar to the sort of moral dilemmas that psychologists and philosophers have used for years to study moral decision-making. One of the best known and most frequently used of these dilemmas is usually referred to as the "trolley problem."[4] In this situation, the research participant is asked to imagine that he or she is driving a trolley car that is approaching a split in the tracks. On one of the tracks, there are five workers who will be killed if the trolley hits them, and it is not possible to apply the brake in time. The only way to save the lives of the five men is to flip a switch that will divert the trolley onto the other track, where there is one worker. If this option is selected, then that person will die. Participants are then asked whether it would be morally right to flip the switch; that is, to kill one person in order to save five.

Most people respond to this dilemma by saying that killing one person in order to save five is moral.[5] However, other variations of this scenario can produce different outcomes. If the person would have to push a man off a footbridge onto the track to stop the trolley and save five others, most people do not believe that would be moral.[6] Those who study *moral psychology* (a subfield of social psychology that overlaps with philosophy in the study of how humans approach issues of morality), describe the decision most people make in the trolley problem—to sacrifice one life in order to save five—as *utilitarian* or *consequence-based*. This approach gives more weight to the outcomes of an action and how it contributes to the greater good. The opposite, for example, that choice made in the footbridge dilemma to not cause one person's death even to save five others, is called *deontological* or *principle-based*. Deontological decisions focus on the act itself, regardless of context, assuming that some things are simply morally wrong. In Lando's case, betraying Han would be the utilitarian course of action, benefiting the entire population of Bespin, while acting on his notion of friendship and not agreeing to Vader's deal would be principle-based.

As fascinating as it would be to know the specific words exchanged when Vader bargains with Lando (i.e., to know how the dilemma he faces is phrased), unfortunately, the only account of this meeting ever reported was not in the films and contains no more than a number of tantalizing tidbits. In the account given in *Galaxy Guide 3: The Empire Strikes Back* (a book of character profiles for a Star Wars role-playing game), Lando claims that his initial response to Vader's offer had been to reject it, but that he then thought about the danger he had been in, the impact his decision would have had on the other inhabitants of Bespin, and the hope that he might be able to do something to help Han at a later point, so he accepted the deal.[7]

Moral Decision-Making

For most of the twentieth century, the few psychologists who thought about such issues took it as a given that morality was based on rational thought processes.[8] Only toward the turn of the millennium did some psychologists begin to assert that emotions were important sources of moral decision-making.[9] The field took off in 2001 with the publication of a neuroscientific finding that certain types of moral dilemmas caused increased activity in brain regions associated with reasoning, while others were more likely to activate regions associated with emotions.[10] This finding led to the development of the *dual-process model,* which states that, when presented with a moral dilemma, the brain checks for strong emotional content (such as the reaction most people have to the thought of pushing someone off a footbridge). If this is present, the decision will more likely be made using deontological principles (e.g., do not push someone off a bridge). If not, then utilitarian reasoning (e.g., one death is better than five) increases in likelihood.[11] Many researchers believe that there is a fixed order to this routine: We first feel our emotional reaction and may then, in some situations, override that reaction using reasoning in order to arrive at a utilitarian decision.[12] This fits neatly with *Galaxy Guide 3*'s version of Lando's meeting with Vader, in which Lando first feels a principle-based impulse to act honorably toward his friend but, upon reflection, is able to reason that he will benefit more people and potentially find a way to help Han as well if he goes along with Vader.[13]

While the dual-process model has come to predominate the research literature in the field of moral psychology, there is a growing trend among researchers to try to find a way to account for moral decision-making using a *single-process model* accounting for both principle- and consequence-based decision-making.[14] However, some assert that there is a danger in taking such a

single-process approach, due to the evidence that deontological
and utilitarian inclinations are independent of one another and
that moral conflict is the result of the simultaneous presence
of and competition between both types of moral inclination.[15]
This suggestion accounts well for the conflict that Lando feels,
and makes it possible to break down some of the emotional and
cognitive factors that may influence Lando's decision.

Getting Inside a Charming Rogue's Head

According to the *Galaxy Guide 3* version of events, Lando's
initial inclination is to act in accordance with the *principle* that
one should not betray one's friend(s). What, then, are some of the
factors that may urge Lando to act on this principle? Research
has found that decision-makers who are experiencing stress
(such as one might experience when a ruthless Sith Lord shows
up unannounced and demands to meet with you) are more
likely to approach moral dilemmas deontologically.[16] Another
factor that may lead one in a deontological direction involves
a region of the brain called the *insula*, which is connected to a
wide variety of neural processes, includingboth gambling (see
sidebar, "Gambling Problem or Professional Gambler?") and
moral decision-making.[17] For instance, the insula seems to be
involved in the *Ultimatum Game* task. In the Ultimatum Game,
the participants are paired and assigned to roles as proposer and
responder. The proposer has a certain amount of money that he
or she must split with the other participant. If, and only if, both
parties are able to agree on how to divide the money, do they
both actually get to keep the amount agreed upon. If an agree-
ment is not reached, neither participant takes home any money.[18]
Clearly, it is in the interest of the proposer to offer as little money
as possible to his or her counterpart, but research has consistently
shown that offers that are considered to be excessively one-sided
are more likely to be rejected, even though the responder would

Gambling Problem or Professional Gambler?

"Cardplayer" and "gambler"[19] Lando obtains his position as Baron Administrator through gambling after losing the *Millennium Falcon* in the same way. The *Galaxy Guide 3* profile of Lando reveals that, while Baron Administrator, he would frequently disguise himself and patronize the casinos on Bespin, often winning vast sums of money before making sure to lose it all on one final bet in order to preserve his anonymity.[20] So, does he have a gambling problem?

Gambling addiction, or gambling disorder, is a problem that affects millions of Americans. It is the only behavioral addiction sufficiently similar to substance abuse disorders that the *Diagnostic and Statistical Manual of Mental Disorders* (DSM-5) groups them together. A diagnosis of *gambling disorder* requires that the individual experience impairment or distress while exhibiting a variety of self-destructive symptoms within a 12-month period.[21]

While Lando's behavior may meet some of the DSM-5 criteria for gambling disorder—for example, spending quite a bit of time thinking about gambling and having lost the *Millennium Falcon* (both a relationship and a business opportunity)—he does not *seem* to attempt to reduce his gambling, nor does he lie about it, and he does not appear to chase his losses (despite giving Han some ribbing about the *Falcon*). Thus, on the whole, Lando's behavior would appear to be more in line with that of a *non*-disordered professional gambler.

also be better off taking something rather than nothing. Due to the fact that both sides come out ahead if the offer is accepted, the responder's decision to accept is analogous to the utilitarian approach to moral dilemmas, while the decision to reject an "unfair" offer can be equated with deontological thinking. The latter decision (to reject the offer) has been linked to an increase in activity in the insula. If fans view Vader's offer to Lando as an ultimatum of this type, it is possible that Lando's disgust (an emotion also linked to both increased activity in the insula [22] and moral decision-making)[23] at the thought of betraying his friend may have led him to consider rejecting Vader's proposal.

Another factor that likely contributes to Lando's decision is fear—Lando fears Darth Vader.[24] Fear activates an entirely different set of brain structures than disgust, particularly the *amygdala*, a structure associated with processing pleasure as well as fear. Thus, it is conceivable that the different patterns of brain activity in fear as opposed to disgust played a role in Lando's consequence-based reasoning in choosing to accept Vader's offer, rather than going with his initial principle-based impulse to reject it.

Other factors that may also have pushed him to accept Vader's offer include self-interest, the power differential between himself and Vader, and his relationship with the citizens he was responsible for as Baron Administrator. In the National Public Radio (NPR) audio dramatization of *The Empire Strikes Back*,[25] Vader directly threatens Lando's life. In this version of the story, it is obviously in Lando's interest to make the decision to accept the deal. Both self-interest and the power differential can affect one's moral decisions.[26] For example, experiments using the Ultimatum Game model have shown that manipulating the relative power of the two participants, so that the proposer has more power than the responder, results in fewer rejections of unfair offers than if both people had equal power.[27] Vader, with the power of the entire Galactic Empire and the Force at his command, clearly has more power than Lando, administrator of a tiny mining outpost, so this too could have been a factor pushing Lando toward a consequence-based decision.

Another factor influencing decision-making—one that may be somewhat less intuitive—has to do with *social connection*, one's sense of having positive social relationships with other beings. People faced with moral dilemmas are more likely to make consequence-based choices if they are in the presence of, or reminded of, a friend or loved one than if they are alone.[28] A threat to people Lando has lived and worked with for some time would probably have impelled him to go the utilitarian route in determining the fate of a friend he has not seen in a long time.

After the Decision

Thus it would appear that, in the case of Lando Calrissian, consequence-based reasoning wins out over principle-based instinct ... at first. Given that Lando's choice can be described as consequence-based, it is important to also look at what happened afterward—the *post-decisional consequences*. While some researchers have considered the decision-making process to be divided only into pre- and post-decision phases, others have suggested that the post-decision phase can be divided still further; that is, after the decision has been made, but during the period when it is still possible to reevaluate the consequences and, perhaps, change one's mind.[29] Star Wars viewers see this played out in Lando's situation, as his deal with Vader is "getting worse all the time."[30]

Viewers first become aware of Lando's dissatisfaction with the deal when he overhears Han's tortured screams and is visibly upset.[31] As Vader then changes the terms of the deal again and again, Lando becomes convinced that he is dealing with a force of evil beyond his reckoning. This serves to confirm Lando's suspicion that he and the other inhabitants of Bespin would not receive any benefits from Vader and his decision was causing-harm to friends and other innocents.[32]

When Lando reevaluates Vader's deal in light of subsequent actions, including torture and betrayal, he finds that the violation of principle is greater than initially anticipated, and there are only negative consequences for Lando and Bespin, the intended beneficiaries of his utilitarian course of action. Thus the moral conflict is resolved and both deontological and utilitarian judgment coincide: Accepting Vader's deal is morally wrong. Lando therefore rejects his previous decision and reverses course,

Transpersonal Psychology

Lando Calrissian may not seem particularly spiritual, and yet his moral crisis—betraying his friends but then turning against the Empire—is akin to Anakin Skywalker's crisis of faith.

Transpersonal psychology looks at all aspects of human nature, including morality.[33] *Transpersonal experiences* are those in which our "sense of identity or self extends beyond (*trans*) the individual (or personal) to encompass wider aspects of humankind, life, psyche or cosmos."[34] In Star Wars, such experiences are attributed to the Force. Through training, Jedi and Sith become able to perform supernatural feats and to strengthen their physical traits. When transpersonal psychology emerged, mainstream psychology often classified spiritual experiences as pathological and dismissed them as unworthy of scientific investigation. Thanks to transpersonal psychologists,[35] "Religious or Spiritual Problem" is listed in the DSM-5 as a condition that may be a focus of clinical attention[36]—which possibly fits Lando and clearly suits Anakin.

—Dana Klisanin

rescuing the princess and the Wookiee, thereby casting his lot with the Rebellion.

Choices and Consequences

Examining the situation through the lens of the dual-process model of moral decision-making, it appears that Lando, who repeatedly protests that he had no choice, is incorrect. A number of factors may have prompted him to choose based on principle and refuse Vader's proposal, but an even greater number influenced him to accept it, and utilitarian moral reasoning won out. Fortunately for Han's friends and the rest of the rebels,

Lando still had time to reevaluate his choice, change his mind, and act accordingly. However, throughout everything, according to a moral decision-making model, he was acting morally in every instance while deciding how to proceed when facing these dilemmas.

References

American Psychiatric Association (2013). *Diagnostic and statistical manual of mental disorders* (DSM-5) (5th ed.) Washington, DC: American Psychiatric Association.

Bluhm, R. (2014). No need for alarm: A critical analysis of Greene's dual-process theory of moral decision-making. *Neuroethics, 7*(3), 299–316.

Conway, P., & Gawronski, B. (2013). Deontological and utilitarian inclinations in moral decision making: A process dissociation approach. *Journal of Personality and Social Psychology, 104*(2), 216–235.

Dedeke, A. (2013). A cognitive-intuitionist model of moral judgment. *Journal of Business Ethics, 126*(3), 437–457.

Glut, D. F. (1980). *The Empire strikes back.* New York, NY: Ballantine.

Greene, J. D. (2015). The rise of moral cognition. *Cognition, 135*(1), 39–42.

Greene, J. D., Nystrom, L. E., Engell, A. D., Darley, J. M., & Cohen, J. D. (2004). The neural bases of cognitive conflict and control in moral judgment. *Neuron, 44*(2), 389–400.

Greene, J. D., Sommerville, R. B., Nystrom, L. E., Darley, J. M., & Cohen, J. D. (2001, September 14). An fMRI investigation of emotional engagement in moral judgment. *Science, 293*(5537), 2105–2108.

Grof, S. (2005). A brief history of transpersonal psychology. *The Inner Door, 17*(2), 1, 4–9.

Haidt, J. (2001). The emotional dog and its rational tail: A social intuitionist approach to moral judgment. *Psychological Review, 108*(4), 814–834.

Kirkebøen, G., Vasaasen, E., & Teigen, K. H. (2013). Revisions and regret: The cost of changing your mind. *Journal of Behavioral Decision Making, 26*(1), 1–12.

Koop, G. J. (2013). An assessment of the temporal dynamics of moral decisions. *Judgment and Decision Making, 8*(5), 527–539.

Lammers, J., & Stapel, D. A. (2009). How power influences moral thinking. *Journal of Personality and Social Psychology, 97*(2), 279–289.

La Rosa, A. O., & Mir, J. R. (2013). On the relationships between disgust and morality: A critical review. *Psicothema, 25*(2), 222–226.

Lucas, B. J., & Livingston, R. W. (2014). Feeling socially connected increases utilitarian choices in moral dilemmas. *Journal of Experimental Social Psychology, 53*(1), 1–4.

Lukoff, D. (1998). From spiritual emergency to spiritual problem: The transpersonal roots of the new DSM-IV category. *Journal of Humanistic Psychology, 38*(2), 21–50.

Moore, A. B., Clark, B. A., & Kane, M. J. (2008). Who shalt not kill? Individual differences in working memory capacity, executive control, and moral judgment. *Psychological Science, 19*(6), 549–557.

Palmer, C. J., Paton, B., Ngo, T. T., Thomson, R. H., Hohwy, J., & Miller, S. M. (2013). Individual differences in moral behaviour: A role for response to risk and uncertainty? *Neuroethics, 6*(1), 97–103.

Sanfey, A. G., Rilling, J. K., Aronson, J. A., Nystrom, L. E., & Cohen, J. D. (2003, June 13). The neural basis of economic decision-making in the Ultimatum Game. *Science, 300*(5626), 1755–1758.

Starcke, K., Ludwig, A., & Brand, M. (2012). Anticipatory stress interferes with utilitarian moral judgment. *Judgment and Decision Making,* 7(1), 61–68.

Stern, M., & Hidalgo, P. (1996). *Galaxy guide 3: The Empire strikes back.* Honesdale, PA: West End Games.

Wallach, W. (2010). Cognitive models of moral decision making. *Topics in Cognitive Science,* 2(3), 420–429.

Walsh R., & Vaughan, F. (1993). *Paths beyond ego: The transpersonal vision.* New York, NY: Tarcher.

Notes

1. *Star Wars: Episode V The Empire Strikes Back* (1980 motion picture).
2. Greene (2015).
3. Glut (1980). In the movie, Han says that "He conned somebody out of it." Sabacc is a popular card game in the Star Wars universe, with elements of poker and blackjack.
4. Greene et al. (2001).
5. Greene et al. (2001).
6. Greene et al. (2001).
7. Stern & Hidalgo (1996).
8. See Wallach (2010).
9. For example, Haidt (2001).
10. Greene et al. (2001).
11. Greene et al. (2004).
12. Koop (2013).
13. Stern & Hidalgo (1996).
14. For example, Bluhm (2014); Dedeke (2013).
15. Conway & Gawronski (2013).
16. Starcke et al. (2012).
17. Palmer et al. (2013).
18. Sanfey et al. (2003).
19. *The Empire Strikes Back* (1980 motion picture).
20. Stern & Hidalgo (1996).
21. American Psychiatric Association (2013).
22. Wicker, B., Keysers, C., Plailly, J., Royet, J. P., Gallese, V., & Rizzolatti, G. (2003). Both of us disgusted in my insula: The common neural basis of seeing and feeling disgust. *Neuron,* 40(3), 655-664.
23. La Rosa & Mir (2013).
24. Stern & Hidalgo (1996).
25. *The Empire Strikes Back* (1993 audio play).
26. Moore et al. (2008).
27. Lammers & Stapel (2009).
28. Lucas & Livingston (2014).
29. Kirkeboen et al. (2013).
30. *The Empire Strikes Back* (1980 motion picture).
31. *The Empire Strikes Back* (1980 motion picture).
32. Glut (1980)
33. Grof (2005).
34. Walsh & Vaughan, (1993), p. 3.
35. Lukoff (1998).
36. American Psychiatric Association (2013).

» 15 »

Anxiety Disorder's Need for Imperial Control: Was Darth Vader Evil or Scared?

FRANK GASKILL

"Father-son myths attracted huge audiences
in the 1970s and '80s. Men feared being like
their fathers, but they wanted desperately
to bond with them even if they could never
really please them enough to feel anointed."
—psychiatrist Frank Pittman[1]

"Join me and we can end this destructive conflict. . . ."
—Darth Vader to his son Luke[2]

Viewing *Star Wars* for the first time was and is for many
people a life-changing experience. Princess Leia's ship
comes into view with Tatooine in the distance as Darth Vader's
Star Destroyer closes in. This opening sequence is the iconic
memory from Lucas's classic film that we all share. Despite the
power of the opening scene, the image that held me captive

as an eight-year-old seeing *Star Wars* for the first time was the moment when Darth Vader steps through the smoking air lock his troopers blasted open. With his black cape flowing about him, Vader stands to survey the damage in the smoke-filled corridor. Without a word, his mere presence bleeds ultimate power and fear. The only sound we hear is his slow, deep breathing. I knew I liked Vader.

Throughout the next 40+ years of viewing the Star Wars films, I knew Vader was similar to me, but I was unclear initially how that could be. He didn't feel like a villain to be feared and at times seemed almost aspirational in his goal of galactic stability and peace. As the films progressed, he became more and more human. As a little boy, I couldn't understand what I was sensing about Vader. As my dad and I left the theater that night in May 1977, he held my hand. Squeezing it, he looked down at me and said, "You know, that Darth Vader was pretty cool." I looked into his eyes and agreed. Vader was cool. The 54 Darth Vader toys and figures inhabiting my office are a testament to that coolness. But how could a murdering, planet-destroying, princess-torturing (his daughter, I might add) machine of a man be cool? Cool is probably not the right word, but more important, I don't believe Darth Vader was evil. Darth Vader wasn't a bad guy. He was just very scared.

This Present Unconscious Menace

Living under Imperial rule has to be stressful. Freedoms are being undermined, the Senate is dissolved, the existential threat of the Death Star is unleashed, and the knowledge that all the Jedi have been killed or expelled offers little to no hope. The tiny rebellion has little chance against the Imperial Starfleet or the regional governors who hold planets captive on the basis of fear. Other threats are ever present from the Hutts, bounty hunters, slavery, and bribery. Stress is omnipresent under the Empire. As Ben Kenobi tells Luke, there had been a sense of safety and hope when the Jedi were considered "the guardians of peace and justice in the Old Republic, before the dark times . . . before the Empire."[3] In the present day, we may not be living under an empire, but we could be living under another, more sinister menace that is walking among us every day.

In my private practice as a psychologist, I see a lot of scared kids and parents. More accurately, I serve the needs of a lot of anxious people. As a society, we are working harder in our jobs now than at any other time in history. Levels of anxiety are the highest ever reported. Individuals are reporting 40 percent more stress, worry, and panic now than they did in the 1950s.[4] With parents under such intensive pressure and stress, the lives of children are similarly under mounting pressure. Living in such conditions on an ongoing basis raises levels of anxiety to pathological levels. Our innate fight-flight-freeze responses tend to engage in situations in which these responses are not needed. When we lived in caves and jungles, fight-or-flight responses served us well and kept us alive. However, exaggerated or uncontrolled responses to anxiety can have dire consequences in those who have limited awareness of how fear can affect them personally in regard to anger outbursts and rash decision-making. In Star Wars, the Sith are well versed in anger as this emotion is what they use to channel the Force. A deeper human emotion fuels the anger of the Sith. Emotions need to be addressed because without such attention, the dark side awaits.

Cognitive behavioral therapy (CBT) is an approach to psychological treatment that alters thinking patterns and/or behaviors that cause problems in people's lives.[5] CBT is used in an attempt to reduce anxiety-based negative thoughts and behaviors that interfere with successful living. CBT is the state-of-the-art tool for anxiety reduction. Anxiety can be paralyzing. It can make you feel that you are under an existential threat, but CBT can help. Before beginning CBT sessions, my most frequently used tool is an introduction to the true nature of Darth Vader. As he is one of the best-known characters in cinematic history, the majority of my clients, even little five-year-olds, have a good understanding of his story. My first session with anxious and fearful kids begins with a foundational question:

"There is only one difference between the Jedi and Darth Vader. What is it?"

The most common answer to my question is, "Darth Vader is evil and the Jedi are good." But I argue the point that Darth Vader really isn't evil. His actions are clearly bad and should be characterized as evil, but those actions are motivated by something else. He is driven by a magnified emotion we all experience to one degree or another. Darth Vader is motivated by anxiety. Therefore, the correct answer to my question about the difference between the Jedi and Vader is *where they place their sense of control.* Vader attempts to control everything external to him, whereas the Jedi strive to demonstrate self-control and allow for free will. Darth Vader wants peace and justice throughout the galaxy. He aspires to an admirable goal for sure. Vader so much desires and believes in a peaceful galactic future that he implores his son to join him on his quest and to destroy the Emperor. Vader actually wants the same goal as the Jedi, but he pursues that goal in a manner that leads him down a frustrating, failure-ridden, and dark path.

Vader's Childhood: Tell Me About Your Mother . . .

Experiencing so many early life stressors must be very hard on young Anakin. His time on Tatooine probably reinforces within him a deep-seated sense that he is controlled by life circumstances. His ultimate unconscious conclusion could be that he has little control over his own destiny, and this may reinforce his desire to seek control of his own destiny. Control of future events drives him. In its response to being controlled by so many factors, Anakin's nature is to attempt to control as much as possible, even things far outside his ability to control. When under stress, people tend to seek ways of gaining control, sometimes even using magical thinking. Before he leaves his mother to train as a Jedi, we get a clear glimpse into Anakin's heart as he says, "I will come back and free you . . . I promise."[6] Although the sentiment is beautiful, we are able to see the pressure this 10-year-old child places on himself. No child should feel that he is responsible for saving his parent.

Perfectionism has been described as a kind of neurosis that pushes someone to achieve severe and exacting goals. A subtype of perfectionism in children has been identified as "pervasive perfectionism."[7] Such individuals are very well organized and tend to set incredibly high personal standards. However, these individuals often react strongly and very negatively to mistakes in a way that results in anger outbursts or meltdowns. Pervasively perfectionistic children tend to have parents who have high expectations of them or are often very critical (think about the Emperor as Anakin's father figure with unreasonably high expectations). Having such a perfectionist manner of thinking leaves a person with unavoidable failure as nobody can be perfect, not even one who expected to bring balance to the Force. Having repeated experiences of failure plus never feeling a sense of perfect completion can leave one feeling defeated, shameful, and guilty. Individuals who tend toward perfection often develop a dichotomous way of thinking that is very moralistic.[8] Anakin, as he turns to the dark side, surmises his dichotomous manner of thinking by stating, "If you're not with me, then you are my enemy." Obi-Wan responds to the Sith way of thinking by stating, "Only a Sith deals in absolutes."[9]

The Story of Anxiety
and Fear in Vader's Life

Anxiety is a powerful force, one required for survival. Anxiety is a more modern term for a base emotion we know as fear. Fear affects all the parts of our brains but especially the limbic system and a little area called the amygdala. When researchers electrically stimulate the amygdala, individuals can immediately experience a fear response and demonstrate all the symptoms of fear, including sweating and a rapid heart rate. Human beings need this fear response especially when living in caves with lions, tigers, and bears as their adversaries. With the fear response, heart rate goes up, breathing quickens, and blood flow moves to the extremities, placing us in a ready state to fight or run. This state is often called fight or flight. In the physical body's effort to survive, it will attempt to control the external environment in any way possible even if that requires jumping out of the way of a car, fighting off a perceived attack, or jumping onto a robot that hovers over lava. In an increasingly stress-filled world, people's bodies often invoke the fight-or-flight response as the biological self perceives an existential threat despite the absence of such a threat. Examples of this can include public speaking and taking a test, which for some people can result in sheer panic. An underlying propensity for anxiety or a perfectionistic style can fuel the fight-or-flight response and makes us believe in the little "brain lies" that can cause us to think we must control variables that are far beyond our control. Stressed brains seek control over stressors, real or imagined.

Fear and the need to control external events repeatedly arise in Anakin's personality. He fears for his mother and feels the need to return to Tatooine to free her. He also fears the loss and potential death of Padmé, the woman he loves, after a blaster hit causes her to fall from a Republic gunship during the chase for Count Dooku. Ben Kenobi embarrassingly challenges and reprimands Anakin so that his Padawan will remain focused on the mission. Anger and frustration are clearly evident in Anakin's face. His heart is with Padmé and cannot be in two places at once. In this moment, he loses sight of the mission because of his fear for Padmé's safety. A true Jedi would release his fear and not allow emotions to cloud his judgment. A similar display manifests during the Jedi rescue mission against General Grievous's ship. As Ben and Anakin are trying to rescue the Chancellor,[10] Anakin wants to break off the attack to help save the clone pilots who were being slaughtered behind him. At every turn, Anakin demonstrates his core of fear and unreasonable goal setting. He repeatedly experiences the pull to save others to prevent bad things from happening. Ultimately, the variables that he strives to control grow into the most unreasonable and unattainable goal of all: the establishment of peace and order throughout the galaxy.

As Anakin attempts to control seen, unforeseen, and imagined tragic life and galactic events, he experiences failure time and time again. Anakin fits the model of the "pervasive perfectionist." He increasingly responds with anger and ultimately rage. He perceives himself as having failed his mother by not saving her from the Sand People. Imagine the personal sense of failure when she dies in his arms. His response to this perceived self-imposed failure is to react with rage in an attempt to seek moralistic justice by killing an entire village of Sand People, including women and children.

More failures ensue, and Anakin focuses on them, building further on his increasing lack of control. Instead of looking inward, focusing on his emotions, and being mindful of the moment and his purpose, he externalizes and emotionally reacts

Hope of Redemption

I grew up in an abusive household where I would be physically attacked for even minor infractions. For a child struggling to see the best in people, finding coping mechanisms in the midst of this upbringing was incredibly difficult. Seeing *Return of the Jedi* seems to be the only thing that got me through my childhood. Star Wars became a coping mechanism and gave me hope that things could be better.

The familial relationship between Luke and Vader is the most tortured I could imagine, but Luke never gave up hope that there was good within his father. The moment Vader comes back to the light and saves his son was always a teary-eyed catharsis for me. If Vader could come back from such ugliness, maybe my dad could, too.

It took me years to decode why *Return of the Jedi* was my favorite part of the saga, but once I connected the dots, it made sense. I just wish I would have had someone there to point it out to me sooner. That's why I tell this story often, to show that Star Wars helps. And for the little boy I used to be, it was the only help I had.

Bryan Young

with little thought to his underlying fears and anxiety. Over and over he runs into variables he cannot control, and this plants more seeds of anxiety, doubt, and fear.

The culmination of his anger that is based on fear and doubt is a physical assault against his wife. As Anakin's fear increases, his anxiety escalates, resulting in an intensification of his desire for external control. This never-ending cycle is what leads him down the path to the dark side.

Vader on the Psychoanalytic Couch

Our emotions are complicated. Sometimes we don't even have the words to express accurately the way we are feeling. This lack of emotional language can be very hard for kids, particularly for boys.[11] An example of confusing emotions would be when someone is both angry and sad. It would be hard to come up with words to explain the emotion other than "sangry." Even adults can emotionally revert to this childlike feeling. The best visual of such an emotion is when Luke responds to the knowledge that Darth Vader is truly his father. We see and hear shock, anger, sadness, and fear all at once expressed in Luke's face and his tortured scream.

One model of understanding complicated and even competing emotions is to think about our emotions in four boxes: (1) mad, (2) sad, (3) worry, and (4) happy. When mad, we are typically being blocked by something that has been placed in our way. Anakin is mad that he is refused permission to sit on the Jedi Council. The Jedi have blocked his way. But worry is why Anakin ultimately becomes Darth Vader. Worry is seated in a person's desire to control the unknown.

People are unable to control the past or the future, but those who remain firmly rooted in the present can manage their circumstances more effectively. Yoda and many other Jedi stay rooted in the present. Yoda once tells Luke, "Difficult to see. Always in motion the future."[12] I like to rewrite the quote as "Difficult to see. Always emotion the future." Darth Vader's emotions cloud his judgment, and this focuses his mind and heart on the future and the past, not on the present. Anakin was not mindful of the present as Sidious gained greater control over him through lies and deceit. If Anakin had been more aware of his complicated emotions and the way fear ruled his life, he might have become more aware of the dire circumstances that held him within the grip of the dark side. Being mindful of the present may have resulted in the destruction of Sidious rather than the destruction of Vader's own life by his own turning to the dark side.

With You Always

Star Wars is just a movie series, not a real story, but we can still dream it all happened. Although the films have a nice, tidy ending as Anakin returns to the fold and dies in his son's arms, we are left with a complicated picture of a little gifted boy who turned to the dark side. The character of Darth Vader has fascinated us and will continue to fascinate us for generations to come. It is all too easy to cast a blanket commentary on Darth Vader by calling him out as bad or even evil. We similarly can name the white-dressed princess as good and pure. Such simplistic and dichotomous thinking can cause us to miss the great emotional depth of the characters in Star Wars. These characters are complicated, real, and relevant to our lives. Good people can be bad. Bad people can be mean but also have great aspirations. Darth Vader does a lot of bad stuff because he is scared.

And he's really cool, too! Thanks, Dad.

References

Dixon, F. A., Lapsley, D. K., & Hanchon, T. A. (2004). An empirical typology of perfectionism in gifted adolescents. *Gifted Child Quarterly, 48*(2), 95–106.

Pittman, F. (1993/2012). *Fathers and sons.* Psychology Today: https://www.psychologytoday.com/articles/200910/fathers-and-sons.

Rotter, J. B. (1945). *Social learning and clinical psychology.* Upper Saddle River, NJ: Prentice-Hall.

Rotter, J. B. (1966). Generalized expectancies for internal versus external locus of control of reinforcement. *Psychological Monographs, 80* (whole no. 609).

Sorotzkin, B. (1985). The quest for perfection: Avoiding guilt or avoiding shame? *Psychotherapy, 22*(3), 564–571.

Stossel, S. (2014, November/December). *A brief history of anxiety: The invention of a modern malaise.* Psychotherapy Network: http://www.psychotherapynetworker.org/magazine/recentissues/2014-novdec/item/2573-a-brief-history-of-anxiety.

Tolin, D. (2012). *Face your fears: A proven plan to beat anxiety, panic, phobias, and obsessions.* Hoboken, NJ: Wiley.

Verhaagen, D. (2010). *Therapy with young men: 16–24 year olds in treatment.* New York, NY: Routledge.

Notes

1. Pittman (1993/2012).
2. *Star Wars: Episode V The Empire Strikes Back* (1983 motion picture).
3. *Star Wars: Episode IV A New Hope* (1977/1981 motion picture).
4. Stossel (2015).
5. Tolin (2012).
6. *Star Wars: Episode I The Phantom Menace* (1999 motion picture).
7. Dixon et al. (2015).
8. Sorotzkin (1985).
9. *Revenge of the Sith* (2005 motion picture).
10. *Revenge of the Sith* (2005 motion picture).
11. Verhaagen (2010).
12. *Star Wars: Episode V The Empire Strikes Back* (1980 motion picture).

The Skywalker Way:
Values in the Light and Dark

JANINA SCARLET

"Knowing your own darkness is the best method for
dealing with the darknesses of other people."

—psychiatrist Carl Jung[1]

Values—enduring beliefs about what matters most in life—can send people with strikingly similar backgrounds down divergent paths in life. The greater the importance a person places on a particular value, the more it will shape attitudes[2] and therefore influence action.[3] Even those whose values mostly mirror one another's can go different ways and become at odds with one another over a single distortion in the reflection, one glaring dissimilarity in personal priorities. Despite their parallels, their differences make a villain of one Skywalker and a hero of his son, yet a remaining shared value brings them together in the end.

Anakin and Luke Skywalker both start out very poor with few prospects for a future on the planet Tatooine.[4] The two

Skywalkers have comparable origins and initially are guided by similar sets of values: Both are ambitious and have a great sense of adventure, both value protecting others, and both become Jedi Knights. However, whereas Luke remains a Jedi, Anakin eventually becomes Darth Vader, a servant of the dark side. The psychology of values can reveal much about their moral judgments, their ability to tolerate distress, and the external influences they encounter along the way. All these factors may play major roles in their personal development, such as their respective decisions to join or refuse to join the dark side.

Values

Among the most important values that most Jedi adhere to are altruism, mindfulness, and a connection with the Force. *Altruism*, or selflessly helping others,[5] is related to improved mental health.[6] Altruism is also something both Luke and Anakin hold in high regard, although in different ways. For Anakin, his desire to protect others seems to be at least partially related to his sense of ambition. He seems to enjoy doing the impossible, driven at times more by the challenge of the task than by the most sensible outcome. In some cases, a person's drive can become a kind of addiction. In that case, the person may become impulsive, with his or her brain activation being similar to that of someone who is addicted to cocaine.[7] People who are addicted to stimulant drugs such as cocaine, caffeine, nicotine, and amphetamines show higher activity of the brain messenger dopamine.[8] Dopamine is related to reward-seeking behaviors, including substance use, gambling, and other risk-taking behaviors, all of which can become addicting.[9] People who are highly ambitious and seek to excel, as Anakin does, also seem to demonstrate higher levels of dopaminergic activation compared with people who are less driven.[10] Anakin does seem addicted to success and adventure. His frequent risk-taking behavior starts early, for example, when he participates in potentially deadly pod races before he ever meets Jedi.[11]

Like his father, Luke Skywalker values altruism and has a sense of adventure. Luke shows his courage and dedication to helping others whenever he can.[12] Unlike Anakin, though, he does not seem to be driven by his ambition in an addictive sense. More specifically, Luke seems to be able to achieve a balance between his values and his ambitions. When he faces the Emperor, Luke is mindful of his feelings, and that allows him to remain altruistic[13] and true to the light side. He refuses to kill Vader despite the amount of pain his father has caused him and others.[14] Even before finding out about his relationship with Darth Vader and believing Vader to be the one who murdered his father, Luke refuses to kill him, stating that he wants to defeat Vader but not kill him.[15]

Research on altruism suggests that people, like Luke, who remain mindful and true to their values of helping others are more likely to experience positive emotions such as love and joy while helping others.[16] In addition, the research on *mindfulness* (noticing the experiences in the present moment rather than fixating on the past or the future) suggests that people who practice mindfulness are more likely to be altruistic and to exhibit better mental health.[17]

In fact, people who tend to be more mindful and those who follow their values are less likely to develop PTSD[18] and are more likely to recover from addiction,[19] depression, anxiety, and chronic pain.[20] In contrast, people who are more impulsive, such as Anakin, are more likely to be driven by immediate gratification, are more likely to struggle with their academic commitments, and may be more likely to struggle with regulating their emotions.[21]

Distress Tolerance

Distress tolerance refers to an individual's ability to regulate his or her emotions during a stressful event. People who struggle with distress tolerance are more likely to try to avoid unpleasant emotions and have a hard time following through with their goals and values when they are distressed.[22] Painful emotions such as fear can lead to impulsive decisions, self-harm, and aggression.[23] Anakin, who struggles with dreams of his mother's suffering, responds impulsively and very aggressively when he slays all the men, women, and children even remotely associated with her death."[24]

People who are more prone to distress appear to have brain activity different from that of people who are less prone to it.[25] The *amygdala* is the part of the brain that is most related to emotion processing and the fear response. This structure seems to be more active in people, such as Anakin, who are more prone to anxiety as opposed to people such as Luke, who are less likely to struggle with it. In fact, by studying an individual's amygdala activity levels, scientists are able to predict the likelihood of that individual's development of anxiety and depression disorders as far as four years in advance. In light of Anakin's impulsive nature, it is possible that his amygdala activation levels areas are as elevated as his midi-chlorian counts.

Luke, in contrast, seems more calm and collected even in the worst situations. For example, in the novel *Star Wars: Heir to the Jedi*, an enraged Luke momentarily experiences the seductive nature of the dark side: the feelings of anger and invincibility.[26] Because he values mercy and impulse control, however, Luke forces himself to slow down and focus on his breath until he is able to reestablish his connection with the Force. Relaxation techniques that incorporate mindful breathing can reduce the physical sensations associated with a variety of negative emotions, including anxiety, tension, and anger, helping people regulate those emotions.[27] By using a technique integral to many forms of modern therapy,[28] Luke regulates his emotions and regains enough focus to remember his personal priorities. Ultimately, it is Luke's connection with his values that allows him to regulate his emotions over this excruciating loss in order to avoid giving in to temptation and acting impulsively. He is able to control his emotions instead of being controlled by them.

Influences

A person's values and ability to tolerate distress and uncertainty can play a role in whether that individual can be manipulated.[29] In certain circumstances, people who are normally fundamentally good can commit thoughtless or even cruel acts. For example, researcher Stanley Milgram at Yale University found that when people are influenced by an authority figure, they are more likely to commit an act that goes against their moral values than they otherwise would be.[30] (See Chapter 13.) In some ways, this is what happens to Anakin when he overpowers Count Dooku. Anakin, following the Jedi Code, attempts to take Dooku prisoner. However, Chancellor Palpatine commands him to kill Dooku.[31] Anakin reluctantly complies with the demand of the authority even though he knows that this act goes against his training.

Then, as a part of his plan to persuade Anakin to join the dark side, Palpatine manipulates his emotions by offering to teach him how to save Padmé. This technique of emotional manipulation is consistent with theories of psychology of influence and persuasion,[32] which find that when a person is upset, he or she is more likely to be susceptible to a suggested behavior. In fact, the more a person believes that he or she can avoid a negative emotion, the more likely that person is to take the action to reduce his or her distress. Knowing that Anakin is worried about losing Padmé, Palpatine uses the young Jedi's fear to his advantage, suggesting that if Anakin does not join him, Padmé will die. To save his wife, his biggest value, Anakin gives up his other values and joins the dark side.

In contrast, Luke does not succumb to the same fate and remains true to the light side. Why does this happen? Why are some people more vulnerable to external influence than others?

When individuals lose their sense of identity, as Anakin does when he becomes Darth Vader, they are likely to act in accordance with their assigned role.[33] The so-called Stanford Prison Experiment demonstrated that people are more likely to become violent when aggressive behavior is consistent with roles assigned to them than are the individuals who are assigned to play more peaceful roles.[34] (For more on the Stanford Prison Experiment, see Chapter 13.) In some ways, this is what happens to Anakin after he becomes Darth Vader. Having lost his previous identity as a Jedi, he starts killing Jedi, including children, on the Emperor's orders.[35]

After someone makes a decision that goes against his or her moral values, that person may experience emotional discomfort and distress. To ease these feelings, the person may adjust his or her beliefs. To reduce his own distress about going against his values, his *cognitive dissonance*[36] over the discrepancy between moral values and immoral action, Vader justifies his action of sacrificing the Jedi by speculating that they would not have understood his reasoning behind assisting Palpatine in killing Mace Windu and would have prevented him from being with Padmé.[37]

The Emperor tries to use the same strategies with Luke that he had earlier with Anakin: He urges him to give in to his anger and demands that he kill Vader. Luke refuses and instead tries to

How to Resist the Dark Side in Us All

Psychologist Philip Zimbardo, known for his research on the Stanford Prison Experiment,[38] offers guidance on how to resist unwanted influence.[39] The key aspects include being mindful, analyzing consequences, and taking responsibility for one's own actions rather than blindly following authority.

As Yoda reminds Luke, a Jedi's mind must be in the present rather than the past or the future.[40] Sometimes when people are afraid of what the future may bring, they are more likely to make a decision driven by a promise of security than one that is based on their values.

Zimbardo suggests that to withstand unwanted influence, people should remain true to their values and identity. When Anakin joins the dark side, the Emperor gives him a new name: Darth Vader. With that name, Anakin has a new identity and is no longer the person he was and thus no longer has the same values and can act against his former Jedi identity.[41] Luke, by contrast, retains his own identity and is able to stay connected with his values[42] and resist the Emperor's persuasion.

reason with his father. He demonstrates that he would rather die than go against his values. It is only after Vader suggests that he will turn Leia to the dark side that Luke, driven by his desire to protect his sister, fights again.

Holding on to one's values is essential to controlling one's emotions and other, baser instincts. Anakin loses all connection to his values when he chooses the dark side and becomes Darth Vader. However, once he connects with his values once again, including the value of a parent protecting and loving a child, he sacrifices himself to save his son's life. This kind of cooperative process and altruistic behavior is related to the individual's levels of *oxytocin*, a hormone usually associated with love and compassion. People who experience love and compassion toward others are more likely to have higher amounts of this hormone. They are also more likely to be altruistic and cooperative to help others.[43] It is possible that through his love for his father, Luke triggers whatever humanity is left in Vader's mostly mechanical body, prompting Vader to help him.

A Difference in Values

"It's not hard to make decisions when
you know what your values are."
—corporate executive Roy E. Disney[44]

Anakin and Luke Skywalker both quickly become proficient with the lightsaber and the Force, and not surprisingly, both gain Palpatine's interest. Whereas Anakin is highly driven and ambitious, Luke is humble and composed. Those differences strongly influence the path each takes. Palpatine is able to use Anakin's ambition and difficulty with controlling his emotions to his own advantage."[45]

However, Luke, by continuously connecting with his values, staying true to his identity, and being mindful of his emotions, is able to say no and withstand the dark side's influence. His example awakens a similar value in Anakin Skywalker and brings his dark father back to the light.

References

Ball-Rokeach, S. J., Rokeach, M., & Grube, J. W. (1984). *Great American values test: Influencing behavior & belief through television.* New York, NY: Free Press.

Beaver, K. M., Wright, J. P., DeLisi, M., & Vaughn, M. G. (2012). Dopaminergic polymorphisms and educational achievement: Results from a longitudinal sample of Americans. *Developmental Psychology, 48*(4), 932–938.

Burg, J. M. (2011). The healthy qualities of mindful breathing: Associations with rumination and depression. *Cognitive Therapy and Research, 35*(2), 179–185.

Cameron, C. D., & Fredrickson, B. L. (2015). *Mindfulness facets predict helping behavior and distinct helping-related emotions.* Mindfulness: http://http://link.springer.com/article/10.1007/s12671-014-0383-2.

Comings, D. E., Rosenthal, R. J., Lesieur, H. R., et al. (1996). A study of the dopamine D2 receptor gene in pathological gambling. *Pharmacogenetics and Genomics, 6*(3), 223–234.

Congressional Record (2001, March 28). Roy E. Disney Center for the Performing Arts. *Congressional Record, Pt. 4, March 27, 2001, to April 23, 2001*, p. 4936. Washington, DC: U. S. Congress.

Conrad, A., Müller, A., Doberenz, S., Kim, S., Meuret, A. E., Wollburg, E., & Roth, W. T. (2007). Psychophysiological effects of breathing instructions for stress management. *Applied Psychophysiology and Biofeedback, 32*(2), 89–98.

Dagher, A., & Robbins, T. W. (2009). Personality, addiction, dopamine: Insights from Parkinson's disease. *Neuron, 61*(4), 502–510.

Dalley, J. W., Fryer, T. D., Brichard, L., Robinson, E. S., Theobald, D. E., Laane, K., Pena, Y., Murphy, E. R., Shah, Y., Probst, K., Abakumova, I., Aigbirhio, F.I., Richards, H. K., Hong, Y., Baron, J. C., Everitt, B. J., & Robbins, T. (2007). Nucleus accumbens D2/3 receptors predict trait impulsivity and cocaine reinforcement. *Science, 315*(5816), 1267–1270.

Davidson, R. J., Putnam, K. M., & Larson, C. L. (2000). Dysfunction in the neural circuitry of emotion regulation—a possible prelude to violence. *Science, 289*(5479), 591–594.

Di Chiara, G., Bassareo, V., Fenu, S., De Luca, M. A., & Spina, L. (2004). Dopamine and drug addiction: The nucleus accumbens shell connection. *Neuropharmacology, 47*(Supplement 1), 227–241.

Dublin, J. E. (1976). "Beyond" gestalt: Toward integrating some systems of psychotherapy. *Psychotherapy, 13*(3), 225–231.

Feldman, G., Greeson, J., & Senville, J. (2010). Differential effects of mindful breathing, progressive muscle relaxation, and loving-kindness meditation on decentering and negative reactions to repetitive thoughts. *Behaviour Research and Therapy, 48*(10), 1002–1011.

Festinger, L. (1957). *A theory of cognitive dissonance.* Stanford, CA: Stanford University Press.

Gratz, K. L., Rosenthal, M. Z., Tull, M. T., Lejuez, C. W., & Gunderson, J. G. (2006). An experimental investigation of emotion dysregulation in borderline personality disorder. *Journal of Abnormal Psychology, 115*(4), 850–855.

Haney, C., Banks, W. C., & Zimbardo, P. G. (1973). Study of prisoners and guards in a simulated prison. *Naval Research Reviews, 9,* 1–17.

Hayes, S. C., Wilson, K. G., Gifford, E. V., Follette, V. M., & Strosahl, K. (1996). Experiential avoidance and behavioral disorders: A functional dimensional approach to diagnosis and treatment. *Journal of Consulting and Clinical Psychology, 64*(6), 1152–1168.

Hearne, K. (2015). *Star Wars: Heir to the Jedi.* New York, NY: Del Rey.

Hogan, K., & Speakman, J. (2006). *Covert persuasion: Psychological tactics and tricks to win the game.* Hoboken, NJ: Wiley.

Homer, P. M., & Kahle, L. R. (1988). A structural equation test of the value-attitude-behavior hierarchy. *Journal of Personality and Social Psychology, 54*(4), 638–646.

Israel, S., Weisel, O., Ebstein, R. P., & Bornstein, G. (2012). Oxytocin, but not vasopressin, increases both parochial and universal altruism. *Psychoneuroendocrinology, 37*(8), 1341–1344.

Jung, C. G. (1937/1973). Letter to Kendig Cully: 25 September 1937. In G. Adler & A. Jaffe (Eds.), *Letters of C. G. Jung, 1906-1950* (p. 237). London, UK: Routledge.

Kim, S., Roth, W. T., & Wollburg, E. (2015). Effects of therapeutic relationships, expectancy, and credibility in breathing techniques for anxiety. *Bulletin of the Menninger Clinic, 79*(2), 116–130.

Lucerno, J. (2005). *Star Wars: Dark Lord: The Rise of Darth Vader.* New York, NY: Del Rey.

Marshall-Berenz, E. C., Vujanovic, A. A., Bonn-Miller, M. O., Bernstein, A., & Zvolensky, M. J. (2010). Multimethod study of distress tolerance and PTSD symptom severity in a trauma-exposed community sample. *Journal of Traumatic Stress, 23*(5), 623–630.

Milgram, S. (1963). Behavioral study of obedience. *Journal of Abnormal and Social Psychology, 67*(4), 371.

Nock, M. K., & Mendes, W. B. (2008). Physiological arousal, distress tolerance, and social problem-solving deficits among adolescent self-injurers. *Journal of Consulting and Clinical Psychology, 76*(1), 28–38.

Schwartz, C., Meisenhelder, J. B., Ma, Y., & Reed, G. (2003). Altruistic social interest behaviors are associated with better mental health. *Psychosomatic Medicine, 65*(5), 778–785.

Stotts, A. L., Vujanovic, A., Heads, A., Suchting, R., Green, C. E., & Schmitz, J. M. (2014). The role of avoidance and inflexibility in characterizing response to contingency management for cocaine use disorders: A secondary profile analysis. *Psychology of Addictive Behaviors.* Advance online publication http://dx.doi.org/10.1037/adb0000011.

Stover, M. W. (2005). *Star Wars: Episode III: Revenge of the Sith.* London, UK: Century.

Swartz, J. R., Knodt, A. R., Radtke, S. R., & Hariri, A. R. (2015). A neural biomarker of psychological vulnerability to future life stress. *Neuron, 85*(3), 505–511.

Tetlock P. E. (1989). Structure and function in political belief systems. In A. R. Pratkanis, S. J. Breckler, & A G. Greenwald (Eds.), *Attitude structure and function* (pp. 129–151). Hillsdale, NJ: Erlbaum.

Tomer, R., Goldstein, R. Z., Wang, G. J., Wong, C., & Volkow, N. D. (2008). Incentive motivation is associated with striatal dopamine asymmetry. *Biological Psychology, 77*(1), 98–101.

Volkow, N. D., Wang, G. J., Telang, F., Fowler, J. S., Logan, J., Childress, A. R., Jayne, M., Ma, Y. & Wong, C. (2006). Cocaine cues and dopamine in dorsal striatum: Mechanism of craving in cocaine addiction. *Journal of Neuroscience, 26*(24), 6583–6588.

Vowles, K. E., & McCracken, L. M. (2008). Acceptance and values-based action in chronic pain: A study of treatment effectiveness and process. *Journal of Consulting and Clinical Psychology, 76*(3), 397–407.

Wallmark, E., Safarzadeh, K., Daukantait, D., & Maddux, R. E. (2013). Promoting altruism through meditation: An 8-week randomized controlled pilot study. *Mindfulness, 4*(3), 223–234.

Wulfert, E., Block, J. A., Santa Ana, E., Rodrigues, M. L., & Colsman, M. (2002). Delay of gratification: Impulsive choices and problem behaviors in early and late adolescence. *Journal of Personality, 70*(4), 533–552.

Young, J. S. (2010). Breathwork as a therapeutic modality: An overview for counselors. *Counseling and Values, 55*(1), 113–125.

Zimbardo, P. G. (1971, October 25). *The psychological power and pathology of imprisonment.* A statement prepared for the U.S. House of Representatives Committee on the Judiciary, Subcommittee No. 3: Hearings on Prison Reform, San Francisco.

Zimbardo, P. G. (2007). *The Lucifer effect: Understanding how good people turn evil.* New York, NY: Random House.

Notes

1. Jung (1937/1973).
2. Ball-Rokeach et al. (1984); Tetlock (1989).
3. Homer & Kahle (1988).
4. *Star Wars: Episode I The Phantom Menace* (1999 motion picture); *Star Wars: Episode IV A New Hope* (1977/1981 motion picture).
5. Cameron & Fredrickson (2015).
6. Schwartz et al. (2003).
7. Dalley et al. (2007); Tomer et al. (2008).
8. Volkow et al. (2006).
9. Comings et al. (1996); Dagher & Robbins (2009).
10. Beaver et al. (2012); Tomer et al. (2008).
11. *Star Wars: Episode I The Phantom Menace* (1999 motion picture).
12. Hearne (2015).
13. Cameron & Fredrickson (2015).
14. *Star Wars: Episode VI Return of the Jedi* (1983 motion picture).

15. Hearne (2015); Zimbardo (1971).
16. Cameron & Fredrickson (2015).
17. Wallmark et al. (2012).
18. Marshall-Berenz (2010).
19. Stotts et al. (2014).
20. Vowles & McCracken (2008).
21. Wulfert et al. (2002).
22. Gratz et al. (2006).
23. Davidson et al. (2000); Nock et al. (2008).
24. *Star Wars: Episode II Attack of the Clones* (2002 motion picture).
25. Swartz et al. (2015).
26. Hearne (2015).
27. Burg (2011); Conrad et al. (2007); Feldman et al. (2010).
28. Dublin (1976); Kim et al. (2015); Young et al. (2010).
29. Zimbardo (2007).
30. Milgram (1963).
31. Stover (2005).
32. Hogan & Speakman (2006).
33. Zimbardo (2007).
34. Zimbardo (2007).
35. *Star Wars: Episode III Revenge of the Sith* (2005 motion picture).
36. Festinger (1957).
37. Lucerno (2005).
38. Haney et al. (1973).
39. Zimbardo (2007).
40. *Star Wars: Episode V The Empire Strikes Back* (1980 motion picture).
41. *Revenge of the Sith.*
42. *Return of the Jedi.*
43. Israel et al. (2012).
44. Congressional Record (2001).
45. *Attack of the Clones.*

An OCEAN Far Away

IV. Agreeableness versus Disagreeableness

TRAVIS LANGLEY

Writers sometimes describe the personality factor of *agreeableness* as likability[1] as though the two words were synonyms. That description is inadequate. Highly agreeable individuals do tend to be more likable than average, true, but they may not be. Whereas Lando Calrissian charms almost everyone he meets, Jar Jar Binks decidedly does not. This factor has less to do with how much people like them and more to do with how strongly they like others and want to be liked.

The social interaction shown by extraverts differs from the social interest that goes with agreeableness. An extravert might be a lively and helpful friend or might as easily be an outgoing jerk. Agreeable individuals are interested in others as people, not simply for the energy and activity that extraverts find appealing.

Agreeable people have compassion, concern, sympathy, and empathy. Overall, their optimism about human nature makes them trusting, cooperative, and altruistic. They want to help. They want to get along. Strong leaders tend to be somewhat agreeable but not highly so. Compliant individuals at the most agreeable end of the scale are more ready to follow. In their eagerness either to appease or to please, Lando and Jar Jar both make grave mistakes that bring harm to others.[2] Lando, at least, turns against the Empire (once it becomes clear that Darth Vader will take everything from him anyway) and begins to cooperate instead with the Rebel Alliance. When harmony with the Empire becomes untenable, he seeks it with the rebels.

Examples of Agreeableness Traits

Altruism

Compliance

Concern for Others

Cooperation

Empathy

Modesty

Need to Be Liked

Need to Get Along

Optimism about People

Seeking Social Harmony

Softheartedness

Straightforwardness

Sympathy

Tendermindedness

Trust

Disagreeable people—those low in agreeableness—are more insulting, argumentative, hardhearted, and pessimistic about human nature. They show little to no concern for others' well-being. Han Solo is disagreeable much of the time, possibly because of habits he developed to survive in the harsher parts of the galaxy in his younger days,[3] but he reveals his compassionate core.[4] Jabba the Hutt genuinely is disagreeable. At least Jabba is up front and honest about his disagreeable nature.

Senator/Emperor/Sith Lord Palpatine makes a grand show of exuding false modesty as he pretends to serve the Republic for the benefit of all. At heart, the man feels no kindness, no concern for anyone but himself. The heartlessness that goes with extreme disagreeableness runs throughout the Dark Tetrad[5] of sadism, psychopathy, narcissism, and Machiavellianism.[6] Lacking compassion, these four overlapping characteristics can represent the greatest human evil when combined in one person. Palpatine shows them all. He stays disagreeable, evil to the end, whereas compassion redeems the apprentice he calls Darth Vader.

References

Baron-Cohen, S. (2012). *The science of evil: On empathy and the origins of cruelty.* New York, NY: Basic.

Buckels, E. E., Jones, D. N., & Paulhus, D. L. (2013). Behavior confirmation of everyday sadism. *Psychological Science, 24*(11), 1–9.

Chabrol, H., Van Leeuwen, N., Rodgers, R., & Sejourne, N. (2009). Contributions of psychopathic, narcissistic, Machiavellian, and sadistic personality traits to juvenile delinquency. *Personality and Individual Differences, 47*, 734–739.

Crispin, A. C. (1997). *The paradise snare (The Han Solo trilogy, #1).* New York: Bantam.

Hawthorne, J.W. (1932). A group test for the measurement of cruelty-compassion: A proposed means of recognizing potential criminality. *Journal of Social Psychology, 3*, 189–211.

Jakobwitz, S., & Egan, V. (2006). The "dark triad" and normal personality traits. *Personality and Individual Differences, 40*, 331–339.

Paulhus, D. L., & Williams, K. M. (2002). The Dark Triad of personality: Narcissism, Machiavellianism, and psychopathy. *Journal of Research in Personality, 36*, 556–563.

Salgado, J. F., & De Fruyt, F. (2005). Personality in personnel selection. In A. Evers, O. Schmidt-Voskuyl, & N. Anderson (Eds.), *Handbook of personnel selection* (pp. 174–198). Oxford: Blackwell.

Stead, R., & Fekken, G. C. (2014). Agreeableness at the core of the dark triad of personality. *Individual Differences Research, 12*(4-A), 131–141.

Notes

1. See, for example, Salgado & De Fruyt (2005), p. 178.
2. *Star Wars: Episode V The Empire Strikes Back* and *Star Wars: Episode II Attack of the Clones* (1980, 2002 motion pictures).
3. Crispin (1997).
4. *Star Wars: Episode IV A New Hope* (1977 motion pictures).
5. Buckels et al. (2013); Chabrol et al. (2009); Jakobwitz & Egan (2006); Paulhus & Williams (2002).
6. Baron-Cohen (2012); Hawthorne (1932); Stead & Fekken (2014).

5 »

Awakenings

In the Star Wars stories, experiences awaken characters' desires to embark on adventures and to fight for what they want or believe in. In our world, those stories stimulate our feelings and imaginations. The original *Star Wars* awakened popular interest in grand science fiction, incredible special effects, and epic sagas too big to tell in a single film.

» 17 »

Samurai, Star Wars, and Underdogs

JONATHAN HETTERLY

"What good is a reward if you ain't around to use it? Besides, attacking that battle station is not my idea of courage. It's more like suicide."
—Han Solo[1]

"The genius of evolution lies in the dynamic
tension between optimism and pessimism
continually correcting each other."
—psychologist Martin E. P. Seligman[2]

Why do people fight a losing battle? Why do people persist when the odds are against them? George Lucas's Star Wars films and Akira Kurosawa's samurai films join a collection of enduring stories in history, literature, mythology, religion, sport, and cinema that tell the tales of people who were expected to fail or given little hope of victory.[3]

When persons are depicted as underdogs, support for them increases.[4] In 2013, Malcolm Gladwell published an entire book on underdogs and people facing giants titled *David and Goliath*.[5] Much has been written in the field of sports psychology regarding underdogs and sympathizing with the disadvantaged teams and groups, but what about those who have more to lose than a competitive sporting event? What inspires men and women to stand up for what they believe in while staring into the face of death?

Moral Growth

In the original Star Wars trilogy, the Galactic Empire is the powerful governing force of the galaxy and the Rebel Alliance is a small but devoted group of freedom fighters standing up against the tyranny of the Emperor and Darth Vader. In the Kurosawa samurai films that influenced and inspired Lucas (see the sidebar titled "Cinematic and Storytelling Influence," below), the samurai are ronin, masterless warriors left to fend for themselves in a postfeudal society that no longer needs for them. What inspires the collective samurai to fight for causes that almost guarantee certain death? What provokes Luke, Han, and later Lando to join a cause that already has the odds for success stacked against it? Perhaps exploring two distinct fields of psychology can help answer these questions.

Research studies show that our brains automatically evaluate fairness. Humans seem to have a positive or pleasurable response to fair treatment and a disgust or protest response to unfairness.[6] Viktor Frankl, when describing his concentration camp experiences in his book *Man's Search for Meaning*, stated that when beaten by guards or punished severely for no reason or for minor infractions, he found the emotional pain and humiliation of unfair treatment more unbearable than the physical pain.[7] Specific stories and the research results show that unfair treatment seems to be intrinsically aversive and fair treatment inherently pleasurable.[8]

Lawrence Kohlberg was an American psychologist who built on psychologist Jean Piaget's theory of stages of cognitive development to identify specific *stages of moral development*.[9] Kohlberg's theory held that moral reasoning and the basis for ethical behavior exist in identifiable developmental stages. The theory centers on the notion that justice is the essential characteristic of moral reasoning.[10] The primary motivations for sticking with and rooting for the underdog may be concerns with justice and fairness for the disadvantaged.[11]

Kohlberg's six stages are grouped into three different levels, each with two stages:

Level 1: Preconventional Morality

Preconventional morality focuses on self-interest, before the person learns moral conventions.

> **Stage 1:** *Obedience and punishment orientation* ("How can I avoid punishment?"). The first stage, which starts in earliest childhood, focuses on the direct consequences of one's actions on oneself. When R2-D2 leaves the Skywalker farm without permission, C-3PO attempts to hide out of fear that he personally will be punished.
>
> **Stage 2:** *Self-interest orientation* ("What's in it for me?"). The second stage focuses on paying for a benefit. This stage expresses a limited interest in the needs of others, only to a point where it might further the individual's own self-interest. When Han Solo first appears, he openly says that he is looking out only for himself.

Individuals at the preconventional level judge the morality of an action by its direct consequences.

Han and Lando both first appear as characters fitting the criteria for preconventional moral development. Han is a smuggler who uses his skills in the service of the highest bidder. His primary agenda is to look out for himself. Money, not a sense of duty or hatred of the Empire, is all that motivates him to transport Obi-Wan and his group to Alderaan or to help rescue the princess on the Death Star.[12] Those are heroic-seeming actions that he does only for money, as opposed to later heroism that is not about money anymore.

Lando Calrissian's moral outlook is also preconventional, but for different reasons. His primary motive is to avoid punishment or pain. Because he knows that the Empire can take over Cloud City and make his life miserable or end it, Lando believes that he's left with no choice but to betray his friend and aid the enemy.[13] Knowledge leads to belief, and belief leads to action.

Eventually Han and Lando outgrow preconventional moral reasoning and move on to higher levels, although it can be difficult to know which higher level they attain. They depart from their more individualistic outlook and integrate into the Rebel Alliance, making the rebel cause their own purpose. They are confronted with how long a person can tolerate oppression and suffering around him while remaining neutral and avoiding taking a side or stand. Despite the threats of death, suffering, and lack of payment, they have found a cause worthy of elevating their courage, convictions, and virtues. No longer is their purpose to serve only themselves.

Level 2: Conventional Morality

Conventional morality is characterized by an acceptance of society's conventions concerning right and wrong.

Stage 3: *Interpersonal accord and conformity* (good boy/ girl attitude). The third stage involves subscribing to social norms. It concerns individuals who are receptive to approval or disapproval from others as it reflects society's views or even views within a group such as the Rebel Alliance. The first time Han Solo comes to the rescue instead of simply looking out for himself, he may have more advanced reasons, but he may simply feel a need for interpersonal accord with his new acquaintances Luke and Leia.

Stage 4: *Authority and social-order-maintaining orientation* (law and order morality). Stage 4 is guided by the attempt to maintain a functioning society. Palpatine plays on this when he tricks moral people into giving him greater authority.[14]

Level 3: Postconventional Morality

Postconventional morality is marked by a realization that the individual's own moral reasoning may take precedence over society's view.

Stage 5: *Social contract orientation.* In Stage 5, laws are regarded as social contracts rather than rigid edicts.

Stage 6: *Universal ethical principles* (principled conscience). Moral reasoning in stage 6 involves recognizing that laws are valid only insofar as they are grounded in justice. The Rebel Alliance is founded on postconventional morality. Leia is the fully formed character who ascribes to this level of moral reasoning. Although Luke, Han, and Lando have no sympathy for the Empire, it is Leia whose example inspires them to join the cause.[15] In stark

contrast to the period dramas that had both idealized
and mythologized the samurai, Kurosawa's samurai
films depicted a more violent and cruel feudal Japan.
Kurosawa's samurai often face the task of adhering
to their virtuous and principled code in the face of
a society that no longer values their social standing.
For many warriors in *The Seven Samurai*, the first
instinct is often to solicit a bribe or inquire what
benefit they will receive for fighting.[16] In *Yojimbo*,
Sanjuro waltzes into town fueled by his own self-
interest.[17] By the end of those Kurosawa films, the
characters are guided by care, concern, and the safety
of others.

Both Star Wars and Kurosawa's films present stories and worlds
where the characters evolve from primitive or childlike morality
to a fully developed moral code that opens them up to helping
others regardless of the risk or the odds of defeat. Kohlberg's
theory of moral development provides one possible perspective,
but it relies too heavily on justice in interpreting how people
make moral choices.

Perhaps exploring specific values and virtues that are associated with underdogs and lost causes can complement Kohlberg's
findings.

Positive Psychology:
Character Values and Virtues

Positive psychology is the scientific study of the strengths and
virtues that enable individuals, communities, and organizations
to thrive. It is grounded in the belief that people want to lead
meaningful and fulfilling lives, cultivate what is best within

Cinematic and Storytelling Influence

When George Lucas first discovered Akira Kurosawa films in the 1960s, he reports, his life changed forever and the early seeds for the Star Wars universe were planted.[18] Kurosawa's 1958 film *The Hidden Fortress* started it all.[19] The film's two bickering peasants, its storytelling characters, inspired the creation of R2-D2 and C-3PO. *The Hidden Fortress* also involves a general or warrior escorting a princess through enemy territory and culminates in a duel between past adversaries.[20] Kurosawa's 1961 film *Yojimbo* includes a confrontation similar to Obi-Wan's cantina lightsaber battle.[21] In addition to characters and plots, *The Hidden Fortress* and *Star Wars* share filmmaking techniques such as the screen wipe, in which one scene is wiped away to transition to the next.

them, and enhance their experiences of love, work, and play. The field is intended to complement, not to replace, traditional psychology and positions itself as an alternative to the traditional mental health focus on pathology and dysfunction.[22]

The samurai and Jedi share many of the same character strengths associated with *positive psychology*, a branch of psychology that posits that strong character development can increase life satisfaction and psychological well-being and have positive effects on relationships, careers, and personal growth.

What are the specific strengths and virtues of positive psychology that can be attributed to standing against tyranny at all costs, and are these character strengths exhibited in the samurai and Jedi? Two significant qualities exhibited by both are (1) courage and (2) humanity.

Courage

"This is the nature of war. By protecting
others, you save yourself. If you only think of
yourself, you'll only destroy yourself."

—Kambei Shimada[23]

Courage may be a virtue that many people may not develop. It consists of emotional strengths that involve the exercise of the will to accomplish goals in the face of opposition, both external and internal, with neither being dependent on the actual size of the opposition or threat.[24] It requires bravery and perseverance regardless of obstacles. Those without courage most certainly would shrink in the face of mounting opposition or minuscule odds of victory. Courage in battle is important for the majority side and essential for the underdog. The Rebel Alliance is afforded opportunity after opportunity to abandon its cause in the face of setbacks and defeat but continues to fight even when faced with its underdog odds before the climatic trench run. *The Seven Samurai* spends a significant portion of the film setting up the size of the opposition and recruiting the small ragtag group of ronin. Regardless of their superior fighting skills and knowledge, in the end they are woefully outnumbered.[25]

Humanity

A second character value and virtue that may help explain why people continue to fight the opposition in the face of mounting defeat is humanity. Regardless of pain, suffering, or loss, many men and women will not stop helping and caring for others regardless of the risk to their own lives. The Rebel Alliance does not make light of the sacrifice that its spies made to help smuggle information out of the Empire's domain. Luke's initial call to action is his inability to stand by idly while Princess Leia is executed. Both Han and Lando respond and turn their priorities around when the tyranny of the Empire is personalized and someone they know or care about is under threat. Sanjuro's motives shift from self-serving double-crossing of the rival gangs to risking his safety and life when rescues and saves Kohei and his wife.[26]

Although most of the attention is paid to the cinematic and storytelling similarities, Kurosawa's samurai films and Lucas's Star Wars universe both promote similar character traits and virtues for a purposeful and fulfilling life. The codes of conduct for both bear a striking resemblance. Although positive psychology often is associated with cultivating happiness in a person's life, courage, humanity, and altruism provide a strong foundation for those bound to a cause worth fighting for even against tremendous odds.

The Greatest Deterrent

Positive psychology and Kohlberg's theory of moral development may provide insight into the reasons why some people remain steadfast in their devotion to a cause, even a lost cause. What, though, might be the reasons that prevent many from joining or staying committed to a fight in which the odds are stacked against them? And how have the Jedi or samurai conquered those obstacles? If people root for the underdog and have sympathy for just causes, why don't more people join the Davids in their fights against the Goliaths of this world?

Perhaps there is no greater fear among most human beings than the fear of suffering and death. When given the opportunity, most individuals take steps to escape, avoid, or reduce the likelihood of death.[27] So how come the samurai and the Jedi are able to navigate around those problems?

Kambei Shimada: As a matter of fact, I'm preparing
for a tough war. It will bring us neither money nor
fame. Want to join?
Shichiroji: Yes!
Shimada: Maybe we die this time.
Shichiroji smiles.[28]

Both the Jedi and the samurai were well established not only
in their beliefs but also in their role and place in the larger
scheme of life. Samurai viewed death as an inevitability of life.[29]
When an individual took on the samurai occupation, he ended
his human life and entered into death. Upon becoming a samurai, the warrior's life has ended and the moment of eventual
physical death becomes irrelevant. Samurai have accepted their
own deaths as though they already had occurred, and so fear of
the actual moment when their hearts stop beating supposedly
ceases to exist.[30]

For the Jedi, death is not supposed to be an impediment to
duty or courage. Instead, it is a transition from physical life to
spiritual existence. In their lightsaber duel on the Death Star,
Obi-Wan cautions Vader, "You can't win, Vader. If you strike
me down, I shall become more powerful than you can possibly
imagine."[31] As an adherent to the light side, Obi-Wan knows
that his physical death can result in his ascension or transition to
becoming a ghostly figure still capable of communicating with
and advising Luke. Death for the Jedi should not invoke fear and
dread of its eventuality but rather should add a level of meaning
and appreciation for life.[32]

Never Tell Them the Odds

What drives the Rebel Alliance to continue to fight against the odds? What inspires the samurai to stand for what they believe in while staring into the face of death? Quite simply, their moral reasoning is guided by justice, courage, and humanity. They have resolved their own fear of death. Regardless of the outcome, they have what it takes to keep fighting despite the odds being stacked against them.

References

American Psychiatric Association. (2013). *Diagnostic and statistical manual of mental disorders* (DSM-5) (5th ed.). Washington, DC: American Psychiatric Association.

Bergen, D. (2008). *Human development: Traditional and contemporary theories.* Upper Saddle River, NJ: Pearson.

Cleary, T. (2009). *Training the samurai mind: A bushido sourcebook.* Boston, MA: Shambhala.

Frankl, V. (1992). *Man's search for meaning: An introduction to logotherapy.* Boston, MA: Beacon.

Gladwell, M. G. (2013). *David and Goliath: Underdogs, misfits, and the art of battling giants.* New York, NY: Little, Brown.

Kaminski, M. (2008). *The secret history of Star Wars.* Kingston, Ontario, Canada: Legacy.

Kohlberg, L. (1973). *Collected papers on moral development and moral education.* Cambridge, MA: Harvard University.

Peterson, C., & Seligman, M. E. P. (2004). *Character strengths and virtues: A handbook and classification.* New York: Oxford University Press and Washington, DC: American Psychological Association.

Ratti, O., & Cleary, T. (1999). *The code of the samurai: A modern translation of the Bushido Shoshinshu of Taira Shigesuke.* North Clarendon, VT: Tuttle.

Richie, D. (1999). *The films of Akira Kurosawa* (3rd ed.). Berkeley, CA: University of California Press.

Seligman, M. E. P. (2002). *Authentic happiness.* New York, NY: Free Press.

Seligman, M. E, P. (2006). *Learned optimism: How to change your mind and your life.* New York, NY: Knopf.

Seligman, M. E. P. (2007). *What you can change and what you can't.* New York, NY: Knopf.

Tabibnia, G., & Lieberman, M. D. (2007). Fairness and cooperation are rewarding: Evidence from social cognitive neuroscience. *Annals of the New York Academy of Science, 1118*(1), 90–101.

Vandello, J. A., Goldschmied, N. P., & Richards, D. A. R. (2007). The appeal of the underdog. *Personality and Social Psychology Bulletin, 33*(12), 1603–1616.

Wong, P. T. P., & Tomer, A. (2001). *Beyond terror and denial: The positive psychology of death acceptance.* London, UK: Routledge.

Notes

1. *Star Wars: Episode IV A New Hope* (1977/1981 motion picture).
2. Seligman (2006).
3. Kaminski (2008); Richie (1999).
4. Vandello et al. (2007).
5. Gladwell (2013).
6. Tabibnia & Lieberman (2007).
7. Frankl (1992).
8. Tabibnia & Lieberman (2007).
9. Kohlberg (1973).
10. Bergen (2008).
11. Vandello et al. (2007).
12. *A New Hope.*
13. *Star Wars: Episode V The Empire Strikes Back* (1980 motion picture).
14. *Star Wars: Episode II Attack of the Clones (2002); Star Wars: Episode III Revenge of the Sith* (2005 motion pictures).
15. *A New Hope.*
16. *The Seven Samurai* (1954 motion picture).
17. *Yojimbo* (1961 motion picture).
18. *The Hidden Fortress* (1958; motion picture. DVD commentary).
19. *The Hidden Fortress.*
20. *A New Hope.*
21. *Yojimbo.*
22. Seligman (2002, 2007).
23. *The Seven Samurai.*
24. Peterson & Seligman (2004).
25. *The Seven Samurai.*
26. *Yojimbo* (1961 motion picture).
27. Wong & Tomer (2001).
28. *The Seven Samurai.*
29. Cleary (2009).
30. Ratti & Cleary (1999).
31. *A New Hope.*
32. *Star Wars: Episode VI Return of the Jedi* (1983 motion picture).

» 18 »

Yoda: Little Big Mentor

CRAIG POHLMAN

"The true leader is always led."
—psychiatrist Carl Jung[1]

Mentors take many forms and serve many roles in their students' lives. By sharing their experience, not only do they pass on their skill, knowledge, and confidence but they also benefit from the act of mentoring. Psychologist Erik Erikson's theory of psychosocial development—in which he outlined a series of stages by which people grow and personality changes over the course of the lifetime—identified times in life when children are readiest to learn from others, when adolescents most easily follow or rebel, and when adults get the most out of contributing to future generations.[2] In Star Wars, the eldest Jedi is the most renowned mentor of all and provides a useful model for understanding the dynamics of mentoring—Jedi Master Yoda.

What Is Mentoring?

Mentoring involves someone helping another to progress in career and in life. Some key components shape mentoring and differentiate it from other processes, such as didactic training, supervision, and interpersonal relationships, like friendships:[3]

- It is professional in nature, related to work or career.
- Knowledge is transferred through the process.
- The mentor provides psychosocial support and social capital.
- Communication is face-to-face and goes beyond the bounds of a formalized training program (such as a course).
- The relationship is ongoing.
- One participant is the mentor and possesses more relevant knowledge, wisdom, or experience than the other participant, the mentee or protégé.

For a relationship to be considered mentoring, it has to take place outside the confines of traditional classroom learning. Taking classes at the Jedi Academy would not count as mentoring, which is "the most intense and powerful one-on-one developmental relationship, entailing the most influence, identification, and emotional involvement."[4] So if that is what mentoring is, why use it? Wouldn't structured training programs and supervision be more streamlined, efficient, or cost-effective? Organizations like the Jedi Order utilize mentoring because it is the best way to achieve several outcomes.

Mentoring Helps Organizations

Specific advantages of mentoring include organizational social-ization, employee integration, managerial succession, and reduced turnover.[5] The Jedi Council built its whole training model around pairs of Jedi Masters and Padawans. The social-ization provides Padawans, who are effectively orphaned at very young ages, with parental figures and some semblance of family. The model ingrains the ethic of collaboration, rather than push-ing Jedi to act alone all the time. Succession is part and parcel of Jedi mentoring. As for reducing turnover, mentoring works well for the Jedi overall, but they also suffer some colossal failures.

Mentoring Helps Individuals

Research has shown that individuals who are mentored make substantial gains, compared to those who are not mentored, in areas like career progress and professional skills.[6] Not all Force-sensitive individuals join the Jedi or Sith. The movies offer hints of that, such as when Leia telepathically senses Luke.[7] Other Star Wars media, like books and television shows, reveal additional examples. Such individuals might learn a mind trick or two and probably have impressive reflexes, but they will never fully real-ize their promise without a mentor's guidance.

Mentoring Helps Mentors

Mentoring doesn't just help the mentee. First, mentors get the gratification of having developed the next generation. They enjoy respect and recognition from mentees. In addition, mentoring has been shown to advance a mentor's career.[8] The

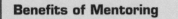

Benefits of Mentoring

Mentoring benefits the mentors themselves in many ways, both practical and personal.

- **Education:** Training someone else reinforces the mentor's own knowledge. This helps the mentor refresh skills and stay sharp.
- **Assistance:** Working with a student or a junior partner helps the mentor get more work done.
- **Legacy:** Mentoring creates a legacy and traditions that will perpetuate the purpose of the mentoring relationship and will enable the mentor's knowledge to live on long after the mentor is gone.
- **Family:** Especially among Jedi, who are not supposed to have families, mentoring can help fulfill paternal or maternal needs.
- **Wish fulfillment:** Vicariously sharing the student's successes can help the mentor enjoy experiences and achievements the mentor has not personally undergone.
- **Identification:** The mentor might connect with a student who reminds that mentor of him- or herself.[9]

—T. L.

Jedi Order is hierarchical, culminating in the Jedi Council and Master status; Yoda reaches the acme as the Council's leader. Stuffing a resume with Padawans-turned-Knights (and Masters) would be a great way to climb that particular corporate ladder. The accomplishments of one generation have to add to the reverence for those who pave the way. Yoda actually boasts to Luke about how many centuries of mentoring he has under his belt.[10] Finally, the current can flow both ways and studies have shown that mentors also learn from their mentees.[11] As an old adage says, the best way to learn something is to teach it. How could a Jedi *not* improve his or her own skills when teaching a Padawan? Yoda tells Obi-Wan that he will teach him how to commune with the deceased Qui-Gon.[12] It's easy to imagine that Yoda achieves some primary gain through that instruction, and improved capacity to telecommute (in essence) would be a handy trick in his long game against Emperor Palpatine.

Phases of Mentorship

Mentoring follows a predictable course. A four-stage model of mentoring has emerged from the literature: initiation, cultivation, separation, and redefinition.[13]

Initiation Phase

During *initiation*, expectations emerge. One example would be setting career objectives for the mentee. For Jedi, this phase would relate to their Code and the ultimate goal of preparing mentees for passing the trials into Knighthood. This is also the time when reverence for a mentor is high, and that reverence is tested during the cultivation phase when reality strikes.

Cultivation

The mentor models and then challenges the mentee. Yoda sets a high bar for Luke (we all know what Yoda says about the difference between trying and doing). The mentor may expose the mentee to difficult circumstances, but with a safety net. Jedi go so far as to take their Padawans into dangerous situations, even combat. The protection they provide only goes so far (talk about trial by fire). The *cultivation* phase is when the interpersonal bond forms between mentor and mentee (trial by fire stuff can pay off).

Separation Phase

Baby birds must fly from their parents' nests. The mentee will not develop fully without achieving independence from the mentor. In the critical phase of *separation*, something happens that significantly alters the relationship. That change could be precipitated by organizational norms (like a Padawan being expected to tackle the trials when reaching a certain age and skill level) or emotional development in mentor or mentee. For Yoda and Luke, the separation phase is brought on by Luke's determination to save Leia, Han, and the others from Vader. The separation phase coincides with turmoil, anxiety, and feelings of loss for many mentors and mentees. The mentee experiences newfound autonomy and an opportunity to test abilities without guidance or support (Luke going to Cloud City without Yoda or Obi-Wan in his corner), but the "equilibrium of the cultivation phase is disrupted."[14] Timing of separation is important. If it happens too early, the mentee may feel abandoned and unprepared. Luke is convinced that he has to leave Dagobah, while Yoda makes it clear that Luke is not yet ready to face Vader.[15] If it happens too late, mentor and mentee may resent each other, as the relationship becomes unresponsive to changing needs and concerns; in other words, it stagnates.

Redefinition Phase

Finally, the *redefinition* phase is about the relationship evolving into something significantly different or ending altogether. Jedi redefine relationships with Padawans to achieve collegial alliances with their former students. Luke's relationship with Yoda ends with Yoda's passing. Or does it? Becoming one with the Force enables Yoda to be a spiritual guide, akin to how Obi-Wan maintains his connection with Luke. Yoda alludes to that when he states, "Rejoice for those around you who transform into the Force. Mourn them, do not. Miss them, do not."[16]

Crash Course: Yoda and Luke

How the mentoring relationship is establishedmayvary—with significant implications. *Formal mentoring* programs are institutionalized to some degree and tend to have prescribed goals.[17] Key characteristics related to effective formal mentoring programs include high mentor commitment, understanding of the program's goals, and mentors addressing both career and personal needs of mentees.[18] The process of matching mentor and mentee is a critical step in formal mentoring programs; introductory experiences often set the tone for the relationship.[19]

The Jedi Academy is set up like a formal mentoring program. The Academy is a key Republic institution with clear goals: to educate those who are Force-sensitive in the use of the light side and to pass the trials to become full-fledged Knights. Masters attend to the career needs of their Padawans and are de facto parents in terms of personal needs. The movies reveal only a little about how the matching of Masters and Padawans occurs, but enough to know that it is not haphazard.

Informal mentoring often is less visible than formal mentoring because the relationship is not overtly labeled or recognized as part of an institution. Informal mentoring is driven by the needs of both parties; goals often are not expressed, and mutual learning and support occurs for both mentee and mentor. The traditional term for the beneficiary of informal mentoring is *protégé*—derived from the Latin word, *protegere*, meaning to protect. An informal mentor's protection and concern goes beyond the protégé's career development, often extending into personal domains, which may or may not be in the best interests of the organization involved (like, say, the Rebellion). By contrast, such protection is generally not recognized as a prime function of formal mentoring. Most formal mentoring programs use the more neutral term *mentee*, rather than *protégé*.[20]

The relationship between Yoda and Luke exemplifies the informal mentoring relationship. It does not occur within the structure of the Academy. There is no strategic matching process. Goals are not overtly expressed. Actually, the fact that their relationship is informal may be a good thing. In our world and in the Old Republic, mentoring usually lasts years. Yoda doesn't have that kind of time with Luke. Ironically, though, the intensity of informal mentoring is generally considered to be much greater than that of formal mentoring because both parties are intrinsically motivated in the informal relationship and the scope of the relationship is not as circumscribed.[21] So Yoda accomplishes more with Luke in a few days on Dagobah than he would have in a comparable period back at the Academy.

The *Other* Redemption in Star Wars

One way to conceptualize Yoda's arc over the course of the Star Wars saga is through the developmental theory of psychologist Erik Erikson. In Erikson's theory, individuals develop psychologically over the course of eight major life stages, each of which is partly defined by a conflict to be resolved in order for growth to occur. Erikson posits that the successful resolution of the conflict at each stage results in the development of a valuable characteristic, a psychological *virtue*.[22]

In Episodes I, II, and III, Yoda acts as though he is in

Erikson's seventh stage, middle adulthood (granted, Yoda's life stages are marked by centuries, not decades). The virtue to be achieved at this stage is *generativity*, "establishing and guiding the next generation," not necessarily through parenthood.[23] As a teacher, mentor, and mentor of mentors, Yoda is fully devoted to the upcoming generations of Jedi. He wields great power, and not only in his Force skills. As leader of the Jedi Council, he holds enormous sway over the affairs of the Republic. But he loses all of that, and a huge amount of suffering occurs, because his leadership and mentoring are lacking. Palpatine's coup takes place on Yoda's watch, largely due to some gigantic screwups in the training of two Jedi. Long before Anakin Skywalker turns to the dark side, Yoda's own Padawan Dooku falls under Palpatine's spell. Count Dooku is a major player in the Clone Wars; without his leadership of the Separatist Alliance, then-Chancellor Palpatine would have been hard-pressed to engineer the Republic's military buildup that formed the infrastructure of his Galactic Empire.

The conflict at Erikson's seventh stage is between generativity (which Yoda certainly accomplished for an extended time) and *stagnation* (self-absorption). Failing to accomplish generativity can lead to "a pervading sense of stagnation and interpersonal impoverishment," as well as the testing of one's faith in the next generation.[24] After his showdown with Palpatine, Yoda tells Senator Organa that he (Yoda) must go into exile because he has failed.[25] To be sure, he fails to defeat Palpatine in the Senate building. Really, though, his failures go back to losing *two* of his progeny to the dark side, not to mention getting blindsided by Palpatine's plot. So even though he had a good run as a Jedi and a Republic bigwig, Yoda's seventh life stage does not conclude very well.

Yoda then transitions to Erikson's eighth stage, marked by the conflict between integrity and disgust or despair during the last years of life.[26] This particular conflict is like the "rocking chair" test in which a person in the twilight of life takes stock of his or her life. While wisdom can result from successful resolution of this conflict (or passing the rocking chair test), despair can manifest in various ways, including anxiety about facing the end of life, contempt of institutions or people, and dissatisfaction with one's own self.

We know very little about Yoda's existence on Dagobah in the years preceding *Star Wars: Episode V The Empire Strikes Back*. He likely does some communing with deceased Jedi and helps Obi-Wan do the same. He uses his powers to keep an eye on Luke. He also probably mopes around a lot, ruing the collapse of the Republic and the Jedi Order. He's more than a little cranky when Luke shows up, demanding Jedi training as if it were his birthright. Yoda being unimpressed with Luke's capricious temperament is reminiscent of how grumpy old folks rant about "kids these days." So while Yoda doesn't show any anxiety about death, he definitely exudes contempt and dissatisfaction.

Despite his misgivings, Yoda is nudged by Obi-Wan and takes Luke on in an informal mentoring relationship. It is short-lived, intense, and ultimately successful, even though Yoda worries that Luke is making a big mistake heading off to Cloud City. But why does Yoda agree to mentor Luke? Well, sure, he recognizes that Luke may be the salvation of the Rebellion and the hope of a New Republic. Putting Luke into play is his final move in his chess match against Palpatine. But here's another explanation: Mentoring Luke is Yoda's path to redemption (and Erikson's eighth stage).

Yoda wants to atone for the sins of his progeny. Obi-Wan is also culpable in Anakin's downfall. During their epic duel on Mustafar, he admits to Anakin that he has failed him as a mentor.[27] "I took it upon myself to train him as a Jedi," Kenobi later tells Luke. "I thought that I could instruct him just as well as Yoda. I was wrong."[28] So both Obi-Wan and Yoda want Luke to succeed as absolution for their mentoring mistakes.

Just before Yoda's physical body vanishes and he becomes one with the Force, Yoda and Luke talk for a moment in his hut on Dagobah.[29] Yoda is contemplative, not cranky. Even though Luke's showdown with Vader and Palpatine looms, Yoda is at peace. He trusts in Luke's abilities and is comforted that he has not turned to the dark side after learning the identity of his father. Yoda also must be content that he did all he could as a mentor to prepare Luke for the challenge ahead. Again, mentoring is a transactional relationship. Mentoring Luke enables Yoda to resolve the conflict of Erikson's eighth life stage. Integrity is achieved in this stage through taking care of people, settling affairs, and adapting to both triumphs and disappointments. Integrity "permits participation by followership as well as acceptance of the responsibility of leadership."[30] Yoda has let go of his misgivings about Luke and accepts him as the torchbearer for the Jedi.

Yoda Wins

Yoda does not defeat Palpatine with his lightsaber or with his Force powers. He defeats him through Luke. He defeats him because he's a great mentor when it counts the most. He helps Luke to break free of limitations he has placed on his own abilities. Under Yoda's tutelage, Luke masters his fear, thus heading off anger, hate, and suffering. Yoda gives Luke the tools to stay grounded in the light side of the Force, even under the direst of circumstances. Luke is then able to choose to risk his own death over striking down his father and joining the dark side. That sacrifice enables Anakin to do what he should have done long ago—destroy the Emperor and restore balance to the Force. Luke and Anakin end the Emperor's evil reign. But none of that is possible without the little big mentor, Yoda.

References

Allen, T.D., Eby, L.T., Poteet, M.L., Lentz, E., & Lima, L.(2004). Career benefits associated with mentoring for protégés: A meta-analysis. *Journal of Applied Psychology, 89(1)*, 127–136.

Baugh, S. G., & Fagenson-Eland, E. A. (2007). Formal mentoring programs: A "poor cousin" to informal relationships? In B. R. Ragins & K. E. Kram (Eds.), *The handbook of mentoring at work: Theory, research, and practice* (pp. 249–271). Thousand Oaks, CA: Sage.

Bishop, P. (1999). Jung in context: A reader. London, UK: Psychology Press.

Blake-Beard, S.D., O'Neill, R. M., & McGowan, E. (2007). Blind dates? The importance of matching in successful formal mentoring relationships. In B. R. Ragins & K. E. Kram (Eds.), *The handbook of mentoring at work: Theory, research, and practice* (pp. 617–632). Thousand Oaks, CA: Sage.

Bozeman, B., & Feeney, M. K. (2007). Toward a useful theory of mentoring: A conceptual analysis and critique. *Administration and Society, 39(6)*, 719–739.

Chao, G.T. (2009). Formal mentoring: Lessons learned from past practice. *Professional Psychology: Research and Practice, 40(3)*, 314–320.

Erikson, E. (1950). Childhood and society. New York, NY: Norton.

Erikson, E. H. (1959). *Identity and the life cycle: Selected papers* (Psychological Issues, Vol. 1, No. 1, Monograph 1). New York, NY: International Universities Press.

Erikson, E. H. (1968). *Identity: Youth and crisis.* New York, NY: Norton.

Erikson, E. H. (1980). *Identity and the life cycle.* New York, NY: Norton.

Erikson, E. H., & Erikson, J. M. (1998). *The life cycle completed* (extended version). New York, NY: Norton.

Kram, K. E. (1983). Phases of the mentor relationship. *Academy of Management Journal, 26(4)*, 608–625.

Langley, T. (2012). *Batman and psychology: A dark and stormy knight.* New York, NY: Wiley.

P-Sontag, L., Vappie, K., & Wanberg, C. R. (2007). The practice of mentoring: MENTTIUM Corporation. In B. R. Ragins & K. E. Kram (Eds.), *The handbook of mentoring at work: Theory, research, and practice* (pp. 593–616). Thousand Oaks, CA: Sage.

Wanberg, C. R., Welsh, E. T., & Hezlett, S. A. (2003). Mentoring research: A review and dynamic process model. *Research in Personnel and Human Resources Management, 22(1)*, 39–124.

Notes

1. Bishop (1999), p. 96.
2. Erikson (1950, 1959, 1968); Erikson & Erikson (1998).
3. Bozeman & Feeney (2007).
4. Wanberg et al. (2003), p. 41.
5. Chao (2009).
6. Allen et al. (2004).
7. *Star Wars: Episode V The Empire Strikes Back* (1980 motion picture).
8. Wanberg et al. (2003).
9. Langley (2012).
10. *The Empire Strikes Back.*
11. Wanberg et al. (2003).
12. *Star Wars: Episode III Revenge of the Sith* (2005 motion picture).
13. Kram (1983).
14. Kram (1983), p. 618.
15. *The Empire Strikes Back.*

16. *Star Wars: Episode VI Return of the Jedi* (1983 motion picture).
17. Baugh & Fagenson-Eland (2007).
18. P-Sontag et al. (2007).
19. Blake-Beard et al.(2007); P-Sontag et al. (2007).
20. Baugh & Fagenson-Eland (2007).
21. Baugh & Fagenson-Eland (2007).
22. Erikson (1980).
23. Erikson (1980), p. 103.
24. Erikson (1980), p. 103.
25. *Revenge of the Sith*.
26. Erikson (1980).
27. *Revenge of the Sith*.
28. *Return of the Jedi*.
29. *Return of the Jedi*.
30. Erikson (1980), p. 105.

A Symphony of Psychology:
The Music of Star Wars

JIM DAVIES AND
JOE KRAEMER

"... once in a while, or more often if we are
fortunate, we hear music that inspires awe,
transfixes us, even stops us in our tracks."

—music theorist Jeanette Bicknell[1]

There are many ways to evaluate the success of a film. One
can cite critical praise, popularity with the public, or simply
how much money the film made. But as with all works of art,
a film's lasting impact is determined in large part by the way it
interacts with human minds. Certain movies click with us, and
it's as if something magical happened. If there is no click, no
magic, a movie fades into obscurity.

John Williams and the Music of Star Wars

The music in Star Wars works because of the way it interacts with psychological processes.[2] In addition to his musical approach, there is the cinematic sensibility that composer John Williams brings to his work. His keen dramatic insight and learned musical articulation enable him to bypass our conscious senses and tap directly into our emotional response centers.

Melody

Williams's themes demonstrate the psychological impact melody can have on a listener. The main title's melody makes several upward leaps, as if it were reaching for new heights again and again.[3] The same thing is true of Ben's Theme, which later grows to encompass "The Force" in general. This is what is heard when Luke is watching the twin sunsets on Tatooine.[4] Now, it's all well and good to talk about upward leaps of melody representing "reaching for greatness," but can we approach this scientifically?

Metaphor and Music

The psychology and cognitive science of music have shown that particular choices in music creativity have predictable effects on audiences. Upward motion is cross-culturally associated with goodness. When forced to choose a direction for a verb (up, down, left, or right), people generally agree that "good" verbs tend to be in the upward direction.[5] Why might this be? When they are full of energy, healthy, awake, and indeed alive, people are more likely to be standing up. People are down when they are sick, asleep, or dead. These very basic bodily metaphors can have a large influence on our understanding of abstract concepts such as goodness.[6]

When Luke's theme goes from low to high over and over, it gives listeners a primal feeling of increasing goodness. Because the high pitches get higher each time, it sounds like the goodness gets greater with each increase.

Why are high pitches associated with verticality in the first place? As intuitive as it feels, there's no real relationship,[7] or it might have something to do with the fact that smaller objects make higher pitches when struck and the fact that smaller objects are more likely to be higher in our visual field (it's easier to throw a small rock than a large one). Other languages use different metaphors, but they all feel about right: What we call high and low pitches are described variously as light and heavy (Kpelle people), young and old (Suya people), weak and strong (Bashi people), and small and large (Manza people), and in Farsi pitches are thin and thick, respectively. Whatever the cause, these associations seem to be inborn. Prelinguistic infants also show sensitivity to the height as well as the thickness metaphors for pitch.[8]

Take Jabba's Theme.[9] Played on a tuba, it gives a ponderous, blobby sound, more like the sound of a heavy desk being pushed across a wood floor than the sound of leaves rustling. Certainly, a tuba sounds more like the voice of Jabba than that of his pet Kowakian monkey-lizard. By comparison, flutes are used in Leia's Theme, first heard when she loads secret plans into R2-D2.[10] The airy, light sound of a flute makes Leia seem fragile, and the combination of chords (in this case C major and F minor) creates a tragic quality. When we look across languages for pitch metaphors, it is natural to think of Leia as being higher, lighter, weaker, younger, smaller, and certainly thinner than Jabba the Hutt. Pitch metaphors are not arbitrary.

Leitmotif

Key to Williams's approach was his use of the traditional method known as *leitmotif*, in which each main character or concept gets

Force Facts: Sounds of Star Wars

You hear a metallic-sounding whoosh. A series of beep-boops. You instantly recognize them as a lightsaber and R2-D2. The rush of the opening strains of *Star Wars: Episode IV A New Hope* sets pulses racing. The music and sounds of the Star Wars universe are as iconic as the look, and the men responsible are Ben Burtt and John Williams.

It's a pretty good bet that you know composer John Williams. He has written, arguably, the most recognizable scores in the history of film. Not all the sounds distinctive to Star Wars are those people would call music, though.

Ben Burtt, the sound designer behind Star Wars (as well as *E.T. The Extra-Terrestrial, The Dark Crystal, Indiana Jones,* and *WALL-E*) created R2-D2's personality by mimicking baby noises into a microphone. The lightsaber noise comes from idling interlock motors in old movie projectors and a TV set near a shieldless microphone. The Sarlaac Pit was created from a recorded burp!

—Jenna Busch

a short, recognizable melody even if that melody is only a few notes long. These melodies can be repeated, stretched, inverted, and played in different keys and at different volumes in different parts of the film. The term *leitmotif* was coined in 1871 to describe its use in opera and found its way into film composing when European operatic composers fled pre–World War II Europe and began scoring movies in Hollywood. Leitmotifs often were used for the scores of adventure stories: the *Flash Gordon* serials, Max Steiner's *King Kong,* and Erich Wolfgang Korngold's *The Adventures of Robin Hood.*[11] That style fell out of favor in the 1960s as films such as *The Graduate,* which principally used the songs of Simon and Garfunkel, paved the way for movies to become vehicles to sell pop records. Williams's music, as it was used in films by Spielberg and Lucas (first *Jaws,* then

Star Wars, followed by *Close Encounters of the Third Kind*, *Raiders of the Lost Ark*, and *E. T. The Extraterrestrial*[12]) brought the use of leitmotif back to Hollywood.

A New Hope includes many themes and leitmotifs:

1. Main Theme.
2. The Rebel Fanfare—brassy action theme.
3. Princess Leia's Theme—romantic theme, often played on flute.
4. Ben's Theme/The Force Theme—stirring, noble theme often played on French horn.
5. The Imperial Theme—military theme.
6. Death Star motif—brassy flourish that usually accompanies shots of the Death Star.
7. Jawa Theme—playful theme featuring oboe and English horn.
8. Medal Theme—majestic theme for the Medal Sequence at the end of the film.

Good musical themes are memorable after people hear them just once, and they function almost like a second language that informs the audience emotionally and intellectually as the film plays.

Music and Emotion

Music may be one of the most abstract art forms. Unlike stories and most visual art, music is often not "about" anything, at least in a way that is detectable by listeners (lacking "explicit referential semantics"[13]). This is remarkable in that there is no human society without a musical tradition.[14]

Most of what music communicates is emotional—people feel surprise, anger, fear, or happiness—and film music is no exception. Research on the psychology of music[15] reflects this, representing emotion on a two-dimensional space of valence (good or bad) and arousal (intensity).[16] That is, music emotionally affects people in two ways: It can make us happy or sad, and it can make us calm or excited. More sophisticated reactions can be created, but for the most part our response to music is some combination of these two emotional variables.

A great example of angry music is what is played after Anakin Skywalker's mother, Shmi, dies.[17] As Shmi dies and Anakin simmers with rage, the violins play jagged rhythms in strongly bowed phrases. The brass crescendos as Anakin bursts out of the hut and slaughters two Sand People. Anger, as in this example, is characterized by high arousal and negative valence on this two-dimensional space. Musically, anger might have a high volume, a fast tempo, high pitch variability, and high-frequency energy content. Happiness, with high arousal but positive valence, typically is produced with a fast tempo, a medium sound level, fast tone attacks, a high pitch level, a major mode, and a bright timbre. Sadness is low arousal and negative valence and is slow; it has a dark timbre, a low pitch level, slow attacks, and a minor mode.[18] It seems that some of the more complex emotions, such as jealousy and guilt, cannot be communicated through music alone. It's hard even to imagine music that would make a listener feel jealous.

Although the two-factor model of music has received a lot of attention, it fails to capture some feelings people claim to get from music, such as tenderness (like sadness but favoring a major key), playfulness, and anxiety. Yoda's theme gives listeners a feeling that is hard to place on a two-dimensional scale of arousal and valence. This theme is composed in what is known as the Lydian mode, which is believed to convey a sense of wonder and magic. (Other songs in the Lydian mode include *The Simpsons'* main title and *The Little Mermaid's* "Part of Your World.") Further light themes in the Star Wars saga include a droid theme, used primarily for R2-D2 and C-3P0 in *Empire*, and the jaunty themes of the Ewoks and Jawas. Additionally, the orchestration often relies on such effects as pizzicato (or plucked) strings, woodwinds (which have a breathy, often comical, sound; for example, the English horn used for the Jawas has a somewhat "ducky" sound), and duets of instruments with an extreme range difference—Jar Jar's Theme in *Phantom Menace* is a duet between tuba (low) and oboe (high). This contrast creates a comic sound. Melodies with large intervallic leaps can also feel comical if combined with the previous techniques.

Darkness in Minor Keys

Key choice, or *mode,* is an important part of communicating feeling. Minor keys have been found in both Indian and Western music to sound sad. Even sad speech tends to produce notes in minor scales.[19] Speech spoken in a low, staccato voice is interpreted as disapproving—even by babies too young to know what is being said.[20] Sad music is associated with minor modes, low pitches, dissonance, and a slow tempo.[21]

A great example of the use of minor key choice is heard in Darth Vader's theme, which sometimes uses bassoons and muted trombones to produce this low effect. If you are watching a movie in which nothing looks strange but you've got a bad feeling about it, you're probably listening to music in a minor key. Williams brilliantly puts major *and* minor elements in Vader's theme. Although the theme is rooted in G minor, the melody actually outlines an E-flat major triad (or chord). Not until Vader dies does Williams harmonize the melody in such a way that its major-sounding quality is emphasized. He reveals a hidden positive quality in the music. The music is bad turned good, mirroring Anakin's redemption.

In a comparable way, the theme for Anakin as a young boy starts in the Lydian mode, evoking the sense of wonder and magic that the child sees in the universe, but ends with a chord progression taken from Darth Vader's theme, alluding to his eventual turn to the dark side.

Dooku's theme is similarly dark, and Williams uses a very similar theme for Anakin and Padmé's love theme in *Attack of the Clones*. The only difference is in the second note of the theme. Dooku's theme follows a chord structure that mirrors the Emperor's theme. This subtly suggests that the theme representing Anakin's growing love for Padmé has something to do with the dark side and Darth Sidious.

Orchestration

How does the main Star Wars theme work psychologically? It follows the logo music for 20th Century Fox, in Bb major, the same key. It opens the films with a crashing, brassy fanfare. The horns and trumpets call to mind a sense of nobility and royalty, married with a military quality, as is appropriate for a film with "wars" in its title.[22]

A B-section follows, with a soaring, sweeping melody in the violins that evokes the vastness of space and the romance of intergalactic travel. The A-theme returns, again in the brass, before the music builds to a crescendo and then settles into a subdued texture as the opening crawl disappears into infinity. There is a delicate texture of tremolo strings, harp, celesta (a sparkly, fairy-tale-sounding keyboard instrument popularized by Tchaikovsky in the *Dance of the Sugar Plum Fairy*), and solo piccolo. This piccolo melody in particular has a distinctive sound of "outer space" as it adheres to a primarily whole-tone scale (a scale made up entirely of whole steps), which has become associated with outer space because of its use in alien invasion movies of the 1950s and 1960s. The camera pans down to the planet Tatooine, and its reveal is accompanied by a flourish of strings, brass, and percussion, especially gong, which convey its huge size across the bottom of the screen.

A rebel spaceship zips down the center of the screen, and its entrance is presaged by a brassy fanfare that leads into a deliberate quotation by Williams of the closing chords from Gustav Holst's *Mars the Bringer of War* from *The Planets*. This quotation further reinforces our psychological association of the music we are hearing with outer space, as it taps into a well-known preexisting musical passage intrinsically linked to the stars. Also, the music feels like it's getting slower and slower as the gigantic Imperial warship takes up the entirety of our view. These loud, thick, slow chords help convey the size and scale of this Star Destroyer. When the camera cuts to a close-up of the smaller rebel craft trying to escape, the music resumes a quick tempo and the brassy Rebel Fanfare before the ship is hit with a laser blast and forced to shut down. At this point, the action cuts to the interior of the ship, and a new piece of orchestral music begins.

The musical palate for the entire saga is virtually defined in the first two minutes or so of *Star Wars: Episode IV A New Hope*. Strong thematic writing, orchestration that penetrates our conscious minds and stirs our emotional responses, and references to well-known works and sounds from our collective history guide our reactions in the direction desired by the filmmakers.

In 1977, the use of a traditional orchestra was a surprising change from the typical music for a science fiction film. Generally, the style of music Williams employs is Romantic, using scales of the late 1800s. But John Williams was a jazz musician as well, and there is a heavy influence of jazz in his chord choices. This combination of approaches gives Williams his unique sound.

Compare it with the weird synthesizer tones of *Forbidden Planet*, the twelve-tone explorations of Goldsmith's score to *Planet of the Apes*, or even the use of Ligetti's atonal choral music for the monolith of *2001:A Space Odyssey*. Instead, in *Star Wars*, Williams contrasts the often strange situations with a classical (rather than futuristic) musical structure and orchestration. Doing so helps ground the film for the audience so that there is a familiar connection underlining the unfamiliar visuals.

Association

A character is introduced, and the audience hears that character's theme. The next time the character appears, viewers hear the theme again, setting up an association between that theme and that character. Now the composer can play the theme when the character is not there, and the audience will be reminded of the character because of the association already established. In the Star Wars prequels, Williams uses Darth Vader's theme in just this way. Whenever he wants to hint at the dark future that lies ahead for young Anakin, he simply drops a few notes from Vader's theme somewhere in the orchestration. When Yoda and Mace Windu sense through the Force that Anakin has given in to the dark side and slaughtered Tusken Raiders, Williams has muted brass sneak an iteration of Vader's Theme in behind the driving strings.

Breaking the Rules

Even if no one in a scene directly talks about the Force, the orchestra can play the Force Theme underneath the dialogue, making the audience associate the scene with a deeper meaning in the Force. When Qui-Gon Jinn asks the Jedi Council if Anakin is to be trained, the first two notes of the Force Theme play before Mace Windu says, "No," derailing the theme and taking it in another (downward) direction.

However, Williams is not a slave to his own style. When Obi-Wan Kenobi dies, Williams uses Leia's Theme. By his own admission, as a piece of music, Leia's Theme has more sweep, scope, and tragedy.[23] Similarly, although most of the scoring for the Star Wars films resembles that of the Romantic period and that of earlier film composers such as Korngold, the music for the Tusken Raiders, for example, is dissonant and very modern. It's more like music that twentieth-century composers such as Ligetti and Corigliano would write. He uses the best music for the scene even if it breaks the rules of leitmotif or the style of the rest of the score.

Williams's themes have been described as "inevitable."[24] They feel eternal, as if they could not have been any other way. His use of a traditional symphonic orchestra lends his work a timeless quality. Williams's great skill and judgment helped make Star Wars what it is. Like all great artists, Williams intuitively knows how to use human psychology to make a movie great.

References

Audissino, E. (2014). *John Williams's film music: Jaws, Star Wars, Raiders of the Lost Ark, and the return of the classical Hollywood music style* (Wisconsin film studies). Madison, WI: University of Wisconsin Press.

Bicknell, J. (2009). *Why music moves us.* New York, NY: Palgrave Macmillan.

Bowling, D. L., Sundararajan, J., Han, S., & Purves, D. (2012). Expression of emotion in Eastern and Western music mirrors vocalization. *PloS ONE, 7*(3), e31942.

Davies, J. (2014). *Riveted: The science of why jokes make us laugh, movies make us cry, and religion makes us feel one with the universe.* New York, NY: Palgrave Macmillan.

Davis, R. (2010). *Complete guide to film scoring: The art and business of writing music for movies and TV.* Boston, MA: Berklee Press.

Deutsch, D. (2010). Speaking in tones. *Scientific American Mind, 21*(3), 36–43.

Dolscheid, S., Hunnius, S., Casasanto, D., & Majid, A. (2012). The sound of thickness: Prelinguistic infants' associations of space and pitch. In N. Miyake, D. Peebles, & R. P. Cooper (Eds.), *Proceedings of the 34th annual meeting of the Cognitive Science Society* (pp. 306–311). Austin, TX: Cognitive Science Society.

Dolscheid, S., Shayan, S., Majid, A., & Casasanto, D. (2013). The thickness of musical pitch: Psychophysical evidence for linguistic relativity. *Psychological Science, 24*(5), 613–621.

Eerola, T. (2012). Modeling listeners' emotional response to music. *Topics in Cognitive Science, 4*(4), 607–624.

Fernald, A., & Morikawa, H. (1993). Common themes and cultural variations in Japanese and American mothers' speech to infants. *Phonetica, 57,* 242–254.

Lakoff, G., & Johnson, M. (1980). *Metaphors we live by.* Chicago, IL: University of Chicago Press.

Lunden, J. (2012). *John Williams' inevitable themes.* NPR Classical: http://www.npr.org/blogs/deceptivecadence/2012/11/10/164615420/john-williams-inevitable-themes.

Mattessino, M. (1997). A new hope for film music. Liner notes for *Star Wars: A New Hope Original Motion Picture Sound Track.*

Miller, R. (1986). *The structure of singing: System and art in vocal technique.* New York: Schirmer.

Pearce, M., & Rohrmeier, M. (2012). Music cognition and the cognitive sciences. *Topics in Cognitive Science, 4*(4), 468–484.

Richardson, D. C., Spivey, M. J., Edelman, S., & Naples, A. J. (2001). "Language is spatial": Experimental evidence for image schemas of concrete and abstract verbs. *Proceedings of the Twenty-Third annual meeting of the Cognitive Science Society* (pp. 873–878). Mahwah, NJ: Erlbaum.

Warrack, J. (1995). Leitmotif. In S. Sadia & N. Fortune (Eds.), *New Grove dictionary of music and musicians,* vol. 10. New York, NY: Oxford University Press.

Winner, E. (1982). *Invented worlds: The psychology of the arts.* Cambridge, MA: Harvard University Press.

Notes

1. Bicknell (2009), p. vii.
2. Davies (2014).
3. Mattessino (1997).
4. *Star Wars: Episode IV A New Hope* (1977/1981 motion picture).
5. Richardson et al. (2001).
6. Lakoff & Johnson (1980).
7. Miller (1986).
8. Dolscheid et al. (2013)
9. *Star Wars: Episode VI Return of the Jedi* (1983 motion picture).
10. *A New Hope.*
11. Mattessino (1997).
12. Audissino (2014); Davis (2010).
13. Pearce & Rohrmeier (2012), p. 475.
14. p. 470.
15. Pearce & Rohrmeier (2012), p. 475.
16. We are speaking, of course, of instrumental music. Lyrical content is not a factor in this discussion.
17. *Star Wars: Episode II Attack of the Clones* (2002 motion picture).
18. Eerola (2012).
19. Bowling et al. (2012).
20. Deutsch (2010); Fernald & Moriwaka (1993).
21. Winner (1982).
22. It is written in B-flat major, the same key as the 20th Century Fox Fanfare music that comes just before it when watching the film, making them sound almost like two parts of the same piece of music (Mattessino, 1997).
23. From the liner notes of the 1977 LP of the *Star Wars* sound track.
24. Lunden (2012).

Shooting, Striking, Returning:
The Universes in Our Heads

DONALD F. GLUT AND
TRAVIS LANGLEY

"Two-thirds of what we see is behind our eyes."

—Chinese proverb

Why do fans argue over who shot first, Han or Greedo? What's the point in debating over plot holes, contradictions, retroactive continuity added in the prequels, changes introduced in reedited Special Editions, or the existence of midi-chlorians? Wasn't Star Wars its creator's story to tell however he chose? Thousands of people contributed, but the idea came from him. So didn't the story belong to him?

Psychologically speaking, no. The creator owned his Star Wars, but he never owned yours. Cognitively, perceptually, and emotionally, you created a saga of your own. You have your own *mental map* of that galaxy.

Throughout this book, we've explored a variety of ways that psychology has influenced the creation of this saga and how the saga impacts us. What about those thousands of perspectives between Star Wars' conception and reception? Everyone designing characters, building machinery, adding their own ideas, and fleshing out the ideas of others has been a world builder, a creator not only of their Star Wars but of ours, too. *The Empire Strikes Back* novelist Donald F. Glut offers a unique perspective on how he mapped out Star Wars' first sequel and shares with us a lesser-known side of the story from the early days of this franchise's creation.

Shooting First in the First Star Wars Film Shot: Constellations of Concepts

TRAVIS LANGLEY

First impressions last.[1] From *Star Wars'* 1977 premiere until its twentieth anniversary Special Edition, some of the first things viewers learned about Han Solo were that he smuggles, he speaks highly of himself and his ship, he has been dodging a debt, and he shoots Greedo before Greedo can fire first.[2] Details from these scenes form the foundation upon which each viewer would build a personal conception of what "Han Solo" means.

Cognitive Maps

Many researchers writing about mental maps mean the *cognitive maps* that we use to keep spatial relations of the outside world in our own minds.[3] The cognitive map is how we understand where things are located relative to each other (distances, positions, angles, whatever lies in between). When you're navigating through the real world, inaccuracies in your understanding of a city's layout can get you lost. When you're imagining a fictional world, a mismatch between the creator's vision and your own rarely matters. So what if you think Luke went southeast to look for the droids when your friend sees the path as northward? This can be fodder for fan fury, of course, if your respective visions do not accord with each other. For the person writing a film novelization, however, the ways in which the writer's mental maps line up differently from the filmmaker's become visible for all to see, as Don Glut touches upon shortly.

Schemas

Renowned developmental psychologist Jean Piaget said that, from infancy onward, we form connections between ideas and experiences.[4] Patterns emerge. A mental structure he called a *schema* (a.k.a. a *scheme*) comes together as an association of related concepts, a more abstract mental map of meaning. A child's "dog" schema evolves as the child learns more about what a dog is (a four-legged animal) and what a dog is not (not the one that meows). The schema can include any associated information, such as dog behaviors, items associated with dogs in general, a shoe that resembles one the child's own dog tore up, people who own dogs, and so much more. New information gets added to the schema (in a process known as *assimilation*), but sometimes the schema must change (a process called *accommodation*) when experience contradicts it. When the child who previously believed all dogs are nice sees one attack somebody, the child may decide the dog must have done it for a good reason or change the schema to view some dogs as bad.

Han Solo is a bit of a bad dog when viewers first meet him. A schema about him might assimilate revelations showing that, yes, he is a bad boy but he also has deeper layers to him with qualities like fierce loyalty to his friends. Accepting that Greedo shoots first, though, means changing the original schema, and accommodation does not happen so easily.[5] Foundations are difficult to rebuild.

Innate Outrage?

Change is stressful. The recurring theme that runs through-out the lists of life's major stressors (winning, losing, marriage, divorce, getting employed, getting fired, etc.) is *change*.[6] Both *eustress* (good stress) and *distress* (bad stress) heap more weight upon our cognitive and emotional loads. Assimilation is easier than accommodation because fitting new information into an existing frame of reference (like accepting Stormtroopers added to a crowd of soldiers in the Special Edition of *Star Wars: Episode IV A New Hope*) involves less change than rebuilding the frame (like accepting antihero Han Solo as more of a traditional "white hat" hero who would never shoot first). A different way to manage the stress, however, is to avoid it entirely, by refus-ing to make the change and retaining the mental represen-tation that makes us more comfortable.

Fan outrage over change therefore arises naturally. Audiences who care enough to be fans (short for *fanatic*, after all) will respond passionately, not passively. Fans are human, and human nature includes wanting to fight for the things we treasure.[7]

—T. L.

Belief Perseverance

People tend to resist accepting evidence that contradicts their beliefs. Sometimes, however, they have no choice. Eventually, people admit that Santa Claus does not exist. *Belief perseverance*, the persistence of notions people already accept, is a powerful thing. Motivated to protect self-esteem and avoid feeling fool-ish for believing incorrectly, people can ignore inconsistencies, make up rational-seeming explanations, reject new evidence, or otherwise justify sticking to their original beliefs.[8] They might be right to do so. The new evidence might be wrong. Beliefs can be wrong, too, though.

With a fictional character, however, why does anything have to be right or wrong? One story has Han shooting first. Another story does not. They're different stories. Why should either be the "real" or "right" one? In that case, it's a difference between whether Han murdered Greedo or fired in self-defense. Only the latter behavior is traditionally heroic. Cowboy heroes in old Westerns could win their duels, but only after the bad guys drew on them.

For some people, the first version of one Star Wars film came from comic book writer Don Glut. He wrote the novelization of *The Empire Strikes Back*.[9] Six weeks before *Star Wars: Episode V The Empire Strikes Back* packed movie theaters, the novelization hit bookstores. Those of us who read the novel knew what Darth Vader was going to reveal to Luke before any fans watched Lord Vader say it on the big screen.

Don once told me about his experiences writing the novelization of *The Empire Strikes Back*. He wondered why people read novelizations of films they also plan to see. The answer that came to him later brings us back to this issue of why fans feel some ownership over forms of entertainment other people created.

Striking: Novelizing
The Empire Strikes Back

Donald F. Glut

The Empire Strikes Back was my first novelization of a motion picture script, in this case that of the second installment of the ongoing Star Wars film saga. By 1980, when most of my income came from writing comic books, I had already written a number of novels and short stories. And although none of my fiction work had been based on some other author's motion

Glut's Behemoth

Don Glut's Star Wars work did not begin with his novelization of *The Empire Strikes Back*. When the original team working on the earliest *Star Wars* comic book left the series before completing work on the tenth issue, Glut scripted the story from their plot.

- Publication: *Star Wars* #10.
- Title: "Behemoth from the World Below."
- Plot: Roy Thomas and Howard Chaykin.
- Script: Don Glut.
- Art: Howard Chaykin, Tom Palmer, and Alan Kupper-berg.
- Publisher: Marvel Comics.
- Cover date: April 1978.

—T. L.

picture script, I had converted quite a few prose pieces—mostly stories by Robert E. Howard featuring his swashbuckling hero Solomon Kane—to the comic book format.

I was already involved, in one way or another—albeit indirectly—with the Star Wars universe. I had on my résumé several of the original stories published by the Marvel Comics Group following the company's multi-issue adaptation of the first Star Wars movie, written and edited by Roy Thomas. I'd been discussing writing some original scripts for the *Star Wars* newspaper comic strip being drawn by Russ Manning, with whom I'd already worked on various *Tarzan* projects.

About that time, somehow, I don't remember how, I connected with an editor and the head of the Star Wars company's Publications Department, who told me to stop immediately whatever Star Wars–related projects I might already be working on to write the novelization of *The Empire Strikes Back*. This book was already an instant best seller, having sold a million advance copies. With no hesitation, I humbly accepted.

First, I had to receive, read, and mentally digest the script by Lawrence Kasdan and Leigh Brackett. Just *having* that script in my house became a minor nightmare. Most of my friends in those days were Star Wars fans, some of whom regarded the characters and situations almost religiously, so I was constantly bombarded with requests, even bribes and threats, to divulge the secrets that would eventually unfold within the new story line. Yet I was sternly warned that if the script were copied or shown to anyone else, legal action would be taken against me. In the realm of Star Wars, I could only imagine Darth Vader showing up at my door one night and grabbing my throat, had I succumbed to temptation and shared that damned script with anyone! Secretly I locked the script inside a metal filing cabinet and began counting the days until I could finally return it to the company.

Having read the Kasdan–Brackett script, I met with the executive producer twice to get firsthand answers to a number of questions I had about the script. For example, how large was this ship compared to that ship, what did Boba Fett's ship look like (an elephant, I was told)—that sort of thing. I was also confused about the rather vague way the ending had been scripted. Although I'd heard for years that Darth Vader was actually Luke Skywalker's father, a fact somehow revealed years earlier at a comic book or science fiction convention where the first as-yet-unreleased Star Wars movie was being promoted, it was unclear just *what* occurred at the end of the Vader versus Luke battle at the climax of *The Empire Strikes Back*.

I was informed that, yes, that was how the movie would end, with the Big Revelation of Luke as the son of the black-clad villain. However, that denouement was to be known only by a select few before the movie's release, when the secret would be out. Moreover, I would frequently get fake pages from the Publications Department offices to insert into the script in my possession—some in which Vader simply knew or killed Luke's father. Meanwhile, I would continue to write and rewrite the ending, accommodating those new pages, until the book's manuscript was officially done and sent off to the printer.

As the movie was being shot and as I was writing the novelization, I suggested more than once that maybe, to ensure accuracy in what I wrote, the company send me to Europe to observe some of the filming and "soak in" some on-location atmosphere. The company did not buy my reasons for going, so all my writing was restricted to the office inside my North Hollywood home.

Thus far, since the movie was still being shot, there was no complete set of still photos to use for reference. These stills—along with the film's conceptual artist Ralph McQuarrie's preproduction paintings of characters, locations, hardware, and costumes, and also copies of storyboards depicting various intended scenes—were all locked inside a trailer parked outside the company's Publications Department offices on the Universal Studios lot. The trailer was off-limits to most employees of the company and to visitors. I was surreptitiously admitted to the trailer and locked inside, where I—among a *very* select few—was allowed access to all the existing visuals.

I was given only about an hour to take in all those sights and, not knowing what I would be getting into that day, had not come prepared. Finding in the trailer several pieces of lined notebook paper and a ballpoint pen, I started copying, with my limited artistic skills and as fast as humanly possible in the allotted time, whatever images I thought might be relevant to describing things in the novel, including Yoda's physical appearance (he would look quite different in the movie than in McQuarrie's depiction), Boba Fett's clothing and gear, and the sky city. Not everything was labeled, so I had to guess which things were based on descriptions in the script.

Upon my release from trailer prison, and not realizing the high levels of secrecy and the resultant paranoia that permeated the company, I casually and innocently showed one of my drawings to someone and asked if the figure I'd hastily sketched was Yoda. The assistant tensed up and sharply looked away, explaining that some staffers were allowed to read the script, others to see the photos, and still others to view the McQuarrie art and storyboards—but almost none of them were permitted to see all three! I guess I should have felt honored to be among the privileged few.

Armed with all the ammunition I was likely to get, I drove home, sat down at my electric typewriter, and started to write my novelization of *The Empire Strikes Back*. In approaching the novelization, I attempted to mentally envision a movie that did not yet exist, based on the images I'd quickly perused while shut away inside that trailer, and also on memories retained from the first Star Wars movie.

I was instructed that the book, as opposed to the movie, should open with Luke saying something, to personalize the character in the reader's mind—hence, his line about it being cold.

Aside from that, the novel was to be as accurate a reflection of the movie as possible, so that the reader could mentally reexperience the film while reading the text. I thought I'd take that need for accuracy a step further. I knew that actor Mark Hamill, who played Luke in Star Wars, had been in an automobile accident that required him to have reconstructive surgery on his face. Thus, after the scene in which Luke is attacked by the snow creature, I wrote in a bit about him not looking exactly as he had before the attack once his wounds had healed. That was one of the first things to be edited out of my first draft.

One problem I had in writing the novel was that the script

Getting Inside Fictional Skin

"Now this is what I call cold!"
—Luke Skywalker[10]

When author Don Glut opens *The Empire Strikes Back* novelization by having the hero comment on the cold, he engages the readers, connecting them to the character and the setting through forced *perspective-taking*. In other words, he immediately makes them take the lead character's point of view. Helping readers vividly imagine someone's perspective makes it easier for them to feel empathy for that person or character.[11] The opening statement primes readers to engage in both *cognitive empathy*, knowing how others feel (because the narrative expresses Luke's opinion about his immediate environment), and *affective empathy*, feeling how others feel (because readers can relate to how he physically feels there).[12]

The scene's freezing temperature may inadvertently prompt greater empathy among readers as well because cold temperatures promote perspective-taking.[13] Perhaps because the cold makes people more willing to huddle together, it also makes them more receptive to getting close in other ways, too.

—T. L.

kept changing, sometimes on a daily basis. Even through post-production, scenes were being added to and deleted from the script, and I had to make changes in the novelization accordingly. This required additional work and time at my end of the project. I think the only artifact of an earlier script that remained in my finished book was a brief early scene involving the herding of ice creatures into pens.

There was one issue with which I had a sizable problem: Scenes occurring during Luke's training by Yoda on Hoth were cross-cut in the script with other scenes simultaneously showing Han Solo and his friends on Bespin. The scenes seemed to occur at the same time, but in my mind they could not have happened that way. I struggled for days and nights trying to reconcile what to me was a kind of chronological paradox. Finally, figuring that if no one involved in making the movie had a problem with my perceived temporal conflict, neither should I.

I wrote my first draft of *The Empire Strikes Back* novelization in a more "literary" style than the version that finally wound up in bookstores. That is, I intended it to read as a richer work of prose fiction, with a lot more text devoted to getting inside a character's head. However, the editors wanted a more "pulp fiction" kind of style, more action-oriented, and since it was their baby and they were paying me, I complied with their wishes. In all I wrote, from page one to the end, three complete drafts of *The Empire Strikes Back*, each stylistically quite different from the others, in a total of six weeks.

The final manuscript was due on a Monday morning. Sunday night of that week I was sitting behind my typewriter, banging away at the keys, making no carbon copies, of the last chapters. My then-wife would come into my office and, as I finished each page, pull it away and rush it into the living room, where an assistant editor sat on our couch going over the final pages.

Upon typing the last page, I returned the script to the assistant editor and was more than glad to get the thing out of my house. We made the Monday morning deadline! *The Empire Strikes Back* became a national best seller, remaining in its number one position for approximately six weeks, the same length of time it took me to write all three drafts.

Frankly, I never really understood just why people read novelizations of movies. If you've already seen the movie, subsequently reading the novel offers few or no surprises, unless—and this has happened more than once—the author of the book introduces new original scenes or takes the story off in an entirely different direction. If, however, you read the novel *before* seeing the movie,

Familiarity versus Novelty: Why Reread, Rewatch, and Read What We've Watched?

Because change is stressful, people find some comfort in familiar stimuli. Hundreds of experiments have shown that, rather than breeding contempt, familiarity fosters fondness.[14] Recognition reduces *threat detection*—the conscious or unconscious search for signs of danger—when scrutinizing unfamiliar situations.[15] Neutral stimuli—people, places, music, items, symbols, and events—tend to be viewed in a positive light and evoke more favorable responses through repetition.[16]

A person does not become a fan as a result of familiarity. A person becomes fanatic over stronger feelings than that. A behavior's consequence is *reinforcement* when it strengthens the likelihood that the person acting that way will repeat that action.[17] Viewers who watch a Star Wars movie over and over again do so in order to receive reinforcement, usually seeking excitement greater than mere comfort. While increasing comfort by reducing the stress of the unknown, repeated exposure also reduces sensitivity to other emotional responses as well through *desensitization*.[18] To recapture the original excitement, viewers can search for nuances they missed before, rewatch with different people or in different circumstances, look up bloopers or deleted scenes, or try many other means to reexperience the sense of novelty while also hanging onto familiarity.

For some viewers, the Special Editions and other reedited editions lend a freshness to their movie-viewing experiences, but not everyone responds well to those. A novelization, however, brings back the novelty.

—T. L.

you know *in advance* what is going to unfold on the screen. Again, no surprises.

When I first saw the movie *The Empire Strikes Back*, of course I knew up front what was going to happen and when. But there was something else going on during that screening, something

I hadn't really expected to happen. As I wrote the book, I could visualize and hear the entire film in my mind. When, at that initial screening, the first shot faded in, I distinctly remember slinking into my chair and thinking, "Ulp! It's different!" In fact, the movie itself was different in countless ways from what I had envisioned while sitting behind my typewriter.

That memory yields another involving Irv Kershner, the director of *The Empire Strikes Back*. I encountered Kershner at a lavish Cinema School reunion party at our alma mater, the University of Southern California. I told him that there were *two* versions of his movie. When he looked puzzled, I said, "There's the version that you directed and everyone saw on the screen, and the version I saw in my head as I wrote the novelization."

Then it struck me. There are, when you consider how many people read my novelization before seeing the motion picture, myriad versions of *The Empire Strikes Back*, each with their own camera angles and compositions, each with their own performances, special effects, and so forth. Every reader of the novel saw his or her own version of the story before actually witnessing the work that was eventually projected on movie screens.

And so it is for any novelization of a movie yet to be seen.

Returning to the Psychology: Head Canon

TRAVIS LANGLEY

Those "myriad versions" that Don Glut talks about are not limited to those that his readers created when they read his book. Every viewer who first discovered *The Empire Strikes Back* on a screen, big or small, created a different, personal version as well. Two people who see the same cloud can argue whether it's a bunny rabbit or a clown car, and that's a single stimulus. Multiply that by how many stimuli fill a film. Every friend who tried to bribe Don into revealing secrets had a version. The people working behind the scenes to give him fake pages to insert into his copy of the script created multiple versions, some of which they may have personally preferred. When readers and viewers imagine what happened between scenes, they expand the versions in their heads and may form their own personal canon that makes the story more fun for them.

A schema can be a solar system, a constellation, an entire galaxy. A viewer's schema for Han Solo is part of a greater schema about all Star Wars heroes. That schema orbits through a greater schema about Star Wars itself. It also exists within other schemas about rebels, adventurers, movie characters, science-fiction characters, and more.

We build universes in our heads. They are complex, and they belong to us. That means they're part of the schemas we form when we think about ourselves.

References

Anderson, C. A., Lepper, M. R., & Ross, L. (1980). Perseverance of social theories: The role of explanation in the persistence of discredited information. *Journal of Personality and Social Psychology, 39*(6), 1037–1049.

Bornstein, R. E. (1989). Exposure and affect: Overview and meta-analysis of research, 1968–1987. *Psychological Bulletin, 106*(2), 265–289.

Chambers, J. R., & Davis, M. H. (2012). The role of the self in perspective-taking and empathy: Ease of self-simulation as a heuristic for inferring empathic feelings. *Social Cognition, 30*(2), 153–180.

Cleary, A. M., Ryals, A. J., & Nomi, J. S. (2013). Intuitively detecting what is hidden with a visual mask: Familiar-novel discrimination and threat detection for unidentified stimuli. *Memory and Cognition, 41*(7), 989–999.

Folkins, C. H., Lawson, K. D., & Opton, E. M., Jr. (1968). Desensitization and the experimental reduction of threat. *Journal of Abnormal Psychology, 73*(2), 100–113.

Glut, D. F. (1980). *The Empire strikes back.* New York, NY: Ballantine.

Guenther, C. L., & Alicke, M. D. (2008). Self-enhancement and belief perseverance. *Journal of Experimental Social Psychology, 44*(3), 706–712.

Holmes, T. H., & Rahe, R. H. (1967). The Social Readjustment Rating Scale. *Journal of Psychosomatic Research, 11*(2), 213–218.

Jones, I. F., Young, S. G., & Claypool, H. M. (2011). Approaching the familiar: On the ability of mere exposure to direct approach and avoidance behavior. *Motivation and Emotion, 35*(3), 383–392.

Kirby, B. (n.d.). *Who shot first? The complete list of Star Wars changes.* Empire Online: http:// www.empireonline.com/features/star-wars-changes.

Kitchin, R. M. (1994). Cognitive maps: What are they and why study them? *Journal of Environmental Psychology, 14*(1), 1–19.

Lewandowsky, S., Stritzke, W. G. K., Oberauer, K., & Morales, M. (2005). Memory for fact, fiction, and misinformation: The Iraq War 2003. *Psychological Science, 16*(3), 190–195.

Myers, D. (2013). *Social psychology* (11th ed.). New York, NY: McGraw-Hill.

Nestler, S. (2010). Belief perseverance: The role of accessible content and accessibility experiences. *Social Psychology, 41*(1), 35–41.

Piaget, J. (1952). *The origins of intelligence in children.* New York, NY: Harcourt Brace Jovanovich.

Piaget, J., & Inhelder, B. (1958). *The growth of logical thinking from childhood to adolescence.* New York, NY: Basic.

Rogers, V. (2015, June 4). *Comic fan outrage? It's part of being human, scientists say.* Newsarama: http://www.newsarama.com/24739-comic-fan-outrage-it-s-part-of-being-human-scientists-say.html.

Ross, L., & Anderson, C. A. (1982). Shortcomings in the attribution process: On the origins and maintenance of erroneous social assessments. In D. Kahneman, P. Slovic, & A. Tversky (Eds.), *Judgment under uncertainty: Heuristics and biases* (pp. 268–283). New York, NY: Cambridge University Press.

Sassenrath, C., Sassenberg, K., & Semin, G. (2014). Cool, but understanding: Experiencing cooler temperatures promotes perspective-taking performance. *Acta Psychologia, 143*(2), 245–251.

Shamay-Tsoory, S. G., Aharon-Peretz, J., & Perry, D. (2009). Two systems for empathy: A double dissociation between emotional and cognitive empathy in inferior frontal gyrus versus ventromedial prefrontal lesions. *Brain, 132*(3), 617–627.

Shih, M. J., Stotzer, R., & Gutiérrez, M. J. (2013). Perspective-taking and empathy: Generalizing the reduction of group bias towards Asian Americans to general outgroups. *Asian American Journal of Psychology, 4*(2), 79–83.

Skinner, B. F. (1938). *The behavior of organisms: An experimental analysis.* New York: NY: Appleton-Century.

Tolman, E. G. (1948). Cognitive maps in rats and man. *Psychological Review, 55*(4), 189–208.

Zajonc, R. B. (1970, February). Brainwash: Familiarity breeds comfort. *Psychology Today*, pp. 32–35, 60–62.

Notes

1. Lewandowsky et al. (2005); Ross & Anderson (1982).
2. Kirby (n.d.).
3. Kitchin (1994); Tolman (1948).
4. Piaget (1952).
5. Piaget & Inhelder (1958).
6. Holmes & Rahe (1967).
7. Rogers (2015).
8. Anderson et al. (1980); Guenther & Alicke (2008); Nestler (2010).
9. Glut (1980).
10. Glut (1980), p. 1.
11. Chambers & Davis (2012); Shih et al. (2013).
12. Shamay-Tsoory et al. (2009).
13. Sassenrath et al. (2013).

14. Bornstein (1989); Jones et al. (2011); Myers (2013).
15. Cleary et al. (2013); Folkins et al. (1968).
16. Zajonc (1970).
17. Skinner (1938).
18. Myers (2013).

An OCEAN Far Away

V. Neuroticism versus Emotional Stability

TRAVIS LANGLEY

eurosis, as Sigmund Freud termed any nonpsychotic mental illness that involves handling distress poorly, is not a modern diagnostic term for many reasons, including the emphasis on anxiety and the shortage of evidence to support Freud's views about many neuroses' hidden causes.[1] Even so, the word *neurotic* remains popular because people commonly have a sense of it describing someone who habitually copes poorly with life. People with trait *neuroticism* tend to handle stress poorly, find minor frustrations hopelessly difficult, feel threatened in everyday situations, and are at greater risk for many common nonpsychotic mental disorders.[2] Neuroticism is the personality factor most consistently associated with negative, unpleasant emotions.[3]

Among the main Star Wars characters, the most neurotic is undoubtedly Anakin Skywalker. Even though C-3PO (who was originally programmed by Anakin[4]) endlessly worries, he does not demonstrate Anakin's extreme negativity and general instability. His daughter Leia is among the less neurotic and more stable main characters, possibly because she did not grow up around her dark father and his turbulent influence. Even though the theorist who originally proposed the two-factor personality theory (neuroticism and extraversion) assumed neuroticism to be largely inherited,[5] and genetic influences do play a role, environment also shapes the development of this set of traits.[6] Stressful life events make neuroticism more likely.[7]

Examples of Neuroticism Traits

Anger Proneness

Angst

Anxiousness

Dissatisfaction

Emotional Expressiveness

Emotional Fluctuation

Envy

Frustration

Hostility

Impatience

Insecurity

Instability

Jealousy

Negative Emotion

Obsessiveness

Poor Emotion Regulation

Self-Consciousness

Tenseness

Trait Depression

Volatility

Vulnerability to Stress

Professionals who focus on the more positive aspects of these personality dimensions often refer to this one by its less neurotic pole: *emotional stability*.[8] No other personality factor correlates as strongly with health. Emotionally stable people are healthier both physically and mentally. That said, though, it is possible to be too stable. Fear and anger serve adaptive purposes. There is even a time to hate, according to Solomon's wisdom, just as there is a time to love. Rather than risk mistiming those feelings, Jedi strive to avoid them, yet they do recognize that there is, as Solomon said next, a time for war and a time for peace.[9] Extreme neuroticism is the internal war, and emotional stability is the peace.

References

Bernd, M., Kibeom, L., & Ashton, M. C. (2007). Personality dimensions explaining relationships between integrity tests and counterproductive behavior: Big five, or one in addition? *Personnel Psychology, 60*(1), 1–34.

Eysenck, H. J. (1990). Genetic and environmental contributions to individual differences: The three major dimensions of personality. *Journal of Personality, 58*(1), 245–261.

Hettema, J. M., Neale, M. C., Myers, J. M., Prescott, C. A., & Kendler, K. S. (2006). A population-based twin study of the relationship between neuroticism and internalizing. *American Journal of Psychiatry, 163*(5), 857–864.

Horwitz, A. V., & Wakefield, J. C. (2007). *The loss of sadness: How psychiatry transformed normal sorrow into depressive disorder.* New York, NY: Oxford University Press.

Horwitz, B. N., Luong, G., & Charles, S. T. (2008). Neuroticism and extraversion share genetic and environmental effects with negative and positive mood spillover in a nationally representative sample. *Personality and Individual Differences, 45*(7), 636–642.

Ormel, J., Jeronimus, B. F., Kotov, R., Riese, H., Bos, E. H., Hankin, B, Rosmalen, J. G. M., & Oldehinkel, A. J. (2013). Neuroticism and common mental disorders: Meaning and utility of a complex relationship. *Clinical Psychology Review, 33*(5), 686–697.

Riese, H., Sneider, H., Jeronimus, B. F., Korhonen, T., Rose, R. J., & Kaprio, J. (2014). Timing of stressful life events affects stability and change in neuroticism. *European Journal of Personality, 28*(2), 193–200.

Spinhoven, P., Penninx, B. W., Hickendorff, M., & van Hemert, A. M. (2014). Reciprocal effects of stable and temporary components of neuroticism and affective disorders: Results of a longitudinal cohort study. *Psychological Medicine, 44*(2), 337–348.

Tmka, R., Balcar, K., Kuška, M., & Hnilca, K. (2012). Neuroticism and valence of negative emotional concepts. *Social Behavior and Personality, 40*(5), 843–844.

Wang, L., Shi, Z., & Li, H. (2009). Neuroticism, extraversion, emotion regulation, negative affect and positive affect: The mediating role of reappraisal and suppression. *Social Behavior and Personality, 37*(2), 193–194.

Wilson, M. (1993). DSM-III and the transformation of American psychiatry: A history. *American Journal of Psychiatry, 150*(3), 399–410.

Notes

1. Horwitz & Wakefield (2007); Wilson (1993).
2. Hettema et al. (2006); Ormel et al. (2013); Spinhoven et al. (2014).
3. Tmka et al. (2012); Wang (2009).

4. *Star Wars: Episode I The Phantom Menace* (1999 motion picture).
5. Eysenck (1990).
6. Horwitz et al (2008).
7. Riese et al. (2014).
8. See, for example, Bernd et al. (2007).
9. Ecclesiastes 3:8.

Final Word:
Never Our Last Hope

"Help me, Obi-Wan Kenobi. You're my only hope."
—Princess Leia[1]

> "Hope is both the earliest and the most
> indispensable virtue inherent in a
> state of being alive. If life is to be
> sustained hope must remain,
> even where confidence is
> wounded, trust impaired."
> —developmental psychologist Erik Erikson[2]

The original Star Wars trilogy is about hope. Characters in the prequels don't talk about it overtly because it has not yet turned scarce. The film titled *Star Wars* in 1977, before anyone knew if it would ever have sequels (much less prequels), became *A New Hope* in 1981. Long after Anakin Skywalker, the Jedi Order, and the Republic itself fall, Obi-Wan Kenobi and others fear that there is little hope. The Empire prepares a superweapon designed to crush the spirit of rebellion through destructive demonstrations, to destroy what hope is left by destroying worlds. Rebels like Princess Leia grow desperate. She sees Obi-Wan Kenobi as her only hope and Kenobi sees her brother Luke as the last hope for them all, but Yoda brings it full circle back to Leia.

Obi-Wan Kenobi: That boy is our only hope.
Yoda: No. There is another.[3]

Hope is not simply a wish or a dream. People can wish and dream for things they know will never happen. Hope is a belief or expectation that things *can* happen. The mere existence of a rebel network means there are plenty of people who believe that fighting to make things better is worthwhile. Leia is not making a random gamble when she sends R2-D2 to find Obi-Wan. She has faith that the old Jedi definitely can and hopefully will make a difference. He doesn't see himself that way, though. Disheartened by betrayal and past tragedies, he has placed his faith in someone else. Even after Yoda says there is another, Ben still focuses on the boy whose upbringing he has monitored from a distance. He has so little hope that he never considers that Darth Vader might be redeemed. He thinks Vader's life must end. When Luke says he cannot kill his father, ghost-Ben says, "Then the Emperor has already won. You were our only hope."[4] Luke has more hope and compassion than Ben does. Luke believes more options exist. He has confidence in Leia, but he also has confidence that good still exists in his father, the former student whom Obi-Wan thinks must die. Deep in Vader's darkness, Luke sees light.

> "Only when it is dark enough can you see the stars."
> —civil rights leader Martin Luther King, Jr.[5]

Hope can become a *self-fulfilling prophecy*, an expectation that causes itself to come true.[6] Children expected to misbehave more often make trouble than those who aren't. Students expected to succeed academically more often make progress than those who aren't.[7] Events don't always turn out as we hoped, of course. Qui-Gon Jinn places his hope in a boy who grows up to destroy the Jedi Order. Then again, Qui-Gon dies and leaves a more cynical Obi-Wan Kenobi to train Anakin instead, under the direction of a Council that has never welcomed the child. Hope by itself cannot fix everything, but it improves the odds. It creates possibilities in our world and an imaginary galaxy.

Throughout this book, we have looked at the healthy and unhealthy aspects of Jedi, Sith, Imperials, rebel scum, and more. With all the talk of light side and dark side, it is easy to make the mistake of thinking the Star Wars stories teach that people are easy to dichotomize as good or evil. And I do mean dichotomize, not just categorize. Certain characters see things that way, but the one who is ultimately proven to be correct sees people as being a lot more complicated and nuanced than that.

When Anakin Skywalker becomes Darth Vader, his dark armor becomes the outer shell that people see in everyday light. Within the darkness inside that armor dwell his better qualities. The dark side of the mind holds hidden potential and less obvious aspects of personality. Star Wars characters keep demonstrating that people should look beyond the surface and not simply embrace existing expectations. The farmboy is a hero. The damsel in distress takes charge of her own rescue. The smuggler risks everything he has to save others. The roaring Wookiee is the group's most nurturing, helpful member, and the teddy bear–like Ewoks end up as some of the most effective killers of all. After the mischievous imp rummaging through Luke's bags turns out to be the most powerful Jedi, he cautions Luke several times to look beyond appearances. Oddly analogous to Darth Vader's own journey, charming Lando betrays his old friend, and yet that traitor has other layers to him beyond that.

The great lesson of Star Wars may be this: There is never just one hope. Hope in Star Wars, while ostensibly about grand events on a galactic scale, requires hope for the individual person. It's about believing a person can find a light, however deep it may be, in the dark side.

References

Erikson, E. (1994). *Insight and responsibility*. New York, NY: Norton.

King, M. L., Jr. (1968, April 3). *I've been to the mountaintop. Address delivered at the Bishop Charles Mason Temple*. https://kinginstitute.stanford.edu/king-papers/documents/ive-been-moun taintop-address-delivered-bishop-charles-mason-temple.

Merton, R. K. (1948). The self-fulfilling prophecy. *Antioch Review, 8*(2), 195.

Rosenthal, R., & Jacobson, L. (1968). *Pygmalion in the classroom: Teachers' expectations and students' intellectual development*. New York, NY: Holt, Rinehart & Winston.

Notes

1. *Star Wars: Episode IV A New Hope* (1977/1981 motion picture).
2. Erikson (1994), p. 115.
3. *Star Wars: Episode V The Empire Strikes Back* (1980 motion picture).
4. *Star Wars: Episode VI Return of the Jedi* (1983 motion picture).
5. King (1968).
6. Merton (1948).
7. Rosenthal & Jacobson (1968).

About the Editor

 Travis Langley, PhD, editor of *Star Wars Psychology: Dark Side of the Mind* and *The Walking Dead Psychology: Psych of the Living Dead*, is a psychology professor who teaches courses on crime, media, and mental illness at Henderson State University. He received a bachelor's degree from Hendrix College and graduate degrees in psychology from Tulane University in New Orleans. Dr. Langley regularly speaks on media and heroism at conventions and universities. *Necessary Evil: Super-Villains of DC Comics* and other films have featured him as an expert interviewee, and the documentary *Legends of the Knight* spotlighted the way he uses fiction to teach real psychology. He authored the acclaimed book *Batman and Psychology: A Dark and Stormy Knight*. *Psychology Today* carries his blog, "Beyond Heroes and Villains."

Follow him as @Superherologist on Twitter, where he ranks among the ten most popular psychologists. You can also keep up with Travis and the rest of this book's contributors through **Facebook.com/ThePsychGeeks**.

His lightsaber is purple. If you say that Mace Windu, Ben Kenobi, or Yoda died, he will happily explain how they all survived.

About the Contributors

Colt J. Blunt, PsyD, LP, has worked as a forensic examiner throughout his career and serves as a guest lecturer and trainer for a number of organizations and educational institutions. His academic interests include the intersection of psychology and law, including the study of criminal behavior. He previously contributed to *The Walking Dead Psychology: Psych of the Living Dead*.

Jenna Busch is a writer, host, and founder of Legion of Leia, a website that promotes and supports women in fandom. She co-hosted "Cocktails with Stan" with comics legend Stan Lee and has appeared as a guest on *Attack of the Show*, NPR, Al Jazeera American, and *Tabletop with Wil Wheaton*. She's a comic book author, *Most Craved* co-host, and *Metro* weekly columnist. Her work has appeared all over the Web Photo by Kevin McIntyre.

Dr. Jim Davies (jimdavies.org) is an associate professor at the Institute of Cognitive Science at Carleton University. He received a PhD in computer science, specializing in artificial intelligence and cognitive science, from the Georgia Institute of Technology. He is the principal investigator of the Science of Imagination Laboratory, which attempts to re-create human visual imagination in software. He is author of the book *Riveted: The Science of Why Jokes Make Us Laugh, Movies Make Us Cry, and Religion Makes Us Feel One with the Universe*. He lives in Ottawa.

 **Frank Gaskill**, PhD, is a cofounder of Southeast Psych, one of the largest private psychology practices in the United States. He coauthored *Max Gamer: Aspie Superhero* and *How We Built Our Dream Practice: Innovative Ideas for Building Yours.* Dr. Gaskill specializes in parenting, Asperger's, and the way technology affects children, teens, and families. He lives with his wife, Liz, and his children, Olivia and Maddox, in Charlotte, NC. Follow him on Twitter (@drfgaskill).

 Donald F. Glut, a New York Times #1 best-selling author, has written hundreds of books, comic books, screenplays for movies and television, and more in both fiction and nonfiction, although he may be best known for writing *The Empire Strikes Back* novel. Many of his books reflect his interest in movies, monsters, and dinosaurs, including the award-winning *Dinosaur Dictionary*. He made critical contributions to the original development of the Masters of the Universe characters. His efforts in recent years have focused largely on filmmaking.

 Jennifer Golbeck is an associate professor in the College of Information Studies at the University of Maryland. She studies human-computer interaction, social media, and how computer models can discover personal attributes such as personality and other psychological traits by analyzing what we share online. *Psychology Today* carries her blog, "Your Online Secrets," and she has written for the print magazine as well. She has a PhD from the University of Maryland and SB and SM degrees from the University of Chicago.

Jonathan Hetterly, MA, LPC, works with teenage and young adult males, specializing in treating substance abuse, addiction, and failure to launch struggles at Southeast Psych in Charlotte, NC. Follow him at @jetterly or ShrinkTank.com, and hear him on the "Shrink Tank" and "Change Your Tune" podcasts.

Dana Klisanin, PhD, is a psychologist, futurist, and author. Her interdisciplinary research examines the impact of media and digital technologies on the mythic and moral dimensions of humanity. Dana's pioneering research includes the area of integral media, digital altruism, the cyberhero archetype, and collaborative heroism. The American Psychological Association's Division of Media Psychology awarded her the 2012 Early Career Award for Scientific Achievement in Media Psychology. Dana is the CEO of Evolutionary Guidance Media R&D, Inc., where she is currently designing and developing *Cyberhero League*, a twenty-first-century scoutlike gaming adventure. *BBC*, *Time*, *USA Today*, and other media outlets have featured her research and *Psychology Today* carries her blog. Dana serves on the board of the World Futures Study Federation and is the director of the MindLab at c3: Center for Conscious Creativity.

Joe Kraemer (joekraemer.com) is a film composer, songwriter, and musician. He has written music for the films *Jack Reacher*, *The Way of the Gun*, *An Unreasonable Man*, and *Mission: Impossible—Rogue Nation*. He has been studying the music of John Williams and its use in films such as *Star Wars* for decades and has conducted in-depth analysis of the scores to *The Phantom Menace* and *Attack of the Clones* for film music magazines and websites.

 **Elizabeth A. Kus** recently completed a PsyD in clinical forensic psychology. She incorporates her passion for geek topics into her therapeutic process, encouraging clients to process their depression, anxiety, or traumas by connecting to their geeky interests. She manages NerdLush.com, where, with friends, she posts about many favorite TV shows, movies, and nerd topics. Reach her there or through Twitter (@elizabeth_ann).

 **Alex Langley**, MS, authored the *The Geek Handbook* series of books and the YA graph novel *Kill Freshman*. He writes about retro and modern gaming for ArcadeSushi.com and is the gaming section editor for NerdSpan.com. Follow him at @RocketLlama on Twitter. His published works also include academic papers, and he likes your hair like that.

 Craig Pohlman, PhD, is a neurodevelopmental psychologist who has helped thousands of struggling learners. He has written several books, including *How Can My Kid Succeed in School?* which helps parents and educators understand and help students with learning challenges. He has mentored many psychologists and sees mentoring as an important tool in education. Craig is the CEO of Southeast Psych, a private practice and media company based in Charlotte, NC.

 **Clay Routledge**, PhD, is an associate professor of psychology at North Dakota State University and an expert in existential psychology. He has published over 75 scientific papers, coedited a book on the psychology of meaning, and authored the book *Nostalgia: A Psychological Resource*. His research has been funded by the John Templeton Foundation and the Society for

the Scientific Study of Religion and featured in media outlets such as *The New York Times* and CBS News. Dr. Routledge writes a popular online column for *Psychology Today* called "More Than Mortal," has served as a guest blogger for *Scientific American*, and frequently serves as a guest expert for national and international radio programs.

Billy San Juan received a PsyD in 2014 and is working toward a license in clinical psychology. He has spoken on geek culture panels at San Diego Comic-Con International and Stan Lee's Comikaze Expo, and he is a contributor to the blog "Magic: The Gathering Judge." Read his thoughts and insights at Facebook.com/Billicent.

Janina Scarlet, PhD, is a licensed clinical psychologist, a scientist, and a full-time geek. She uses superhero therapy to help patients with anxiety, depression, chronic pain, and PTSD at the Center for Stress and Anxiety Management and Sharp Memorial Hospital and is also a professor at Alliant International University, San Diego. Dr. Scarlet has authored chapters in the Sterling Publishing work *The Walking Dead Psychology*. She authored the book *Superhero Therapy*, illustrated by Dean Trippe (Little, Brown). She can be reached via superhero-therapy.com or on Twitter (@shadowquill).

Jay Scarlet holds master's degrees in psychology and library and information science. He works at Chula Vista Public Library. He is also a past member of the Young Adult Library Services Association (YALSA)'s Research Committee. A long time ago in a movie theater far, far away, upon seeing scenes of Luke Skywalker's home, his father leaned over to his mother and whispered, "I've been there."

Laura Vecchiolla is in the middle of her training to becoming a Jedi Master and is a doctoral student in clinical psychology at the Chicago School of Professional Psychology, Her dissertation research aims at connecting the empowering themes of myth and the hero's journey to the process of trauma recovery. As she begins her career as a psychologist, Laura plans to use her eternal love of myth and story to continue to help others in their own journeys toward growth and healing.

Mara Wood is a doctoral student in school psychology. Her research focus is the educational application of comic books and their therapeutic use with children and adolescents. She has presented research on transportation and identification with comic book characters at the Comics Arts Conference. She regularly contributes to Talking Comics, cohosts "The Missfits" podcast, and writes about psychology, comics, books, and *Dungeons & Dragons* on her blog, marawood-blog.com. Find her on Twitter (@MegaMaraMon).

E. Paul Zehr, PhD, is a professor, author, and martial artist at the University of Victoria, where he teaches in the neuroscience, kinesiology, and island medical programs. His pop-sci books include *Becoming Batman* (2008), *Inventing Iron Man* (2011), *Project Superhero* (2014), and *Beyond Human* (2016). *Maxim*, CNN, NPR, and others have interviewed him for his diverse expertise. Paul writes for *Psychology Today, Scientific American,* and *Digital Journal.*

Special Contributors

 Carrie Goldman is the award-winning author of *Bullied: What Every Parent, Teacher, and Kid Needs to Know about Ending the Cycle of Fear* (HarperCollins, 2012). She is a regular blogger for *The Huffington Post*, ChicagoNow, and *Psychology Today*. Goldman works with schools, corporations, and community groups on bullying prevention, intervention, and reconciliation. Together with Chase Masterson, she cofounded the Anti-Bullying Coalition. Goldman received a BS from Northwestern University and an MBA from the Kellogg School of Management.

 Bryan Young is an author, filmmaker, and Star Wars essayist. His publications include four novels and the nonfiction *Children's Illustrated History of Presidential Assassination*. His work appears regularly in *Star Wars Insider* magazine and on *Huffington Post*, StarWars.com, and Big Shiny Robot. Young hosts the "Full of Sith" podcast, a dedicated safe space for Star Wars fans to discuss the saga. He lives and works in Salt Lake City, Utah, with his family and two cats. Contact him on Twitter (@swankmotron).

Index